Words of Wall Street

2,000 Investment Terms Defined

Words of Wall Street

of

Wall

Street

2,000 Investment Terms Defined

Allan H. Pessin
Joseph A. Ross

DOW JONES-IRWIN
Homewood, Illinois 60430

© DOW JONES-IRWIN, 1983

This publication is designed to provide accurate and
authoritative information in regard to the subject matter
covered. It is sold with the understanding that the
publisher is not engaged in rendering legal, accounting, or
other professional service. If legal advice or other expert
assistance is required, the services of a competent
professional person should be sought.

*From a Declaration of Principles jointly adopted by a Committee
of the American Bar Association and a Committee of Publishers.*

Library of Congress Catalog Card No. 82–73632

Printed in the United States of America

2 3 4 5 6 7 8 9 0 K 0 9 8 7 6 5 4 3

Preface

Every profession centers on three elements:

- The problems that people bring to the professionals
- The words and expressions that are unique to the profession
- The systems and procedures whereby professionals use the tools of the profession to solve the problems of the people who use the services of the profession.

It is no different with the securities profession. People use the services of the securities professional, there are delivery systems, and there are words and expressions unique to the profession.

This is not a how-to-do-it book; instead, it concentrates on the terms and expressions used in the securities industry and it describes many of the delivery systems used in the securities industry.

We have tried to make this book less than a dictionary, but more than a glossary of terms. We have given extensive explanations and, wherever examples will help to illustrate a term, we have added them.

The book is easy to use. Entries are alphabetized letter-by-letter. Before the main glossary, we have placed an alphabetical Table of Cross References, which contains many synonyms, abbreviations, and terms related to the terms in the main glossary. Beside each term in this table is the entry related to it. If you do not find a term in the glossary, check the Table of Cross References.

The book has two audiences:

- The individual investor who wants to learn more about the securities industry: its terms, its delivery systems, and the colorful slang that surrounds the securities industry.
- The industry professional who wants more specific information about a term or expression.

This book will not make you rich. Its goal is not problem solving, nor does it teach one how to pick this or that security. However, it does teach the reader the language of the securities industry—in many cases, this is more than half the problem.

Allan H. Pessin
Joseph A. Ross

Table of Cross References

DEEP DISCOUNT *see* DEEP DISCOUNT BOND

DESIGNATED ORDER *see* DESIGNATED NET *and* DESIGNATED CONCES-
SION

DJIA *see* DOW JONES INDUSTRIAL AVERAGE

DK *see* DON'T KNOW

DNR *see* DO NOT REDUCE

DOT *see* DESIGNATED ORDER TURNAROUND

DTC *see* DEPOSITORY TRUST COMPANY

EARNED SURPLUS *see* RETAINED EARNINGS

EBT *see* EARNINGS BEFORE TAXES

EXERCISE AN OPTION *see* EXERCISE

EXPIRATION MONTH *see* EXPIRATION CYCLE *and* EXPIRATION DATE

FAIL *see* FAIL TO RECEIVE *and* FAIL TO DELIVER

FASB *see* FINANCIAL ACCOUNTING STANDARDS BOARD

FC *see* FIRST CALL DATE

FDIC *see* FEDERAL DEPOSIT INSURANCE CORPORATION

FED *see* FEDERAL RESERVE BOARD *and* FEDERAL RESERVE SYSTEM

FHA *see* FEDERAL HOUSING ADMINISTRATION

FHLB *see* FEDERAL HOME LOAN BANK

FIFO *see* FIRST IN, FIRST OUT

FLB *see* FEDERAL LAND BANKS

FLOOR GIVE UP *see* GIVE UP

FNMA *see* FEDERAL NATIONAL MORTGAGE ASSOCIATION *and*
FANNIE MAE

FOK *see* FILL OR KILL

FOMC *see* FEDERAL OPEN MARKET COMMITTEE

FOREIGN BOND *see* YANKEE BOND

FORWARD *see* FORWARD CONTRACT

FRB *see* FEDERAL RESERVE BOARD

FREDDIE MAC *see* FEDERAL HOME LOAN MORTGAGE CORPORATION

FREE TO TRADE *see* FREED UP

FRN *see* FLOATING RATE NOTE

FUNDS RATE *see* FEDERAL FUNDS RATE

FYI *see* FOR YOUR INFORMATION

GINNIE MAE *see* GOVERNMENT NATIONAL MORTGAGE ASSOCIATION

GNMA *see* GOVERNMENT NATIONAL MORTGAGE ASSOCIATION

GNMA PRODUCTION RATE *see* PRODUCTION RATE

GNP *see* GROSS NATIONAL PRODUCT

GO *see* GENERAL OBLIGATION BOND
GROUP LESS CONCESSION ORDER *see* DESIGNATED CONCESSION
GTC *see* GOOD TILL CANCELLED ORDER
GTD *see* GUARANTEED BOND
HEDGE RATIO *see* DELTA
HUD *see* HOUSING AND URBAN DEVELOPMENT
IA *see* INVESTMENT ADVISER
IB RATE *see* INTER-BANK RATE
ICC *see* INTERSTATE COMMERCE COMMISSION
IDB *see* INDUSTRIAL DEVELOPMENT BOND
IMM *see* INTERNATIONAL MONETARY MARKET
INDUSTRIAL REVENUE BOND *see* INDUSTRIAL DEVELOPMENT BOND
IOC *see* IMMEDIATE-OR-CANCEL ORDER
IRA *see* INDIVIDUAL RETIREMENT ACCOUNT
ISO *see* INCENTIVE STOCK OPTION
ISSUE PRICE *see* PUBLIC OFFERING PRICE
ITC *see* INVESTMENT TAX CREDIT
ITS *see* INTERMARKET TRADING SYSTEM
JTWROS *see* JOINT TENANTS WITH RIGHT OF SURVIVORSHIP
KCBT *see* KANSAS CITY BOARD OF TRADE
LEGALS *see* LEGAL TRANSFER
LETTER STOCK *see* LETTER SECURITY
LIFO *see* LAST IN, FIRST OUT
LIVING TRUST *see* INTER VIVOS TRUST
LOIS *see* LIMIT ORDER INFORMATION SYSTEM
MIT *see* MARKED IF TOUCHED ORDER *or* MUNICIPAL
    INVESTMENT TRUST
MUNICIPAL SECURITY *see* MUNICIPAL BOND
NET WORKING CAPITAL *see* NET CURRENT ASSETS
NEW HOUSING AUTHORITY BONDS *see* PUBLIC HOUSING
    AUTHORITY BONDS
NYSE *see* NEW YORK STOCK EXCHANGE
OPEN BOX *see* ACTIVE BOX
PFD *see* PREFERRED STOCK
PRICE SPREAD *see* VERTICAL SPREAD
RECEIVER IN BANKRUPTCY *see* RECEIVER
REGISTERED BOND *see* REGISTERED SECURITY
REGULAR SPECIALIST *see* SPECIALIST

REVERSE REPO *see* REVERSE REPURCHASE AGREEMENT
RP *see* REPURCHASE AGREEMENT
RW *see* REGULAR-WAY SETTLEMENT
S & P *see* STANDARD & POOR'S; *also its* INDEX *and its* RATING
SALLIE MAE *see* STUDENT LOAN MARKETING ASSOCIATION
SBA *see* SMALL BUSINESS ADMINISTRATION
SDR *see* SPECIAL DRAWING RIGHTS
SEC *see* SECURITIES AND EXCHANGE COMMISSION *and* SEC RULES
SEC REGULATIONS *see* SEC RULES
SEP *see* SIMPLIFIED EMPLOYEE PENSION PLAN
SF *see* SINKING FUND
SIA *see* SECURITIES INDUSTRY ASSOCIATION
SIAC *see* SECURITIES INDUSTRY AUTOMATION CORPORATION
SIMULTANEOUS TRANSACTION *see* RISKLESS TRANSACTION
SIPC *see* SECURITIES INVESTORS PROTECTION CORPORATION
SMA *see* SPECIAL MISCELLANEOUS ACCOUNT
SOP *see* STATEMENT OF POLICY
SROP *see* SENIOR REGISTERED OPTION PRINCIPAL
STANDARD & POOR'S INDEX *see* S & P INDEX
STOCKHOLDERS' EQUITY *see* SHAREHOLDERS' EQUITY
SUBCHAPTER S *see* SUBCHAPTER S CORPORATION
TAB *see* TAX ANTICIPATION BILL
TAN *see* TAX ANTICIPATION NOTE
T-BILL *see* TREASURY BILL
T-BOND *see* TREASURY BOND
TIME SPREAD *see* CALENDAR SPREAD
TTV *see* TRADING TO TOTAL VOLUME
TVA *see* TENNESSEE VALLEY AUTHORITY
UNDERWRITERS' RETENTION *see* RETENTION
UNDIVIDED ACCOUNT *see* EASTERN ACCOUNT
UNIFIED MORTGAGE BOND *see* CONSOLIDATED MORTGAGE BOND
UNITED ACCOUNT *see* EASTERN ACCOUNT
UPTICK *see* PLUS TICK
USASLE *see* UNIFORM SECURITIES AGENT STATE LAW EXAMINATION
VISIBLE SUPPLY *see* THIRTY-DAY VISIBLE SUPPLY
WAREHOUSING *see* PARKING
WARRANT *see* SUBSCRIPTION WARRANT
WD *see* WHEN DISTRIBUTED

WI *see* WHEN ISSUED
WORKING CAPITAL RATIO *see* CURRENT RATIO
WOW *see* WITH OR WITHOUT
YTM *see* YIELD TO MATURITY

Glossary

A

A
1   Lowercase: used in newspaper stock transaction tables after dividend to designate that extra cash dividends were paid during previous year. For example, 2.40a.

   Formerly used in option transaction table to designate that no trades in an option series occurred that day.
2   Uppercase: used in the newspaper reports of a corporation's earnings to designate that the principal marketplace for the corporation's securities is the American Stock Exchange. For example, Atlas Van (A).

ABC AGREEMENT
New York Stock Exchange term to designate this situation: a member uses borrowed funds to purchase an exchange seat. So called because the exchange-approved agreement has three provisions: the member may (1) retain the seat and purchase another seat for a designee of the lender's choice, (2) sell the seat and remit the proceeds to the lender, (3) transfer the seat, at a nominal consideration, to another person in the employ of the lending member firm.

ACCOUNT
General industry term for:
1   The bookkeeping record of a client's transactions and credit or debit balances of either cash or securities with the member firm. The term also is used of the conduct of such business relationships. For example, "Our firm emphasizes accounts productive to the firm and to client."
2   The books of an investment syndicate that indicate contractual relationships, the securities owned and sold, and the final financial balance between a participant in a syndicate and the syndicate.

ACCOUNT EXECUTIVE

Commonly used term for an employee of a broker-dealer who has been registered with the NASD and/or one of the exchanges. Such employees are permitted to solicit buy and sell orders for securities and, in general, to handle client accounts.

Technically, the term applies to a registered representative, although some member firms use other designations for registered employees.

ACCOUNT STATEMENT

General name for the periodic statement that gives the status of a client's account with a broker-dealer. Such statements, which must be sent at least quarterly to clients with open accounts, give a summary of all transactions during the previous period, plus a recounting of debits, credits, and long and short positions.

In practice, most broker-dealers send account statements monthly if the client has bought or sold during the previous month.

Also used of the option agreement that must be signed when a client opens an option account.

ACCREDITED INVESTOR

Term used by SEC in Regulation D of private placements.

Concept: although 35 is the upper limit of persons who may purchase a private placement, accredited investors are not included in this number.

General definition of accredited investors: institutional-type accounts and persons of wealth (persons with a net worth of $1 million or more; persons with an annual income of $200,000 or more; persons who purchase $150,000 or more of the offering and this does not represent more than 20% of their net worth).

ACCRETION

Technical term for the upward adjustment of the cost of acquisition of a bond purchased at an original issue discount. Internal Revenue rules adopted in July 1982 give precise provisions for this upward adjustment. The difference between the adjusted cost basis in successive tax years is considered interest income for the tax year in which the adjustment is made.

ACCRUAL BASIS

Designation of an accounting procedure whereby debits and credits are entered in the books of the company on the date they are incurred, rather than on the date they are paid or received. For example, ABC Corporation sells an item worth $20 on credit. It would debit inventory and credit accounts receivable by $20. Then, when the $20 is actually received, it will credit cash and debit accounts receivable.

ACCRUED INTEREST

Term designating the interest due on a bond or other fixed-income security that must be paid by the buyer of a security to its seller. Usual computation: coupon rate of interest times elapsed days from prior interest payment date (i.e., coupon date) up to but not including settlement date. Principal exceptions: money market securities that are sold at a discount do not have accrued interest.

Antonym: flat (i.e., without accrued interest).

Synonym: and interest (used as a qualifier). For example, The trade was made "and interest" (i.e., the accrued interest must be added to the contract price).

ACCUMULATION AREA

Term used by technical analysts if the market price of a security tends to move sideways. The term implies that buyers are willing to purchase at present prices.

Because prices tend to reflect the accumulated decisions of buyers and sellers, it is difficult to tell in practice whether a sideways price movement results from buying (accumulation) or from selling (distribution).

See also DISTRIBUTION AREA.

ACCUMULATION UNITS

Term used of annuities if a person buys an annuity, either fixed or variable, through a lump-sum purchase for future payout or by periodic purchases (i.e., accumulation). When the purchaser elects a payout method, these units will be converted to annuity units.

Basic concept: accumulation units remain the property of the purchaser; upon election of a payout method, the annuitant surrenders the property and, in exchange, receives a right to future payments from the insurance company. These payments are fixed if the annuity is a fixed annuity; variable if the annuity is variable.

ACID-TEST RATIO

A measurement of corporate liquidity. Accepted measurement: subtract inventory from current assets; divide the remainder by current liabilities. For example, a company has current assets of $10 million and inventory of $3 million. Net: $7 million. It has current liabilities of $3.5 million. Its acid-test ratio is:

$$\frac{\$7 \text{ million}}{\$3.5 \text{ million}} = \frac{2}{1}$$

Ratios below 1 to 1 are considered low. However, ratios that are extremely high may indicate that a company is not using assets effectively, may be cash rich, and is subject to a takeover by other companies.

ACQ
Abbreviation used on the consolidated tape for a transaction that represents an exchange acquisition (i.e., a block trade initiated by a buyer with all transaction costs paid by a purchaser). Such transactions are infrequent.

ACTING IN CONCERT
Basic concept: two or more persons who, either collectively or through a common agent, endeavor to achieve an investment goal.

Basic restrictions against acting in concert: such persons may not (1) exceed the position and exercise limits set by the option exchanges, (2) work to change the management of a registered corporation without filing with the SEC, (3) accumulate a control position in the security of a corporation without reporting to the SEC, (4) manipulate the price of a security. Each of these restrictions also applies to individuals.

ACTIVE BOND CROWD
New York Stock Exchange term for the combination of these two ideas: (1) the bond floor members who (2) most frequently trade in actively traded bonds. Antonym: the can, or cabinet crowd.

In practice, all NYSE members who trade on the bond floor act as agents. Therefore, the distinction between active-crowd and can-crowd brokers refers more to the securities traded than to the designation of the NYSE members who trade on the bond floor. For example, if you were to trade bond A you could be in the can crowd, and if you trade bond B you could be in the active crowd.

See also CABINET CROWD.

ACTIVE BOX
Jargon for location of securities, held in the vault of a broker-dealer, that are eligible for use as collateral for broker or customer account financing. To be eligible for broker financing, the securities must be owned by the broker-dealer. To be eligible for customer account financing, the securities must be customer owned but held as a pledge for margin loan made by the broker to the customer.

ACTIVE MARKET
Term used to describe either a marketplace or the buying and selling of an individual security that is so marked by: (1) frequent transactions

with (2) reasonable volume and (3) relatively narrow spreads between the bids-offers that successive transactions are made at moderate price changes.

The term is relative; thus, no precise definition can be given. In practice, what is active for security A may be inactive for security B.

A/D

Often used to abbreviate advance(s) versus decline(s) in a particular marketplace or of equity securities in general.

See also ADVANCE DECLINE INDEX.

AD HOC

Latin: for this purpose. Commonly used of an action that is taken to solve a particular problem. For example, "Let's appoint an ad hoc committee." Or, "Joe, this is an ad hoc solution." The term may imply a permanent or a temporary solution. For example, "This is a very complex situation, but—ad hoc—let's concentrate on the financial effects of Plan A."

ADJUSTED DEBIT BALANCE

The ledger debit balance (i.e., the dollar amount a client owes a broker) plus any available special miscellaneous account (SMA) adjusted by any paper profits on short accounts. The ADB determines whether a client's margin account is subject to the retention requirement.

In practice, following the Regulation-T adjustments made in February 1982, the term adjusted debit balance is meaningless, with this exception: withdrawals of cash or securities based on the SMA entries are not permitted if the client's account would thereby be in violation of margin maintenance requirements.

ADJUSTED EXERCISE PRICE

Term used of GNMA put and call options. Contract is for $100,000 unpaid principal balance on a GNMA pass-through security with an 8% nominal coupon. If GNMA pass-throughs with higher coupon rates are delivered, the exercise (strike) price will be so adjusted that the yield is the same. For example, the strike price on a GNMA call is 56. The yield will be 11%. If the call is exercised and the writer delivers a GNMA pass-through with an 11% coupon, the adjusted exercise price will be par, or 100.

ADJUSTMENT BOND

Bond, issued in exchange for other bonds, that promises to pay interest only if earned or to the extent earned. Authorization for the exchange must come from the bondholders who accept the adjustment bonds. Normally, the exchange will be made only if the company will otherwise be bankrupt—and bondholders give their authorization in an endeavor to avoid liquidation of the company.

Also called INCOME BOND.

ADMINISTRATOR

1 Person responsible for the supervision of state securities laws.
2 Court-appointed person to oversee the distribution of the estate of a person who dies intestate.

The feminine term administratrix is occasionally used.

AD VALOREM

Latin: according to the value. Used both of the assessed valuation of property and of the tax on such property. For example, the Township of Southhold has an ad valorem tax of 76 mills ($.076) per dollar of assessed valuation.

See also ASSESSED VALUATION.

ADVANCE DECLINE INDEX

Often used as a measurment of market sentiment (i.e., relative bullishness or bearishness of the stock market).

One frequently used formula: divide number of advancing issues by number of declining issues on a market day. For example, if 900 issues advance and 450 decline on a market day, the A-D index is 2. Numbers greater than 1 are bullish, numbers less than 1 are bearish.

Another formula: divide number of advances plus one half of stocks unchanged by number of issues traded. Numbers above 50% are bullish, numbers less than 50% are bearish.

ADVANCE REFUNDING

Term used to describe this situation: A municipality has outstanding bonds that are not yet callable (e.g., the earliest call date is 1988). If general interest rates drop, the municipality may find it advantageous to issue new bonds at a lower rate. The proceeds are invested in government securities that will mature in 1988, at which time the money will be used to call the earlier issue.

Also called prerefunding.

ADVERTISEMENT

In securities industry usage, any material for use in a newspaper or magazine, or on radio or television, or with another public medium. Substantially identical letters to 10 or more people are considered advertisements.

Industry rules require: truthfulness and good taste; approval by a designated person within the issuing firm; and adequate record keeping of all advertisements. Also, the National Association of Securities Dealers requires that advertising copy be filed with the association within five days of use (three days if the advertisement pertains to investment company securities).

AFFIDAVIT OF DOMICILE
Statement by executor or administrator of an estate attesting to the domicile of a decedent at the time of death. The affidavit is important for the transfer of securities from an estate because it, together with the tax waiver from the state of domicile, shows that no tax liens are outstanding against the securities about to be transferred.

AFFILIATED PERSON
General name for a person who can influence the management decisions of a corporation. Although legal advice may be needed in specific situations, the term includes: holders of 10% or more of the outstanding stock of a corporation, directors, elected officers (chairman, president, vice presidents, secretary, and treasurer), and members of their immediate family.

Also called control person.

AFTERMARKET
General name for the trading activity in a security during the period of its initial offering to the public, and immediately thereafter, until the syndicate account is closed.

More popular name: secondary market.

AFTERTAX BASIS
Used to identify an investor's average rate of return on a bond purchased at a discount (i.e., the return after federal tax on the income and on the capital gain). Normally based on a corporate holder paying the maximum corporate tax on income and capital gains.

Often given by government bond dealers on their offer sheets so prospective purchasers can compare directly the aftertax yield with the nontaxable yield on municipal bonds selling at par.

AGED FAIL
Industry jargon for a contract between two broker-dealers that remains unsettled after 30 days from the time that delivery and payment should have been completed. Term is important because aged fails severely affect the capital of the affected firm, in that an aged

fail may no longer be considered an asset because the chances of its successful completion are negligible.

AGENCY
1   A security, almost always debt, issued by a corporation sponsored by the U.S. government. Examples: bonds of the Federal Intermediate Credit Banks (FICB) or the Tennessee Valley Authority. Agency securities are exempt from registration under the Securities Act of 1933.
2   The act of buying or selling for the account and risk for another person.
See also BROKER.

AGENT
1   A person who buys or sells for the account and risk of another. Generally, an agent takes no financial risk and charges a commission for his services.
2   In state securities law, any person who represents an issuer or a broker-dealer in the purchase or sale of securities to, or for, a person domiciled in that state.

AGE OF MAJORITY
Age at which a person may legally contract. Depending on state law, the age of majority is from 18 to 21.

AGGREGATE EXERCISE PRICE
Term in security options: the exercise (strike) price times the number of securities involved in the contract. For example, a call is purchased at 50 for 100 shares. The aggregate exercise price is $5,000. Exception: GNMA options and T-bill, T-note, and T-bond options, in which the aggregate exercise price is the strike price times the face value of the underlying contract. For example, a GNMA call at 68 is 68% times $100,000, the face value of the underlying contract.

See also ADJUSTED EXERCISE PRICE.

AGGREGATE INDEBTEDNESS
Term used by the SEC in the computation of broker-dealer compliance with the SEC's net capital requirements. Best definition: the total of the broker-dealer's indebtedness to customers. For example, a broker-dealer owes $200,000: $50,000 is owed to a partner in the business and $150,000 is owed to customers for their credit balances in their accounts. The broker-dealer's aggregate indebtedness is the $150,000 owed to customers.

AGGRIEVED PARTY
Industry term for:

1   A person who accuses a member or a person associated with a member of a trade practice complaint under the National Association of Securities Dealers' (NASDs') Rules of Fair Practice.

2   A person who requests arbitration of a controversy between himself and a member through the arbitration facilities provided by the NASD, the Municipal Securities Rulemaking Board (MSRB), or any of the exchanges.

AGREEMENT AMONG UNDERWRITERS
The formal contract between the members of an underwriting, or syndicate, account.

In general, the agreement among underwriters appoints one or more syndicate managers, defines the powers of the manager(s), and sets the rules for the conduct of the account.

ALLIED MEMBER
New York Stock Exchange term for a senior officer of a member firm who is not a member of the exchange. For example, the chairman, the president, or a vice president of a NYSE member firm is not a member of the exchange; such a person is an allied member. Allied members must register with the NYSE, must pass a special examination, and are bound by the rules of the exchange.

ALLIGATOR SPREAD
Slang for an option spread position that offers more in commission dollars to an account executive than to a client who accepts the risks of the spread. In effect, the client's potential profit on the position is eaten up by the cost of the transaction.

ALL OR NONE
1   Used of an underwritten offering: it is conditional to a total subscription of the shares offered. If every share is not subscribed, issuer has the right to cancel the offering. For example, the Women's Bank offered shares on an all-or-none basis.

2   Used of an order ticket by a buying or selling customer: buy or sell the entire amount on a single transaction. Do not execute a partial transaction. Order entry symbol: AON. All-or-none instructions that require immediate execution must be marked fill or kill (FOK). Thus, AON restricts the size but not necessarily the time of the transaction.

ALL YOUR MARKET

Jargon in the over-the-counter market. Situation: An OTC broker-dealer asks another dealer for a quote. The response: "It's all your market." Meaning: The only interest in the security seems to be localized in the area from where the dealer in Little Rock calls a dealer in Chicago for a quote on the stock of a bank in Fayetteville, Arkansas. Response: "It's all your market."

ALTERNATIVE ORDER

Exchange order that combines a limit with a stop order for the same security. Because limit orders and stop orders are entered on opposite sides of the market (e.g., a buy limit should be below the current market, and a buy stop above), the execution of one side of the alternative order requires the cancellation of the other side of the order. Alternative orders may not combine a buy with a sell order for the same security.

Also called an either-or order.

AMERICAN DEPOSITORY RECEIPT

Negotiable receipt, registered in the name of the owner, for shares of a foreign corporation held in the vault of a foreign branch of an American bank. The receipt may or may not be on a share-for-share basis with the underlying security. ADRs if sold in the United States are subject to the securities laws of the United States, and many foreign corporations sell their securities in the United States in the form of ADRs. Because of ease of transfer and resale, ADRs are a popular form of domestic equity ownership of foreign corporations.

AMERICAN MUNICIPAL BOND ASSURANCE CORPORATION

This insuror guarantees payment of principal and interest on insured municipal bonds. The insurance premium is paid by the issuer of the bonds.

AMBAC-insured bonds generally are rated AAA by Standard & Poor's.

AMERICAN STOCK EXCHANGE

Located in New York City, the American Stock Exchange is the second largest of the securities exchanges in the United States. Prior to 1921, the exchange was known as the New York Curb Exchange—hence its popular name as the Curb.

Both ASE and AMEX are commonly used as abbreviations for the American Stock Exchange. Listed stocks, bonds, and options are traded on the AMEX.

AMICUS CURIAE

Latin: friend of the court. Term used of briefs filed by parties who are interested in a court trial but who are not participants in the trial. For example, there is a trial between the United States and a company that imports pianos, with the government charging that the importer is violating import laws. Another manufacturer of pianos files an amicus curiae brief to show that the importing of pianos does violate certain U.S. laws.

AMORTIZE

Accounting method whereby the cost of acquisition of an asset gradually is reduced to reflect the theoretical resale value of the asset.

As a noun: method is amortization.

Uses:

1 A company purchases a fixed asset that, over time, decreases in value because of use or obsolescence.
2 An investor purchases a security at a premium over its par (or redemption) value. For example, an investor buys a municipal bond at a premium over its redemption value.

Tax advice is needed if government or corporate securities, purchased at a premium, are amortized.

See also DEPRECIATION.

AMOS

Acronym for Amex Options Switching System. A computerized options order-routing system that will transmit incoming options orders to the appropriate trading posts and—if the orders are executed—report the executions to the member who entered the order.

ANNUAL REPORT

Popular term for the yearly report made by a company to its stockholders. Federal law requires all registered corporations to make such reports. They usually contain a balance sheet, an income statement, a list of changes in retained earnings, and how income of the corporation was used.

The report form filed annually with the SEC is called Form 10-K, which expands on items in the annual report. Shareholders may request Form 10-K from the corporate secretary for additional information.

ANNUITANT

Legal designation for a person who receives benefits from an annuity.

Technically, the term is used of a person who has elected the type of payout to be made on the annuity.

The term also is used of a person who is currently purchasing accumulation units in an annuity plan or who has made a lump-sum purchase but has not yet elected a method of payout.

See also ANNUITY; ANNUITY UNIT; and ACCUMULATION UNITS.

ANNUITY

An investment contract sold by a life insurance company in which the annuitant receives regular payments for life, or for a fixed period, in exchange for the immediate or installment deposit of a specified number of dollars.

Technically, the premium paid by the annuitant purchases accumulation units. At the time when the annuitant elects a payout method, the annuitant gives up ownership of the accumulation units and, in exchange, receives the right to a guaranteed payout in accordance with the payout method elected.

ANNUITY UNIT

An accounting device used to convert accumulation units of an annuity into units upon which the payments to an annuitant will be based. Used both of fixed and variable annuities. For example, over the years a contributor to a variable annuity has accumulated x accumulation units. Upon election of a payout method, the annuitant will receive y annuity units. This number is fixed. Because it is a variable annuity, however, the monthly payment will vary. The monthly payouts would not vary if the annuitant had been accumulating units of a fixed annuity.

ANNUNCIATOR BOARD

A mechanical paging device—prominently displayed on the walls of the New York and American Stock Exchange—that was formerly used to summon floor brokers, or other members, to a prearranged location for order executions or messages. Now, electronic paging devices are used.

APPROVED PERSON

Exchange term for a person who is: (1) not an employee of a member firm, but who is (2) in a control capacity. For example, a member of the board of directors of a member corporation who is not an employee of the corporation.

Approved persons must agree to be bound by the constitution and rules of the exchange and be approved by the board of governors of the exchange.

ARBITRAGE
1 As verb: the act of buying and selling the same security in different marketplaces to profit from a disparity in market prices.
2 As verb: the act of buying one security coupled to a short sale of the same security to profit from a disparity of prices.
3 As noun: an offsetting security position that has a built-in profit.
4 As adjective or as past participle: to describe a security position that establishes a profit. For example, "His long position was arbitraged by a short sale."
See also ARBITRAGEUR.

ARBITRAGE BONDS
IRS term for bonds issued by a municipality if the proceeds of the sale are invested in other bonds paying a higher rate of interest than the municipality pays on its own bonds. If bonds are classified as arbitrage bonds, the IRS may revoke the tax exemption on the interest income the municipality pays on its bonds.

In practice, a municipality must clear with the IRS a bond issuance used for the prerefunding of their outstanding issues.

See also PREREFUNDING.

ARBITRAGEUR
A person who endeavors to profit from offsetting long and short security positions or from a disparity in market prices on different markets.

Although the term can be used of private individuals, the term generally is used of broker-dealers or their employees who conduct the arbitrage operations.

See also ARBITRAGE.

ARBITRATION
Industry-sponsored method to adjudicate controversies between members or between members and nonmembers. Arbitration provides a final, binding decision—provided the parties to the arbitration agree to abide by the decision before the arbitration proceedings begin. Each of the exchanges, the NASD, and the MSRB have provisions for the arbitration of industry disputes.

ARREARAGE
Term used of unpaid dividends on cumulative preferred shares. Although such unpaid dividends are not owed to the preferred shareholders—only bond interest is owed—the company promises that it will not pay any dividend to common shareholders until such arrearages are paid. For example, a company passes two $3 dividends

on its cumulative preferred shares. The company will not pay any dividends to its common shareholders until it has paid the $6 arrearage.

AS AGENT
A person who acts as a broker in a transaction and who assumes no financial risk. For example, "Today, we purchased 1,000 shares of XYZ at $55 as agent for your account."

The term often is used as a synonym for subagent. For example, Bill Smith works as a broker for Smythe & Sons. Smythe & Sons usually acts as a broker. Technically, Bill Smith is a subagent for his employer.

ASE INDEX
Index of all common stocks listed on the American Stock Exchange.

Because it weights price changes to reflect the number of outstanding shares for individual stocks, the index is rather a measurement of the average value change than a measurement of average price change. For example, company A has two shares outstanding at a price of $50. Company B has four shares outstanding at a price of $53. Total value: $312; average value $52. Today, A goes down 1 point; B goes up 1 point. Average price change is zero. Average value change is $+\frac{1}{3}$. New total value is $314 for six shares, or an average value of $52-\frac{1}{3}$. The ASE index will reflect this change in average value.

ASIAN CD
Certificate of deposit issued by a bank located in Asia. Most common locations: Tokyo, Hong Kong, or Singapore. Unless otherwise stated, it may be presumed that the CD is denominated in U.S. dollars.

CDs denominated in yen or in Singapore or Hong Kong dollars, although they enjoy relative safety of principal, are subject to currency exchange risks.

ASKED PRICE
Commonly accepted industry term for the lowest price at which a dealer is willing to sell a security. Presumption: The asked price is for the accepted unit of trading, although on exchanges the number of shares available at the asked price normally is given. For example, a security is bid 29, asked 30.

Also shortened to asked.

Synonym: offering price. For example, the bid is 29, the offer is 30.

ASSESSED VALUATION
The value, often arbitrarily assigned, of property in a taxing municipality. The tax then is assigned in mills per dollar of assessed

valuation. For example, a taxpayer's house and lot are assigned an assessed valuation of $10,000. If the ad valorem tax is 76 mills ($.076) per dollar of assesed valuation, the tax on the property will be $760. Concept of assessed valuation is important in analyzing municipal bonds whose debt service will be paid from property taxes.

See AD VALOREM; LIMITED TAX BOND.

ASSET

Any item of value owned by an individual or a corporation. Most common differentiations:
1   Current asset: an item of value that will be turned into cash within a year.
2   Fixed asset: an item of value that is used in the conduct of a business that, ordinarily, will not be converted into cash within a year.
3   Intangible asset: an item of value whose resale value is difficult to determine.

ASSET FINANCING

General term: a loan made to the owner of an asset who, in turn, segregates the asset as collateral for the loan. For example, a corporation borrows against the collateral value of an asset, such as land, property, or plant.

Basic concept: rather than looking at a loan from the viewpoint of the lender, asset financing looks at a loan from a viewpoint of the borrower. For example, a corporation looks at its assets and asks: "How can I turn these assets into cash for the operation of my business?"

ASSIGN

1   General term: to sign, to sell, to transfer, or to give away.
2   Specific term: to impose an obligation on someone else. For example, the Options Clearing Corporation—upon notice of an option exercise by the owner of the option—assigns the obligation of complying with the terms of the option (e.g., a call, to deliver the security; a put, to purchase the security) on a member firm whose client wrote the option.

Also used as a noun: assignment.

ASSIGNMENT (1)

Technical term for a form whereby a registered owner of a security transfers ownership. Generally, a registered security provides a form on its reverse side whereby the registered owner may assign ownership. Ownership also may be assigned on a separate piece of paper.

See also BOND POWER; STOCK POWER.

ASSIGNMENT (2)

Form whereby the Options Clearing Corporation notifies a member firm that an option has been exercised against one of its clients who wrote a security option. The member firm, in turn, must assign the exercise against one of its clients on either a random or a first-in, first-out (FIFO) basis.

Also called assignment notice.

ASSOCIATED PERSON

General term: any person associated with a broker-dealer as a proprietor, partner, officer, director, branch office manager, investment banker, or salesperson. Persons who perform ministerial or clerical functions are not associated persons.

ASSOCIATE MEMBER

American Stock Exchange term: a person who has purchased from the exchange the right to execute orders through a regular member of the exchange. Such members may trade and clear orders through the regular member but have no right of access to the floor of the exchange.

ASSOCIATE SPECIALIST

Exchange members who act as assistants to regular specialists. Associate specialists are, in effect, in training. They may execute orders as agents for regular specialists—but only under the supervision of the regular, or relief, specialist.

AT RISK

Tax law term used as a criterion for a deduction against a tax liability.

General concept: to provide a deduction, the money invested in a business—either personal capital or borrowed money—must be at risk (i.e., able to increase or decrease in value). For example, a person invests in a business, and the general partner guarantees the return of all money invested. The investor's money is not at risk. Hence, no deduction will be allowed for depreciation. Tax advice is needed.

AT THE CLOSE

Customer instruction on a market order that is to be executed on an exchange.

Basic concept: 30 seconds before the close, a bell signals the last half minute before the close. This at-the-close order should be executed during this time. The order is a customer instruction; no guarantee can be given that an execution will be obtained. The customer should understand the provisional nature of the order.

AT THE MONEY

Term used of a security option if the strike (execution) price and the market price are the same. For example, a put at 35 on ABC if the market price of ABC is 35.

The term abstracts from premiums paid or received and from the cost of executing the option contract. Thus, at the money should not be confused with the client's break-even point—either as holder or seller—on the option contract.

AT THE OPENING

Customer instruction on a limit order that is to be executed on the initial transaction in an exchange-traded security. If the instruction cannot be implemented, the order is to be cancelled.

Note: This instruction should not be placed on a market order. All market orders received before the initial transaction must be included in the initial transaction; this is exchange regulation.

AUTEX SYSTEM

A communications network using electronic screens to enable broker-dealers and other subscribers to show their trading interest in specific blocks of stock. If a mutual interest is found, the transaction is completed on a securities exchange or in the over-the-counter market.

AUTHORIZED SHARES

The maximum number of shares, either common or preferred, that a corporation may issue. The number of authorized shares is stated in the charter of the corporation. Corporations may issue fewer shares. Permission to issue more shares requires amendment of the corporate charter, based on the approval of the company's shareholders.

AUTOMATIC REINVESTMENT

Feature that permits an equity owner to receive dividend distributions in the form of new shares in lieu of a cash distribution. The feature is common to most mutual funds, which also permit the reinvestment of capital gains on fund portfolio transactions.

About 800 NYSE-listed corporations also have dividend reinvestment programs.

Since both programs are voluntary, the equity owner is liable to taxation in the year the distribution is made. However, under the Economic Recovery Tax Act, reinvestments of dividends from qualified utility shares in new shares of the same company are tax exempt: $750 on a single return, $1,500 on a joint return. This feature expires in tax year 1985.

AUTOMATIC WITHDRAWAL
Feature of many mutual funds that permits fundholder to receive a fixed-dollar amount each month or quarter. Check is sent to the holder, and dividends, capital gains, or share liquidation is used to pay for the withdrawals.

Also known as check-a-month plan.

AVERAGE
1 As noun: a measurement of general price movement of a security or a group of securities. For example, the measurement of the Dow Jones Industrial Average.
2 As verb: to make purchases at various prices to achieve an advantageous price for an entire lot of securities. For example, "Let's buy over time to average the price."
3 As adjective: a qualifier for a noun implying normative performance. For example, a mutual fund's performance last year was average in terms of performance that was measured against the Standard & Poor's Index.

AVERAGE DOWN
Investment strategy often used by purchasers of securities.

Concept: Do not buy all at once; instead, buy multiple holdings at various prices as a security falls in market value. For example, a client wants to buy 10,000 shares of a stock. Instead of buying all at once, the client buys 2,000 shares; then, if the price falls, the client will purchase additional lots of 2,000 shares—up to 10,000—to attain an average price that is lower than the original purchase price.

Strategy can be profitable if stock is going through a sideways movement with up-and-down price variations.

AVERAGE LIFE
The number of years required for one half of a debt to be retired through a sinking fund, serial maturity, or amortizing payments. For example, the company issued 25-year bonds with a sinking fund that will begin in 5 years. The average life of the bond issue is 18 years and 7 months.

AVERAGE UP
Term describing the purchase of the same security at various times and prices above the lowest price paid. For example, an investor buys

100 shares at $22, $24, $26, and $28. The investor has averaged up 400 shares at an average price of $25.

Term also is used of sales at various times at prices above the lowest price received.

AVERAGING THE DOLLAR

Term inaccurately used of dollar cost averaging.

See also DOLLAR COST AVERAGING.

AWAY FROM ME

Term used by a market maker to identify a quotation, transaction, or market in an issue that did not originate with the market maker. For example, in response to a customer enquiry, a trader may respond, "The bonds sold at par, away from me." Meaning: Someone else sold the bonds at par.

AWAY FROM THE BLUE

Jargon for an offering of municipal securities by a dealer who has not previously advertised it in the Blue List (book).

AWAY FROM THE MARKET

Term describing an order that cannot be executed because it contains a limit bid below, or a limit offer above, prevailing quotes for the security. For example, the quote for a security is 25 to 25-½. A limit order to buy at 24 is away from the market.

Unless the order stipulates immediate cancellation (e.g., fill or kill, or immediate or cancel), such orders are given to the specialist for later transaction if the limit can be met.

B

B
1 Used lowercase in stock tables to signify that dollar dividend is annual plus payment of stock dividend. For example, 2.45b.
2 Used lowercase in older option tables to signify option series not offered. Curent practice is to use an s.

BABY BOND

A bond with a face value of less than the usual $1,000. $100 and $500 are common face values of baby bonds.

BACKDATING
Mutual funds permitting a fundholder who did not originally sign a letter of intent to sign one with a prior date (up to 90 days) on it. This permits prior purchases, together with a present large purchase, to qualify for a reduced sales charge.

BACKING AWAY
Market maker fails to honor a firm bid for the minimum quantity. Action violates the Rules of Fair Practice of the National Association of Securities Dealers (NASD).

BACK OFFICE
Those departments of a broker-dealer organization that are not directly engaged in sales or trading activity.

Back office functions are cashiering, accounting, various communications, and the record keeping of the clients' cash or margin accounts.

BACKUP LINE
Line of credit by commercial bank to issuer of commercial paper if placement of the paper is slow or is difficult to accomplish.

BALANCED MUTUAL FUND
A management investment company that endeavors to minimize capital risk by investing in a portfolio with a varying percentage of bonds, preferred stocks, and common stocks.

BALANCE OF PAYMENTS
Difference in dollars between total payments made for goods and services imported from, and receipts for goods and services exported to, foreign countries. Often a gross figure or computed on a country-by-country basis.

BALANCE OF TRADE
Dollar difference between a country's merchandise imports and its exports. Differs from balance of payments in that it does not include money paid for services or funds spent by citizens of one country traveling in the other.

BALANCE SHEET
Simplified financial statement showing the nature and amount of a company's assets, liabilities, and net worth (shareholders' or stockholders' equity) on a given date.

BALLOON INTEREST
Feature of serial bond issue in which earlier years' coupons are lower than coupon interest rates for later serial maturities.

BALLOON MATURITY
Feature of serial bond issues in which dollar amounts of earlier maturities are smaller than dollar amounts of later maturities.

BANKER'S ACCEPTANCE
Time draft that becomes a money market instrument when payment is guaranteed; that is, accepted by a bank. Used extensively in international trade.

Manufacturer accepts a discounted amount from the bank for the goods; importer pays face amount. The discount becomes in effect the interest to the purchaser of the accepted time draft because the purchaser will receive the full face value at maturity. Most BAs mature within 9 months, although shorter maturities are common.

Also called BA, BAs.

BANK FOR COOPERATIVES
Supervised by Farm Credit Administration, a government-sponsored corporation, to make and service loans to agricultural cooperative associations.

BANK QUALITY
Refers to a debt security that has been assigned one of the top four credit ratings: AAA, AA, A, BBB.

Synonymous with bank grade.

See also LEGAL LIST.

BANKRUPTCY
Designates insolvency of corporation or individual.

BARRON'S CONFIDENCE INDEX
Weekly index prepared by the publishers of Barron's. Index compares yields of higher-grade to lower-grade corporate bonds. As yields on lower-grade bonds fall, it shows that investors are more confident about the economy. Used for an insight into possible market sentiment about equity securities.

BASE MARKET VALUE
Average value of traded securities at a certain time, used in construction of a market index. Movement is in terms of dollar change or percentage change from original base. For example, NYSE Index had an original base of 50.00 as of December 31, 1965.

BASIC

Acronym for Banking and Securities Industry Committee. Promotes standardization of securities operations and of certificate processing systems.

BASIS BOOK

Published by Financial Publishing Company of Boston, book contains coupon interest rates and time remaining to maturity. From these, one can compute yield to maturity given dollar price, or dollar price given yield to maturity.

BASIS POINT

By common agreement, .01% of yield on a fixed-income security. For example, if a bond's yield to maturity changed from 9.05% to 10.35%, there was a change of 130 basis points.

Also used with yield changes for securities sold at a discount from face value.

BASIS PRICE

1 Noun: Arbitrary price set by floor official that will be used to execute certain odd-lot orders.
2 Noun: Also used to designate a taxpayer's cost of acquisition for the computation of capital gains or losses.

BD FORM

Document that broker-dealers must file with SEC. Contains information about principals, net capital compliance, and financial statements about firm. Must be constantly updated.

BEARER FORMAT

Security is not registered in the name of the owner; instead, it is presumed to be the property of the holder, and transfer is completed by giving security to new owner.

Many older bonds were issued only in bearer format, although current trend is to issue bonds in registered format.

Many foreign equity securities are in bearer format; this gives rise to American Depository Receipts.

See also COUPON BOND and COUPON.

BEARISH

Having the opinion that securities will fall in market value. Used of persons or of general market conditions. For example: "Mr. Smith is bearish," or "The market is bearish."

The term may have arisen from an 18th-century slang expression on the London exchange, "To sell a bear (skin)." The implication was that the skin was sold before the bear was caught because the dealer thought the price would fall. In contemporary English slang, stock is often called a bear skin.

BEAR RAID
Manipulation of the price of a security by short selling at prices lower than previous transaction prices. When the price was sufficiently low, the manipulator profited by repurchasing the security sold short at a lower price.

The practice is now illegal. Current SEC rules require that short sales of exchange-traded securities be made at a price that is higher than the last different price in the security. In effect, short sellers may not depress the price of a security by their short sale.

BEAR SPREAD
Option strategy that combines a long and a short call, or a long and a short put. Called a bear spread because the call or put spread will become profitable if the underlying security declines in price.

For example: Client buys an October 50 call and sells an October 40 call when the underlying stock is at 44. The premium on the short call will be much more than the premium on the long call; this will give the client a net credit on the spread. If the underlying stock goes down in value, the value of the short call will also go down and the client will profit from the net credit received when the spread was put on.

Bearish put spreads also rely on a drop in the value of the underlying security but imply that the drop in value will cause the spread, put on at a debit, to increase in value. Thus, the client can take off the spread at a net profit.

BELL
Trading on the exchanges begins and ends with a recognized signal, often a bell.

See also AT THE CLOSE.

BELLWETHER
One who assumes a position of leadership. Said of a security or industry that seems to lead a market movement or economic trend.

BENEFICIAL OWNER
The person entitled to all benefits of ownership even though a broker or bank holds the security. For example, a fundholder leaves shares

of a mutual fund with the custodian bank, or a brokerage client leaves stock with his broker.

See also STREET NAME.

BENEFICIARY

Person who will receive the financial benefits of an asset, subject to certain conditions. Asset may be an insurance policy, an annuity, a trust, or other property.

BEST EFFORTS

Term used of an underwriting conducted on an agency basis. The distributor promises to do his best to sell the security but does not guarantee the sale by purchasing the security from the issuer. If the security is not sold, the underwriter receives no fee, but he has no further financial obligation to the issuer.

See also BOUGHT DEAL.

BETA

An analysis of price volatility of a security in terms of Standard & Poor's Index. The S&P Index is given a value of 1. Securities with a beta greater than 1 have in the past been more volatile than the S&P; those with a beta less than 1 have been less volatile. It is anticipated that this trend will continue, although the beta is subject to factual revision in terms of current comparisons of the security and the S&P Index.

BID

Price at which someone is willing here and now to purchase a security.

Synonymous with bid price.

See also QUOTE.

BID WANTED

Signifies that someone who is willing to sell securities wants someone else to give a price at which he is willing to buy. Bid need not be specific because seller is willing to negotiate the final price. Often used on published market quotation sheets.

Common abbreviation is BW.

BIG BOARD

The New York Stock Exchange.

BILLS

Short-term securities of the U.S. Treasury sold at a discount from their face value. Difference between purchase price and face value represents interest income if held to maturity.

Other governments also use bills for short-term financing.

Bill is synonymous with bills.

See also TREASURY BILL; TREASURY BILL AUCTION.

BLACK MARKET BONDS

Trading in SEC-registered bonds by dealers outside the offering syndicate between the effective date and the date pricing restrictions are removed from members of the account. Often detrimental to distribution efforts of the syndicate.

BLANKET CERTIFICATION FORM

NASD Form FR-1. Given by foreign brokers or dealers who purchase new-issue securities, which begin trading at an immediate premium, for their customers from NASD members. The form states that the foreign broker understands the NASD rules on hot issues and will abide by them.

See also HOT ISSUE.

BLANKET FIDELITY BOND

Insurance coverage required of brokers to protect firm against fraudulent trading, check and securities forgery, and security misplacement or loss. Minimum coverage is required by industry rules and varies with firm's SEC net capital requirement.

Synonymous with blanket bond.

BLANKET RECOMMENDATION

Securities recommendations made to all customers regardless of their financial capability and investment objectives.

BLOCK

A purchase or sale of a large number of shares or dollar value of bonds. Although term is relative, 10,000 or more shares, or any quantity worth over $200,000, is generally considered a block. The use of a block for bond purchases and sales varies with the user and with normal market round-lot practices.

BLOCK POSITIONER

A dealer who, to give liquidity to a seller, will take the opposite side of a trade. Block positioners must register with the SEC and, if members of the exchange, with the NYSE. Block positioners hope to profit by a rise in the value of the security, but they often offset a portion of their risk by arbitrage: the sale of calls or the purchase of puts.

Block positioners also sell securities to buyers of stocks or bonds. In many cases, they will sell short.

BLOWOUT
An offering of securities that is almost immediately sold out.
See also GOING AWAY and HOT ISSUE.

BLUE CHIP
A widely known company that is a leader in its industry and has a proven record of profits and a long history of dividend payment.

In poker playing and in casino play, the blue chip is usually the one with the highest value.

BLUE LIST
A list published each business day by Standard & Poor's that contains the par value, issuer, coupon rate, yield to maturity, and the dealers who make markets in municipal bonds. The Blue List also contains some corporate bond offerings and prerefunded municipal bonds offered by the same dealers.

Also called Blue Book.

BLUE ROOM
An ancillary trading room that is part of the New York Stock Exchange floor complex. Distinguished by its color, hence the name.

BLUE-SKYING
General term used for the qualification of securities for sale in any of the United States under their securities laws. Also used for the registration of broker-dealers or their agent.

The expression blue sky means lacking in substance (e.g., right out of the blue—having no worth). These state laws provide that new securities issuers qualify by providing information about the issue and the issuer so buyers may judge the issue's value.

Generally, issues senior to securities already blue-skied (or a further issuance of securities already listed on a national exchange) are exempt from blue-sky procedures. Legal advice is needed.

See also UNIFORM SECURITIES AGENT STATE LAW EXAMINATION.

BOARD BROKER
An employee of the Chicago Board Option Exchange who makes a memorandum of option orders that are away from the market and

thus not capable of execution at the present time. The board broker may execute orders on an agency basis, and if this is done, the board broker notifies the member who entered the order.

See also ORDER BOOK OFFICIAL.

BOARD OF ARBITRATION

The arbitrators who are chosen to decide a controversy in the securities industry. Three or five members from the board hear individual cases requiring arbitration.

See also ARBITRATION and CODE OF ARBITRATION.

BOARD OF DIRECTORS

The group of persons, elected by vote of the stockholders, who make important management decisions and who elect the officers of a corporation. Members of the board of directors are control persons under the securities laws of the United States, and the securities they own are restricted.

Frequently abbreviated BD.

Often used interchangeably with board of governors for governing body of exchanges and associations of broker-dealers.

BOARD OF GOVERNORS

1 Chief elective body of the National Association of Securities Dealers.
2 Board of Governors of the Federal Reserve System.

BOILER ROOM

Place where brokers, often illicitly, conduct high pressure—hence the name—telephone sales campaigns for highly speculative securities.

BONA FIDE ARBITRAGE

An arbitrage in good faith; that is, offsetting buy and sell transactions that have a built-in profit.

BOND

1 Any debt security, such as an IOU or a corporation promissory note.
2 A debt security with a maturity of more than 7 to 10 years. Used in distinction to note, a debt security with a shorter time to maturity. Often an issuer will describe a debt security as a bond that other issuers would call a note.
3 Money or property depositied as a pledge of good faith.
4 Usually, bonds are secured by a mortgage.
5 One's word given as a pledge of future performance. For example, "My word is my bond."

BOND ANTICIPATION NOTE
Short-term municipal note used as interim financing. Principal and interest on the BAN will be repaid from the proceeds of a forthcoming bond issue.

BOND BROKER
1 Brokers who transact bond orders on the floor of the exchanges.
2 Brokers in the over-the-counter corporate municipal or U.S. Treasury bond markets who do agency transactions for market makers and institutional clients.

BOND BUYERS INDEX
An index that measures yield levels of municipal bonds. The index contains two measurements of yield. The 20-bond index contains bonds that have an average rating of A+; the 11-bond index contains bonds that have a rating of AA. Each index is of newly issued municipal bonds selling at par. Both the trend of yields and the spread between the two indices gives dealers, underwriters, and institutional buyers an insight into interest rate trends and their accompanying market risk. The index also contains the aftertax yield of 20-year government bonds as a measure of comparative yield.

BOND POWER
A separate form for an owner's assignment and power of substitution which, when signed, transfers ownership of a registered bond to a new owner.

BOND RATIO
A measurement of a corporation's leverage. The ratio is found by dividing the total of a corporation's bonds with more than one year to maturity by the total of those bonds plus the stockholders' equity. For example, if the total of bonds is $10 million, and the stockholders' equity is $30 million, the bond ratio is:

$$\frac{\$10 \text{ million (bonds)}}{\$40 \text{ million (bonds + equity)}}$$

Except for utilities, where higher bond ratios are usual, bond ratios in excess of 33% are considered highly leveraged.
See also LEVERAGE.

BOOK
1 The record of either indications of interest for a proposed underwriting or the record of the syndicate activity of the members of an underwriting account. For example, ABC Brokerage is managing the book.
2 See also SPECIALIST'S BOOK.

BOOK VALUE

Take total assets minus intangibles, subtract all liabilities and the par value of preferred stock. Divide by the number of outstanding common shares. Quotient is the book value.

Although book value can be a deceptive measurement, it is used by many to make a gross selection of common shares that may be underpriced. Book value should not be an ultimate criterion for security selection.

Also called the net tangible value or the liquidating value per common share.

BOSTON STOCK EXCHANGE

A regional securities exchange organized to facilitate trading in New England firms' securities as well as in many securities listed on the stock exchanges in New York City.

The acronym is BSE.

BOT

BOT is often used to abbreviate bought.
See also BALANCE OF TRADE.

BOUGHT DEAL

Synonym for a firm commitment underwriting in which the syndicate (the group of underwriters) guarantees performance by buying the securities from the issuer.

The expression implies financial risk for the syndicate. Underwritings that do not imply financial risk are called best efforts.

BOX

Industry term for the physical location of securities in safekeeping. Because of federal and industry rules on safekeeping and segregation of customer securities, there are many boxes. Some boxes are eligible for stock loans or for repledging to a bank to finance customer margin accounts.

Also called stock box.
See also HYPOTHECATION and REHYPOTHECATION.

BRANCH OFFICE MANAGER

A person in charge of one or more of a member firm's branch offices. Such persons must pass a special exchange examination. Exchange rules also require that persons who actually supervise the sales activities of three or more registered representatives, or who have compliance responsibilities within their organization, must pass the BOM examination.

BREADTH OF THE MARKET

A comparison of the number of issues traded with the number of issues listed for trading. For example, if 2,000 issues are listed and 1,600 are traded on a given day, the breadth of the market is 80%. Market trends are considered to be corroborated only if there is a reasonable breadth of the market.

BREADTH OF THE MARKET INDEX

A measurement of the number of issues advancing versus the number of issues declining on a given day or as a moving average.

Many measurements are used: advances divided by declines, as a percentage; advances minus declines, as a net positive or negative number. The measurement, consistently followed, is an insight into investor sentiment and is used extensively by market analysts.

Also called Advance Decline Index.

BREAK

1 Bookkeeping imbalance either within a brokerage firm or between two brokers.
2 Sudden, significant price decline of a security.
3 Sudden good fortune.

BREAK EVEN

A transaction in which the income received equals the expenditures made.

BREAK-EVEN POINT

Dollar value at which transaction will neither gain nor lose. Generally computed on gross prices without commissions, although accuracy requires that adjusted cost of acquisition be compared to net proceeds of sale.

See also BREAK-EVEN POINT ON OPTIONS.

BREAK-EVEN POINT ON OPTIONS

1 Long call break even is strike (or exercise) price plus premium.
2 Long put break even is strike price minus premium.
3 Short uncovered call break even is strike price plus premium.
4 Short covered call break even is purchase price minus premium.
5 Short put break even, if covered by short stock, is price at which underlying stock was shorted plus premium.
6 Short uncovered put break even is strike price minus premium.

BREAKING THE SYNDICATE
Termination of the agreement among underwriters (a syndicate) for a specific offering of securities. Members are then free to dispose of unsold securities and are no longer bound by restrictive price agreements.

BREAKOUT
Price of a security emerging from a previous trading pattern. The new price "breaks out" above the high (or below the low) trading pattern lines that enclose all other prices for that security in the preceding period. Breakouts are used by technical analysts to predict substantial upside or downside movement.
See also TRADING PATTERN.

BREAKPOINT
Dollar level of purchases, either lump sum or by accumulation, which qualifies mutual fund holder for reduced percentage sales charge.
See also LETTER OF INTENT and RIGHT OF ACCUMULATION.

BREAKPOINT SALES
Unethical practice. Soliciting mutual fund purchases in dollar amounts that are slightly below eligibility for reduced sales charge. Sales within $1,000 of breakpoint may be considered breakpoint sales.

BRIDGE LOAN
Short-term financing provided while borrower seeks longer-term loan.

BROAD TAPE
Common name for a subscription news service that provides timely financial information. So called because tape provides detailed information, as opposed to narrow tapes of stock exchange transactions.
Often used for Dow Jones tape, although expression may include Reuters, Munifacts, Associated Press, or United Press International.

BROKER
Person or firm acting as intermediary between buyer and seller.
See also AGENT.

BROKER LOAN

Short-term secured loan made by broker from commercial bank to finance customer security positions.

The expression also is used of loans made by a bank to specialists or to broker-dealers to carry proprietary accounts.

See also CALL LOAN and REHYPOTHECATION.

BUCKET SHOP

An establishment whose brokers accept customer orders but who does not immediately execute them. Later, the order is executed at a price that is advantageous to the broker but is confirmed to the customer at the earlier prevailing price. Practice is illegal under Securities Exchange Act of 1934 and is forbidden by industry regulations.

BULK SEGREGATION

Customer-owned securities held in street name but kept separate from firm-owned securities. Securities are not individually registered in name of customer nor otherwise identified as belonging to individual person.

BULLISH

Used of persons or of the market. State of believing that price will rise or will continue to rise. For example: "We feel that the market will turn bullish within the next two months," which means "we" think there is an advancing market.

BULL SPREAD

General name for an option strategy whereby a customer who owns a class of option (a call or a put) writes an option of the same class and will profit if the underlying stock goes up in market value.

For example, a client owns a Monsanto 50 call. He sells a Monsanto 60 call when Monsanto is selling at 53. Provided the short call does not expire after the long call, he will profit if Monsanto rises in market value. Reason: The value of the long call will tend to rise faster than the value of the short call because the long call is in the money and the short call is not. Yet, even if both calls go in the money, the client can exercise the long call at a profit that represents the difference between the strike prices minus the net debit paid by the client when the spread was put on. If the stock drops in value, the client's loss is limited to the debit incurred when he bought the call and sold the higher-priced call.

Put spread can also be bullish; that is, the client will profit if the stock rises.

For example, a client owns an IBM 70 put and sells an IBM 75 put when IBM is at 71. Provided IBM goes up in value, the maximum gain is the net premium received when the client bought the lower priced put and sold the higher priced put. His maximum loss is the difference between the strike prices minus the premium received.

BUNCHING
1 Combining round-lot orders for convenience in executing them on the floor.
2 Combining odd-lot orders, with permission of customers, to save odd-lot differential.

BUSINESS CONDUCT COMMITTEE
Organized under National Association of Securities Dealers rules in each of 13 districts. Acts as court of first instance for trade practice complaints made under Code of Procedure. Determines facts and imposes discipline. Decisions may be appealed to Board of Governors of NASD.

Also called District Business Conduct Committee.

BUSINESS CYCLE
1 Term used of time from top of one rise in gross national product through one fall in GNP back to original base line. In past, business cycles have tended to average about 2-½ years.
2 Time it takes a manufacturing company to turn raw materials into sold finished products.

BUSINESS DAY
Day on which the principal securities marketplaces are open for trading.

See also REGULAR WAY TRANSACTION.

BUTTERFLY SPREAD
Option strategy. Client sells two calls, then buys two calls, one with strike (exercise) price higher and one with a strike price lower than short calls. Client is partially hedged in either direction and hopes to profit from call premium received and restricted movement of underlying stock.

BUY
As noun, a synonym for bargain. For example, "It's a buy." Also used as an adjective. For example, "It's a buy situation."

BUY IN

Follows a failure by seller to deliver securities. Broker must buy in to obtain the securities which the contra party did not deliver in accord with industry rules. Term used of broker-to-broker transactions. Industry rules set times for buy in procedures.

See also CONTRA BROKER.

BUYING CLIMAX

A sudden upward movement in the market value of a security characterized by a gap in the prices between one trading session and the following. Used in technical analysis, and often considered an indication that a security has been overbought and price will fall.

BUYING POWER

Used for general margin accounts. The dollar value of securities that may be purchased in terms of the special miscellaneous account entry without generating a margin call. If marginable equity securities are purchased, buying power is two times the SMA entry under Federal Reserve rules in effect in 1982. For example, client has SMA entry of $1,000. Client may buy marginable securities worth $2,000 without generating a margin call. If a security is not eligible for margin purchase, the special miscellaneous account entry may be used on a dollar-for-dollar basis.

BUY-IN PROCEDURE

The buyer's remedy if the selling broker-dealer fails to deliver the purchased security. Two business days after giving written notice of intent to the delinquent seller, the buyer may purchase the promised amount of that security in the market and hold the delinquent seller responsible for any loss that may be incurred.

Also called close-out.

See also SELL-OUT PROCEDURE.

BUY MINUS

Instruction from buyer to purchase only on dips in market price, or at last previous price if that is lower than previous different price.

See also MINUS TICK; DOWNTICK; ZERO-MINUS TICK.

BUY STOP ORDER

Customer instruction on a buy order to broker, or specialist, on the floor of an exchange. If the market price touches this price, or if there is a transaction above this price, the broker is to execute a market order at the best available price. For example: BUY 500 LMN 52 STOP. The customer is giving the following instruction: if there is a transaction at 52 or above, immediately buy 500 LMN at the best available price. The transaction at 52 or above is said to elect, activate, or trigger the stop and thus turn it into a market order to buy.

BUY THE BOOK
Instruction from trader or institutional account to buy all shares available from specialist's book at current offer price. Trades also will be made with other members in the crowd who are willing to sell at that price.

C

CA
Abbreviation often used in bond tables and in offering sheets for callable.

CABINET CROWD
Term for members of the New York Stock Exchange who trade in inactive bonds (those that are seldom traded). The term derives from the practice of filing all orders for such bonds on cards in metal racks called cabinets. Orders are removed only if canceled or if a contra party is willing to accept the stated bid or offer.
See also ACTIVE BOND CROWD.

CABINET SECURITY
Exchange-trade securities that do not have an active market, principally stocks that trade in 10-share units and many inactively traded bonds. Name arises from practice of placing orders, according to buy-sell and limit prices, on small cards in assigned places in metal cabinets on the floor of the exchange. Orders remain in cabinets until broker who entered them removes them from cabinet, or contra broker accepts bid or offer.

CAGE
The cashiering function of a member firm or of one of its branch offices.

CALENDAR
Industry term for list of upcoming securities offerings. Usually preceded by type of security. For example, municipal calendar, corporate bond calendar.

CALENDAR SPREAD

Option spread endeavoring to profit from the purchase of an option in a farther month and from the sale of an option of the same class in a nearer month. For example, buy October 50 call, sell closer July 50 call; or buy October 45 put, sell closer July 45 put.

Called horizontal spread if strike (exercise) prices are the same. Called diagonal spread if strike prices are different.

Calendar spreads are bullish if investor will profit from upward movement of underlying stock; bearish if investor will profit from downward movement of stock.

CALL

1 Verb: The action whereby a company elects to redeem a security prior to its maturity date.
2 Noun: An option to buy a stated number of shares of a security at a stated price on or before a specified date.

CALLABLE

Security which, at option of the issuer, may be redeemed prior to maturity for bonds or be repurchased by issuer if security is preferred stock. Early call often requires issuer to repurchase security at a premium above par value.

See also CALL PREMIUM; CALLABLE BOND.

CALLABLE BOND

Bond that may be called by issuer on or after a specified date.

CALLED AWAY

1 A security that is called by the issuer from a client's account.
2 A security that a client must deliver because a short call is exercised against a client's account.

CALL FEATURE

Bonds accompanied by call date and redemption price. For example, ABC 9% bonds have a call feature on February 1, 1985, at 105.

CALL LOAN

Loan made by broker, upon deposit of appropriate collateral, to finance margin activities of customers. Loan is callable at any time by either party.

Also called broker loan, or broker's collateral loan.

See also BROKER LOAN; REHYPOTHECATION.

CALL LOAN RATE

Interest rate charged by banks for call loans. Often used as base for minimum margin interest charge.

Also termed call money rate.

See also TRUTH IN LENDING LAW.

CALL OPTION

Privilege given to holder of option to purchase a specified number of shares, or dollar face value of bonds, at a specified price on or before expiration date of option. Option comes into being when buyer, or holder, and writer, or seller, agree upon a premium for the privilege.

See also CALL; PREMIUM; EXPIRATION; STRIKE PRICE.

CALL PREMIUM

1   Dollars, or points, paid by issuer if preferred stock or bonds are redeemed at option of issuer prior to maturity.
2   Dollars per share paid by buyer of an option for privilege of buying a call for a specified number of shares at a specified price on or before expiration date.

The premium paid for selling a put for a specified number of shares at a specified price by a certain date is known as a put premium.

See also INTRINSIC VALUE and TIME VALUE.

CALL PRICE

Money a corporation must pay to redeem its senior securities. For bonds, the call price usually is a percentage of par value. For preferred stock, the call price is the dollar price per share.

CALL PROTECTION

Time between original issue date of security and earliest date when issuer may exercise right to redeem security prior to original maturity date.

Also called cushion.

CANCEL

Instruction to void a prior order to buy or sell, or price, or amount. May or may not be accompanied by new instruction.

CAN CROWD

Slang expression for bond brokers who trade cabinet securities.

See also CABINET SECURITY.

CAPITAL GAIN

Securities transaction in which the proceeds of the sale exceed the adjusted cost of acquisition. May arise from prior purchase and subsequent sale, or prior sale and subsequent purchase (short sale), or sale of a gifted security above the basis price, or sale of a security received from a bequest at a price above fair market value established by administrator or executor.

See also CAPITAL LOSS; LONG TERM; SHORT TERM.

CAPITALIZATION

General term for sources of a company's funds that are evidenced by either longer-term bonds or stock. Current liabilities (in which bonds that will mature in one year or less are numbered) are excluded from capitalization. In addition to the par value of outstanding preferred and common stock, paid-in surplus and retained earnings are included in capitalization.

See also CAPITALIZATION RATIO.

CAPITALIZATION RATIO

Measurement of longer-term sources of funds used by a corporation in terms of funded debt (bonds), preferred stock, and common stock.

Normally stated as a percentage. For example, company has longer-term debt of $10, preferred stock of $5, and common stock of $35 (including surplus). Total capital $50. Bond ratio is 20%, preferred stock ratio 10%, common stock ratio 70%.

See also DEBT-TO-EQUITY RATIO; LEVERAGE.

CAPITAL LOSS

Securities transaction in which proceeds of sale is less than adjusted cost of acquisition.

CAPITAL STOCK

Term often used of all sources of equity capital for a corporation. Common usage: synonym for common stock. For example, American Telephone and Telegraph issues capital stock but everyone will call them common shares.

Also called capital shares.

See also COMMON STOCK.

CAPITAL SURPLUS

Dollar amount by which price paid by original purchaser exceeds par value of securities. For example, issuer sells stock at $15 that has a par value of $5. The $5 is entered in common stock account on balance sheet, and $10 is entered in capital surplus account. Same principle used if company sells stock reacquired and held in the treasury above par value.

Also called paid-in capital.

CARRYOVER
Provision of tax law of United States that permits individual taxpayer, who sustains net capital loss in excess of annual deduction of $3,000 against income, to carry over the remainder into the subsequent tax years until it is offset against either capital gains or income.

CASH BASIS
1 Accounting method that credits money only as it is received.
2 Optional method allowed to holders of Series EE savings bonds. Holder may elect to pay tax on increased redemption value only when it is received at redemption. For example, client buys Series EE bond at 50% of face value and bond will mature in eight years. Client may elect to pay tax on 6.25% of face value each year or pay tax on 50% of the face value when bond matures.

CASH FLOW
Acccpted measurement is earnings after interest and taxes, and preferred dividend if applicable, to which the annual depreciation charge for fixed assets is added.

The cash flow measurement is indicative of the earning power of a company, but can be deceptive. Many recent articles in scholarly journals dispute accepted measurement standards.

Cash flow is calculated as follows: company has annual aftertax earnings of $50 million. Company also had depreciation charge of $5 million and preferred stock dividend of $2 million. Cash flow is:

$50,000,000	
− 2,000,000	For preferred dividend
$48,000,000	For common stockholders
+ 5,000,000	Depreciation
$53,000,000	Cash flow

CASHIERING DEPARTMENT
Function within a broker-dealer organization that is responsible for the physical handling of securities and maintenance of inter-broker records.

This department also handles receive and deliver functions, transfer responsibilities, dividend and interest records, the vault and its safekeeping function, proxy statements and proxy reports, reorganization, and all other responsibilities that center on broker-customer and broker-broker financial relationships.

CASH ON DELIVERY

Used typically on buy orders entered by institutional investors, many of whom are prohibited from delivering cash unless an asset is received in its place. For example, if I give you $1 million you must give me something worth $1 million.

Also called delivery against cash (DAC).

CASH RATIO

Measurement of a corporation's liquidity. Compares cash and marketable securities to current liabilities. Indicator of company's ability to meet immediate claims of creditors.

See also ACID-TEST RATIO; CURRENT RATIO; NET CURRENT ASSETS.

CASH TRANSACTION

Securities transaction, usually negotiated, that settles on the same day as the trade. Cash transactions are frequent in Treasury bill market but uncommon in other markets where regular way transactions prevail.

Also called cash sale.

CENTRAL BANK

Bank organized for benefit of government of a country. Issues currency and administers monetary policy. U.S. counterpart is the Federal Reserve System.

CENTRAL REGISTRATION DEPOSITORY

Computerized record-keeping system for registrations of representatives and broker-dealer principals and agents under state securities laws. Greatly simplifies paperwork because multiple filings are not required if applicant is to be registered with many authorities.

CERTIFICATE

Evidence of security ownership. In most cases, the evidence is a piece of paper, properly inscribed, that states the name of the issuer and the conditions under which the issue was made. Generally, the certificate is fully transferable. In recent years, there has been an increasing trend to book-entry security ownership; that is, the evidence of ownership is kept on the books of the issuer and transfer is made by offsetting journal entries. For example, security options, and many issues of Treasury bills, notes, bonds, and agency securities.

CERTIFICATE OF BENEFICIAL INTEREST

Used instead of term common stock to designate equity security that is nonvoting and where underlying assets of a corporation are debt securities of other corporations or issuers. For example, a company, whose principal assets are mortgages, issues shares representing a pro rata ownership of these debt securities. Such shares could be called CBI.

Also called SBI, share of beneficial interest.

CERTIFICATE OF DEPOSIT
Debt instrument issued by commercial bank. Promises to pay principal and fixed rate of interest at maturity, normally one year or less. Amounts of $100,000 or more with 30 or more days to maturity are exempt from interest ceiling imposed by Regulation Q of Federal Reserve and are negotiable and actively traded in money market.

CHARTER
Common term for certificate of incorporation, a state-validated document giving legal status to a corporation.

Also called certificate of incorporation.

CHARTIST
Market technician who makes buy-sell decisions based on plotted price movements of a security.

See also POINT AND FIGURE CHART.

CHECKING THE MARKET
Canvassing market makers to determine best bid or offer for a security. May be done by telephone, telex, or other electronic media.

CHECK KITING
Issuing a check without sufficient funds in the account, in the hope of depositing money into the account before the first check is presented for payment.

CHICAGO BOARD OF TRADE
Nation's largest exchange for trading of futures contracts. Well known for grains and metals futures, CBT also trade futures in fixed income securities and currencies. Parent organization of Chicago Board Options Exchange (CBOE).

CHICAGO BOARD OPTIONS EXCHANGE
Nation's first and largest organized marketplace for the exchange trading of specific put and call options.

CHICAGO MERCANTILE EXCHANGE
Second largest commodities exchange. Specializes in futures in poultry, eggs, live cattle, and other agricultural commodities. Parent of International Monetary Market, specializing in currency futures.

CHURNING

Excessive trading in an account, with connotation that buy-sell activities are against financial interests of customer. Unethical activity and often actionable at law by offended party. Courts judge degree of control over the account, broker profits versus customer profits, and turnover of original capital to decide if churning has occurred.

CINCINNATI STOCK EXCHANGE

The nation's first fully automated stock exchange. Transactions are arranged by members via the computer facilities of Control Data Corporation without benefit of a physical trading floor in a central location.

Abbreviated CSE.

CIRCLE

Industry term for indications of interest taken while security is in registration. Registered representative makes list of potential clients for new issue and circles those who are interested.

CLASS

1 Used of securities with similar features. For example, bonds are a class of security.
2 Used of options with similar features. For example, all calls of an underlying security are one class, all puts are another class. Definition is important because option position and exercise limits generally are determined by class.

CLEAN

Term used by block positioners if they are able to match buy-and-sell orders from customers without the need to take the security into inventory. For example, "We did a clean trade for 50,000 ABC." In other words, they had a seller of 50,000 and found a buyer without taking inventory risk.

Clean on the tape is often used if the transaction appears on an exchange tape.

The term natural is often used as a synonym for clean. For example, "We did a natural for 50,000 ABC."

CLEAR

1 Comparison and verification of details of a securities trade as preparation for final settlement.
2 Performance of clearing function for another brokerage firm. For example, ABC clears for XYZ.

CLEARING HOUSE FUNDS

Monies represented by a personal or a corporate check that must go through local or regional bank clearing function before an account credit is given to payee. Used in distinction to federal funds, which are immediately usable by payee. Most securities transactions outside of money market are payable in clearing house funds.

See also FEDERAL FUNDS.

CLIFFORD TRUST

Temporary inter vivos trust (between living persons). Assets are pledged for 10 or more years. Income from assets is paid to a specified party. At end of trust, assets revert to grantor. IRS considers income a gift to recipient, so legal advice is needed.

See also INTER VIVOS TRUST.

CLOSE

1 Final transaction in listed security on a business day.
2 Next-to-last column in financial report of stock and bond transactions. Final transaction price given.
3 Last 30 seconds of market trading. Time is marked by continuous ringing of bell on NYSE and ASE.
4 As verb: transfer of money and securities following an underwriting. For example, "They close the deal on Tuesday."

CLOSE A POSITION

To remove the risk inherent in an investment by making an offsetting transaction that gives the client no further risk or options. For example, a client owns 500 shares of ABC. The client is at risk if ABC declines in value. The client sells 500 ABC and delivers the shares to the new owner. The client has closed the position and has no further risk. Offsetting transactions that exclude risk but leave other optional decisions open (e.g., a short against the box) are not considered as closing a position.

CLOSED-END MANAGEMENT COMPANY

Management investment company that issues a fixed number of shares. Generally, shares are not redeemable at option of shareholder. Redemption, therefore, takes place through secondary market transactions. Most closed-end management company shares are listed for trading on exchanges.

CLOSED-END MORTGAGE

Provision of indenture of mortgage bond that prohibits issuing corporation from repledging same collateral without permission of first mortgage holders who have the prior claim on pledged assets in the event of default.

CLOSELY HELD
Term refers to a company whose common stock is predominantly held by a few owners, but there are sufficient shares held by others to form a base for secondary market trading. If this latter case is not true, the company is said to be privately held.

See also FLOAT.

CLOSING PURCHASE
Writer of an option makes a purchase of same series, thereby giving the writer a net zero position. For example, writer of five XYZ April 45 calls subsequently buys five XYZ April 45 calls.

CLOSING QUOTE
Market maker's or specialist's final bid and offer at time trading ceases on a particular trading day.

CMV
Frequently used abbreviation for current market value in ledger displays of margin accounts.

CODE OF ARBITRATION
National Association of Securities Dealers' rules for submission and arbitration of controversies involving money or securities transactions between members or members and customers.

See also ARBITRATION and BOARD OF ARBITRATION.

CODE OF PROCEDURE
National Association of Securities Dealers' rules for the adjudication of trade practice complaints in violation of the Rules of Fair Practice.

COD TRANSACTION
Frequently used designation on institutional client buy orders. Broker buys for client's account and will deliver to client's agent. Upon delivery, agent will pay for cost of purchase.

Also called DVP, deliver versus payment, and DAC, deliver against cost.

COINCIDENT INDICATOR
A measurement of economic or financial activity that tends to move in the same direction and at the same time as the gross national product (GNP).

COLLATERAL

An asset pledged by a borrower to a lender. If there is a default, the collateral may be taken or sold by the lender to repay the loan.

COLLATERALIZE

To put up an asset as a pledge that a loan will be repaid. For example, to collateralize a margin loan by the deposit of stock with the broker.

COLLATERAL TRUST BOND

Corporate debt security which pledges a portfolio of securities, usually held in trust by a bank, as protection for the purchasers of the bond. Securities may be those of subsidiaries or of other corporations and may be either debt or equity securities.

Also called collateral trust certificate.

COLLECTION RATIO

Number of days it takes a corporation to turn a dollar entered under accounts receivable into a dollar entered under cash.

Formula: divide accounts receivable by average daily sales. For example, if accounts receivable entry is $1,500,000 and average daily sales are $50,000, collection ratio is 30. It takes this company an average of 30 days to turn a sale dollar into a cash dollar.

COMBINATION

Long call and long put, or short call and short put, on same underlying security having different expiration months or different strike prices. For example, buy XYZ April 50 call, buy XYZ July 45 put. Order ticket will give the net debit, on long combination, or the net credit, on short combination, that is acceptable to customer. Order will be executed only if conditions can be met.

COMEX

A commodity exchange in New York City. Formed by merger of four prior exchanges, Comex trades futures in metals, petroleum, coffee, sugar, and financial instruments.

COMMERCIAL PAPER

Unsecured promissory notes of corporations, issued to provide short-term financing, sold at a discount and redeemed at face value. Exempt from registration if maturity is 270 days or less. Highly competitive with other money market instruments.

COMMINGLING
Using customer securities in same loan agreement with member firm securities. Prohibited by federal law and by industry regulations.
See also SEGREGATE.

COMMISSION
Fee charged by a broker for buying or selling securities or property for the account of a customer.

COMMITTEE ON UNIFORM SECURITIES IDENTIFICATION PROCEDURES
Its numbering system—9 characters, 7 numbers, and 2 letters—permits a standardized computer identification of any security issued in the United States after 1970. For example, the CUSIP number 4375542AF applies only to the XYZ 5-½% bonds that will mature in 1994. CUSIP identifiers for stocks have 9 numbers.
Also called CUSIP number.

COMMODITIES FUTURES TRADING COMMISSION
Federal regulator of commodities exchanges and futures trading, headquartered in the District of Columbia.

COMMON STOCK
Class of ownership, or equity, security with residual claims on assets of corporation after claims of bondholders, other creditors, and preferred stockholders are settled. Charter of corporation defines the rights of common stockholders. Generally, common stockholders control management and company policy through voting rights.

COMMON STOCK EQUIVALENT
Name given to securities that may, with or without the addition of money, be exchanged for common stock. Convertibles, rights, warrants, and long calls are typical common stock equivalents, but only under certain conditions.

COMMON STOCK RATIO
That percentage of a corporation's relatively permanent capital that comes from common stock, paid-in surplus, and retained earnings. Bond ratio, preferred stock ratio, and common stock ratio total 100%.

COMPARISON
Notice exchanged between brokers who are parties to a trade to verify and confirm details of the trade prior to settlement.

Also called comparison sheet.

See also DK.

COMPETITIVE BID

Price and terms offered to an issuer by an underwriter. Issuer will award securities to underwriting syndicate that provides highest bid or most advantageous terms, in accord with prearranged conditions for the award. Many municipal, utility, and railroad securities offerings are competitive.

COMPETITIVE TRADER

A member of an exchange who trades in stocks on the floor for an account in which he has an interest.

Also known as a registered trader or floor trader.

COMPLIANCE REGISTERED OPTIONS PRINCIPAL

Person registered as options principal who is responsible for a firm's compliance with options rules and regulations. Must make periodic reports and suggestions to senior management following periodic audits of option transactions and their supervision. Generally, a CROP may not have any sales functions.

CONCESSION

1   Corporate underwritings: dollar remuneration per share or per bond given to members of selling group who successfully market the securities.
2   Municipal underwritings: dollar discount from public offering price. Given to members of the Municipal Securities Rulemaking Board (MSRB) who are not members of the account if they purchase bonds for their own or the accounts of customers.

CONDUIT THEORY

Nickname for IRS treatment of income received by qualified investment organizations, principally regulated investment companies. Interest and dividends received, as well as net capital gains, are passed along to investors for their personal tax liability without subjecting the investment company to federal and local taxation. Hence, term conduit or pipeline.

CONSENT TO SERVICE

Legal document authorizing someone to act as attorney to accept orders of any lawful process or proceeding brought against person who signs the document. Filing of consent to service is required with each application for registration as broker dealer or agent under Uniform Security Agent rules.

See also BLUE-SKYING.

CONSOLIDATED MORTGAGE BOND

Term bond with a single coupon rate of interest issued to obtain funds to refund previously issued mortgage bonds at different interest rates and maturities.

CONSOLIDATED TAPE

Process whereby all transactions in listed stocks, whether made on principal exchange, other exchanges, or in OTC market, are reported on the tape of the principal exchange. At present there are two networks: Network A for NYSE issues, Network B for ASE issues. Process is sponsored by Consolidated Tape Association, made up by exchanges and the National Association of Securities Dealers (NASD).

CONSTANT DOLLAR PLAN

Method of formula investing. Client determines number of dollars in stocks and number in bonds in a fully invested portfolio. At stated periodic intervals, buy-sell action in either portfolio will bring accounts back to prestated dollar level.

Called constant ratio plan if percentages rather than dollar amounts are used.

CONSUMER PRICE INDEX

Government-sponsored index of change in prices for consumer goods and services over time. Components include foods and beverages, transportation, housing, medical care, and entertainment. Uses preestablished base of 100; thus, changes are in percentages up or down. Also used as measurement of inflation or disinflation. Many labor contracts and changes in social security payments are based on changes in CPI.

CONTINGENT ORDER

Order for the purchase or sale of a security and the sale or purchase of another if the swap can be made at a stipulated price difference.

See also SWAP.

CONTINUOUS NET SETTLEMENT

Prevalent method of clearing and settling securities transactions. National Securities Clearing Corporation interposes itself between brokers, thereby establishing a securities balance account. Broker's balance account is adjusted upward or downward each day, depending on whether the firm was a net buyer or seller on that day. Money balances are adjusted similarly, and shares or funds can be withdrawn according to net balance.

Opposite: window settlement whereby seller delivers securities to buyer and receives payment.

CONTRA BROKER

Broker on the other side of the transaction. Thus, buying broker has selling broker as contra broker.

Also spelled as one word.

CONTRACT SHEET

Prepared daily by Securities Industry Automation Corporation (SIAC) from information given by brokers and contra brokers. Brokers compare their transaction records to prepare for settlement. Items not in agreement with records are DKd, slang for don't know, or marked QT, questioned trade. Discrepancies are usually resolved quickly so settlement may be made on proper day.

CONTRACTUAL PLAN

Method of periodic accumulation of mutual fund shares through the use of a plan company or a participating unit investment trust. Client agrees to purchase a fixed dollar amount of the fund by periodic investments over a 10-year or 15-year period. In return, client receives certain plan features and often receives decreasing term life insurance as part of program of financial planning.

Also called prepaid plans.

See also FRONT-END LOAD; LOAD SPREAD OPTION; PLAN COMPLETION INSURANCE; PLAN COMPANY.

CONTROLLER

In brokerage firms, officer responsible for preparing firm and customer financial reports, compliance with SEC net capital rules, and internal auditing function.

CONTROL PERSON

Generic term for someone who can influence corporate decisions. Control can arise from voting power, because person owns 10% or more of corporation's voting shares, or because person is director or elected officer of corporation.

Also called affiliated person in certain contexts.

See also CONTROL STOCK.

CONTROL STOCK

Voting shares owned by a control person. Shares may have been acquired by private purchase, purchase in the public marketplace, or by bequest or gift. Concept usually applies to the aggregate shares held by family members.

See also CONTROL PERSON.

CONVENTIONAL OPTION

Put or call contract negotiated outside a listed option marketplace. Because of limited secondary market, few conventional options are negotiated.

CONVERSION

1 Feature permitting owners of certain bonds and preferred stock to exchange these securities for a fixed number of common shares.
2 Feature of many mutual funds whereby owners of one fund may exchange shares for shares of other funds under same management without additional sales charges.
3 Illegal use of assets held in trust for another for one's personal advantage.

See also CONVERSION RATIO and FAMILY OF FUNDS.

CONVERSION PARITY

Mathematical statement of equality between value of underlying common stock and theoretical value of convertible security. For example, if a bond is convertible into 40 shares of common stock and stock has market value of $22 per share, conversion parity is $880; that is, 40 times $22.

See also CONVERSION PREMIUM and CONVERSION RATIO.

CONVERSION PREMIUM

Dollars in excess of market price of a convertible security over conversion parity. May also be stated as a percent. For example, convertible bond is selling at $990. Conversion parity is $880. Premium is $110, $990 minus $880. Or, premium is 12.5%, $110 divided by $880.

Percent of conversion premium provides critical insight into risk of ownership of convertibles. Low premium centers risk on changes in market value of underlying common stock; high premium centers risk on convertible as a fixed income security.

CONVERSION PRICE

Fixed dollar value often used by corporation to state conversion ratio of convertible securities. For example, a bond is convertible into common shares at $40 per share. Thus, conversion ratio is par value, $1,000, divided by $40, or 25 shares.

Conversion price is theoretical and presumes convertible selling at par. Conversion feature goes with security, and convertible may be exchanged for common stock at option of holder.

As a general rule, if company splits stock or pays a stock dividend, the conversion price will change because convertible will be exchangeable for a larger number of shares.

CONVERSION RATIO

Statement of the relationship between a convertible bond and the number of common shares into which it is convertible. For example, a bond with a face value of 000 is convertible into 40 shares of common stock. As a ratio:

$$\frac{1\ (\text{bond})}{40\ (\text{shares})} = \frac{\$1,000}{x}$$

This shows that the theoretical conversion price of the common stock is $25.

See CONVERSION PARITY to find the practical application of conversion ratio to the actual market prices of the convertible bond and the underlying common stock.

CONVERTIBLE

Class of corporation securities that is convertible into a fixed number of shares of other securities of same corporation. Convertibles usually are debentures or preferred shares that may be exchanged for a fixed number of common shares.

COOLING-OFF PERIOD

Commonly used expression for statutory 20-day period that 1933 Act interposes between filing of preliminary registration and effective date of public sale. SEC may shorten or lengthen period. Time is used by SEC to review registration and by issuer and underwriter to examine issue and registration statement more closely.

Also called cooling period.

CORNERING THE MARKET

A person, or group of persons working in concert, acquires such a large position in a security that persons who have made short sales of the security cannot cover without paying sharply inflated prices.

CORPORATE EQUIVALENT YIELD

Yield on a corporate bond selling at par that must be achieved to equal the yield on a government security selling at a discount. Cash flow on discounted government security reflects tax on interest income and maximum corporate tax on capital gains.

Used by government bond dealers in their offering sheets to show possible advantage, or disadvantage, of an investment in government bonds at the offered price.

CORPORATE FINANCING COMMITTEE

Standing committee that assists Board of Governors of National Association of Securities Dealers. It examines documents filed with SEC by underwriters to determine the fairness of the markup.

CORPORATE INCOME FUND

A fixed unit investment trust. Portfolio usually contains fixed-income securities. Most CIFs feature monthly payment of net investment income. Portfolio is supervised but not managed.

CORPORATION

An assocation, usually of many persons, chartered by a state to conduct business within that state. Federal government also charters corporations.

Corporation is a legal person and thus is independent of life of underlying persons and provides owners with limited personal liability for debts of the corporation.

Difference between corporation and partnership is often very close. Legal advice is required for appropriate tax treatment of income.

CORRESPONDENT

A financial organization (e.g., a securities firm or bank) that on a regular basis performs services for another organization in a market or place where the other doesn't have direct access (e.g., a foreign country or another exchange).

COST OF CARRY

Out-of-pocket expense paid by investor during period that a security position is maintained. For example, client with long margin position has a cost of carry in margin interest; client with short margin position has cost of carry in dividends paid to the lender of the borrowed securities. Although cost of carry does not include the possible investment value of funds tied up in accrued interest or equity tied up in a short account, these must be considered in computing true return on an investment.

Also called carry.

COUPON

1 Interest rate, expressed as a percentage of par or face value, that issuer promises to pay over lifetime of debt security. Coupon rate is annual. Normal practice is to pay half the amount semiannually.
2 Small, detachable certificate that is removed from main certificate and presented for payment of bond interest.
See also BEARER FORMAT.

COUPON BOND

Bond with small detachable certificates to be presented as evidence of interest payments due that is not otherwise registered in name of owner.

Industry rules presume that corporate and municipal bond transactions are for coupon bonds unless otherwise agreed before completion of trade.

COVENANT

Those portions of indenture or bond resolution in which issuer promises to do, or not to do, certain activities. Covenants are for benefit of bondholders and may, with permission of bondholders, be voided or changed.

Also called restrictive covenant.

COVER

1 Of corporations: the ability to pay fixed charges on debt securities by earned income. Important in ratings of bonds.
2 Of clients who have sold short: the act of buying an equivalent number of shares or bonds and instructing broker to deliver against short position. Also used of short against box when client instructs broker to deliver box securities against short position.
See also BOX.

COVERED OPTION

If option writer has another security position that protects the broker against financial risk, the short option is said to be covered. For example, owner of 300 shares that are held by broker sells 3 call options against long stock position. Cover may not fully protect broker; in which case, broker will mark to the market. Short covered option itself, however, requires no margin.

See also NAKED OPTION and UNCOVERED OPTION.

CREDIT BALANCE

1 In cash accounts: monies on deposit with broker or uninvested proceeds of sales. May be withdrawn at will.
2 In margin accounts: proceeds of short sales. If margin account is

mixed, that is, account contains both long and short positions, broker usually nets credit and debit balances.

3 Free credit balances may be withdrawn at will. Additional credit balances required by Reg-T on short sales are not free credit balances.

See also SECURITIES INVESTORS PROTECTION CORPORATION (for treatment of credit balances).

CROSS

Broker acts as agent for both a buyer and a seller in a completed transaction. For example, a floor broker with both a buy and sell order for the same amount of shares, after following proper floor procedures, completes both transactions by having her customers buy and sell to each other.

CROSSED MARKET

If any broker's bid is higher than the lowest offer of another broker, or vice versa, the market is said to be crossed. This occasionally happens. The rules of the National Association of Securities Dealers (NASD) for NASD Automated Quotations (NASDAQ) forbid dealers to cross the market intentionally.

CROWD

Exchange term for those members who come to the post to seek an execution and who, because no execution is currently available, remain there. They, together with the specialist, form a crowd.

See also TRADING POST.

CUM DIVIDEND

Cum is Latin for with. Securities are sold with a dividend if the current buyer is entitled to the next dividend to be paid. Normally, securities are sold with a dividend if the trade is made on or prior to the fifth business day before the company's preestablished record date. Transactions for cash (i.e., same-day settlement) and for mutual funds are exceptions to the general rule.

CUM RIGHTS

In Latin, cum means with. Normally, buyers will receive rights accompanying the purchase of securities if the trade is made on or prior to the date on the prospectus accompanying a rights distribution.

CUMULATIVE PREFERRED

A feature of certain preferred shares, established by the issuing corporation, assuring the holder that if any preferred dividends are passed by the corporation, such passed dividends plus any current dividend will be paid to the preferred stockholder before any dividend is paid to common stockholders. Almost all currently issued preferred shares are cumulative.

CUMULATIVE VOTING
Privilege occasionally given to common shareholders by the corporation's charter. The privilege permits shareholders to allocate their votes in any manner they please. Thus, a holder of 100 shares— if five persons are to be elected to the board—may assign his 500 votes (100 shares times five vacancies) to a candidate of his choice. Through cumulative voting, minority shareholders can, if they act in concert, make sure that at least one or more persons on the board will represent their interests.

CURB
Nickname for American Stock Exchange. Prior to 1921, the ASE was known as the New York Curb Exchange because it worked outdoors on Broad Street—literally on the curb. Oldtimers still refer to the ASE as the Curb.

CURRENCY IN CIRCULATION
A popular misnomer for money in circulation. Currency is only coins and paper money. Money is a broader term and includes demand deposits, which are balances in checking accounts.

CURRENT ASSET
Item of value owned by a corporation that either is cash or can become cash within one year. Most common current asset entries on a corporation's balance sheet: cash, marketable securities, accounts receivable, and inventory.

CURRENT COUPON BOND
Any bond, whether corporate, municipal, or government, whose coupon rate of interest is close to its yield to maturity. For example, if a bond's current coupon is 15% and its yield to maturity is 15.4%, it is said to be a current coupon bond. So called because the bond's cash flow is competitive with other bonds of the same class and it is less sensitive, short-term, to interest rate changes.

CURRENT LIABILITY
Term used in balance sheet bookkeeping and financial statement analysis: the sum of all debts, currently owed, that will become due within one year.

CURRENT MARKET VALUE

Norm used in margin account ledgers for the resale value of securities long in the account. Used as a basis for marks to the market. Closing price for listed securities is used to determine current market value; bid price is used for OTC securities.

Also called long market value if client owns security, or short market value if client owes security.

CURRENT PRODUCTION RATE

Maximum coupon rate of interest that may be placed on currently generated GNMA Modified Pass-Throughs. On these securities the current production rate is ½% below the rate at which the mortgage is issued to the home owner. For example, if the current FHA-VA mortgage rate is 16-½%, the current production rate is 16. The sponsoring bank uses the ½% to cover the clerical cost of processing the mortgage; the 16% passes through to the GNMA pass-through holder.

CURRENT RATIO

Common measurement of a corporation's liquidity. Ratio is computed by dividing current assets by current liabilities. For example, a corporation with current assets of $2.5 million and current liabilities of $1 million has a current ratio of 2.5 to 1. Generally accepted norm is 2 to 1, although utilities are an exception and permit a lower ratio.

CURRENT YIELD

Percentage measured by taking annual dividend interest from an investment and dividing by current replacement cost. Closing price is used on OTC securities.

Most important measurement for security holder who intends to spend the cash flow because it permits her to compare yield with other possible investments of the same amount of money.

Normally, total dollar return for previous year is used. If anticipated dollar return is used in computation, it is called estimated or anticipated current yield. Mutual fund current yield usually is based on average purchase price for a stated period.

Also called current return.

CUSHION

If associated with time, the years between issue date and the earliest callable date of a security. For example, this bond will mature in 20 years, but it has a 5-year cushion. Translation: the bond is callable, but there are 5 years between its issue date and its earliest callable date.

CUSHION BOND

A bond, currently callable, whose market price—in terms of competition with other bonds of similar coupon and rating—is artificially suppressed because of its call price. For example, a bond, callable at 105, that should sell at 120; it is selling at 107, however, because the marketplace fears it will be called. Its price is said to be cushioned.

Although cushioning works against the bondholder as interest rates decline, it works for the bondholder if interest rates rise. In other words, the bond will, in many cases, tend to remain stable during a period of interest-rate changes because the call price and the market price are close.

CUSHION THEORY

Because short sales must be made on upticks, they do not depress the market for a security. Short positions, therefore, have only one future effect: a rise in prices as short sellers buy to cover. A total large short position—while bearish short-term—is bullish long-term. Market analysts look to total short positions that exceed average daily volume by 1-½ to 2 times as quite bullish. This is called the cushion theory.

Because many current short sellers are borrowing to deliver against exercised short calls, most market analysts restrict short sale analysis to that made by members for proprietary accounts.

See also SHORT INTEREST THEORY.

CUSTOMER'S LOAN CONSENT

A written agreement that brokers ask their margin customers to sign. It permits the broker to borrow margined securities, to the amount of the debit balance, for use in delivery against short sales made by other customers and for use by the broker to cover certain fails.

D

D

Used lowercase in stock transaction tables to designate a price that is the low for the past 52 weeks. For example, if the low for today also is the low for the past 52 weeks, the stock transaction table will read d 21. Next day, the new low of 21 will replace the old low in the 52-week range: 43 21.

DAILY BOND BUYER

Trade publication of the municipal bond industry, although it contains news of value to all fixed-income investors. Published daily, Monday through Friday.

See also BOND BUYERS INDEX and THIRTY-DAY VISIBLE SUPPLY.

DAISY CHAIN

Slang, for a pattern of fictitious trading activity by a group of persons buying and selling. The unsuspicious person drawn into the chain bails out the persons who created the manipulation. He, in turn, has no one to whom to sell because the activity was manipulative.

DATED DATE

The date from which accrued interest is calculated on bonds and other debt instruments that are newly offered. For example, if the dated date is May 1 and when issued settlement is May 25, the buyer will pay 24 days of accrued interest to the issuer. This money will be regained when the first interest payment is paid.

DAY ORDER

An order to buy or sell securities that expires at the end of the trading day unless it is either executed or cancelled. All orders are presumed to be day orders unless otherwise designated by the person who enters them.

DAY TRADE

A commitment and a decommitment made on the same day: a purchase followed by a long sale, or a short sale followed by a short cover. Special margin maintenance requirements apply.

DEALER

An individual or firm who, as a matter of regular business, purchases or sells securities for his account and risk.

Also called a principal.

DEALER BANK

1 A commercial bank that makes a continuous market in government and agency securities.
2 A separately identifiable department of a bank that is registered as a municipal securities dealer with the Municipal Securities Rulemaking Board (MSRB).

DEBENTURE

Longer-term debt instrument issued by a corporation that is unsecured by other collateral. Hence, only the good faith and credit standing of the issuer backs the security.

Often called a note if maturity is less than 10 years.

DEBIT BALANCE

Money owed by a margin account customer to a broker for funds advanced for the purchase of securities.

DEBT INSTRUMENT

General name for any certificate that evidences a loan between a borrower and a lender.

Commonly used equivalent terms, although there are differences in the payment of interest on the debt, are bill, note, bond, certificate of indebtedness, certificate of deposit, banker's acceptance, commercial paper, receiver's certificate.

DEBT SECURITY

General term for any security that represents money loaned and that must be repaid to the lender at a future date.

More specific terms are bill, note, bond, debenture, commercial paper, certificate of deposit, banker's acceptance.

DEBT SERVICE

Issuer's required payment of principal and interest on a debt. Usually computed on an annual basis until debt is repaid.

See also LEVEL DEBT SERVICE.

DEBT-TO-EQUITY RATIO

Measurement of leverage in a corporation's financial structure. Formula varies. Less common: total long-term debt divided by stockholders' equity. More common: long-term debt plus par value of preferred stock divided by common stockholders' equity. Use of term, therefore, must be carefully reviewed to make sure which set of figures is being used. Second measurement is more properly a measurement of securities with fixed charges (bonds and preferred) against securities without fixed charges (common).

DEEP DISCOUNT BOND

Term used of a bond originally issued at or near par that is currently selling below 80% of its par value. For example, the American Telephone 3-⅞ of '90 are currently selling at 55. $550 per bond

represents a deep discount from the original par value of $1,000.
Term is not used for bonds sold at an original issue discount.

DEEP IN THE MONEY

Used of options. A call, for example, has a strike (exercise) price 5 or more points below the current market price of the underlying security, or a put has a strike price 5 or more points above the market price of the underlying security. Term, however, is relative to strike and market prices.

See also DEEP OUT OF THE MONEY.

DEEP OUT OF THE MONEY

Used of options. A call, for example, has a strike (exercise) price more than 5 points above market price of underlying security, or a put has a strike price more than 5 points below market price of underlying security. Term is relative and depends on strike and market price of securities.

DEEP SIX

Nautical term for a sunken ship in six fathoms of water; thus, one that will never sail again.

Often used as a verb: to deep six (i.e., to reject something as valueless). For example, we should deep six that idea; or the market deep sixed the news.

DEFAULT

Used of debts if the debtor fails to meet an interest payment or to repay the principal. The debt agreement, however, may define default in other ways.

DEFERRED PAYMENT ANNUITY

Annuity contract whereby annuitant makes a lump-sum or installment deposit of premiums. Annuity payoff does not start until a later date at the election of the annuitant.

DEFICIENCY LETTER

Written statement from SEC to issuer during the registration process. Suggests revisions or addition of other information to the preliminary registration statement. Although a deficiency letter does not necessarily delay the registration, an effective date will not be assigned until the deficiency is corrected.

DELAYED DELIVERY

Settlement of a securities contract after regular way delivery. For example, if regular way settlement is next business day, a contract to settle on the second business day would be a form of delayed delivery.

DELIVERY AGAINST PAYMENT
When delivery is made to the customer's bank, the bank will pay in cash, or by check, for the customer's account. It is a frequently used transaction settlement procedure by institutional accounts.

Also known as delivery versus payment; delivery against cash; or, from the other side of the trade, receive against payment.

DELTA
Greek letter D. Delta, by inference to the proportional change between two quantities in differential calculus, is used of options to state the change in the option premium for each 1 point change in the price of the underlying stock. For example, a delta of .75 means that the premium tends to increase by ¾ point for each point that the underlying stock goes up. For options in the money, delta will always approach 1 as the option nears expiration. Same concept is true of puts as stock goes down.

Also called the hedge value.

DEMAND DEPOSIT
Banking term for customer assets that may be drawn against by check or draft. In its simplest terms, deposits in bank customer checking accounts. The deposit may arise from cash or other deposits in the customer's account or by credit if the bank extends a loan to the customer.

DENOMINATION
Number of shares or principal amount of bonds inscribed on the face of a security.

See also GOOD DELIVERY.

DEVELOPMENT
Department is a frequent guarantor of securities issued to promote middle-income housing and other urban development projects.

DEPLETION
Accounting term for a theoretical pool of funds set aside from a corporation's annual earnings for the replacement of a natural asset that is being used up. For example, oil from a well, ore from a lode. Because it is usually impossible to replace the asset, the depletion is usually given in the form of a credit against taxes due by the corporation.

DEPOSITORY TRUST COMPANY

A central securities certificate depository, and member of the Federal Reserve System, through which members may arrange deliveries of securities between each other through computerized debit and credit entries without physical delivery of the certificates.

The DTC is industry owned, with the NYSE as the majority owner.

DEPRECIATION

Theoretical sum of money that represents the loss of value of a tangible asset over time because of use or of obsolescence. The sum is deducted from purchase price of a fixed asset to give its residual value for balance sheet accounting. A similar sum is deducted from the corporation's income for that year.

See also CASH FLOW; STRAIGHT-LINE DEPRECIATION; DOUBLE-DECLINING-BALANCE METHOD; SUM-OF-THE-YEARS'-DIGITS METHOD.

DEPTH

1 Ability of the market to absorb either a large buy or a large sell order without a significant price change in a security.
2 Degree of general investor interest in the market. For example, the depth of the market index compares the number of issues traded with the number of issues listed. The greater the number of issues traded, the greater the market depth.

DESIGNATED CONCESSION

Order given to a syndicate. The order, for a number of shares or bonds, designates the nonmembers of the account who are to receive the concession for the sale of the securities. For example, an order for 1,000 bonds designates that the concession for 400 is to go to A, 300 to B, and 300 to C.

DESIGNATED NET

Order given to a municipal security syndicate by a nonmember of the MSRB. For example, by an insurance company to a municipal underwriting syndicate. The order, executed at the public offering price, directs that the concession be credited to the accounts of at least three members of the syndicate designated by the insurance company.

Frequently used by institutional municipal investors to reward account members who have presented sales ideas or other valuable research information.

DESIGNATED ORDER TURNAROUND

Electronic switching service provided to NYSE members whereby market orders for 1 to 499 shares are routed directly to the specialist.

The specialist represents such orders in the crowd. If no contra broker is found, the order is executed against the book (i.e., buy orders against the best offer on the book; sell orders against the best bid). The specialist does not charge the member firm for the service if an immediate transaction is made.

On the NYSE, DOT transactions account for more than 50% of all trades—although a much smaller percentage of total volume.

DEVALUATION
Official lowering of value of one country's currency in terms of the exchange rate for another country's currency. For example, if the United States was to state that starting tomorrow $1 will be exchanged for 1,000 Italian lire instead of today's rate of $1 for 1,100 lire, this act would devalue the dollar. Reason: holders of lire could buy more U.S. goods tomorrow than they could today. Devaluation normally is the result of an unfavorable balance of trade. Currency spent abroad returns to the home country in the form of purchases of that country's goods.

DIAGONAL SPREAD
Option strategy based on a long and short position in the same class of option. For example, long a call and short a call, where the strike prices are different and the expiration months are different.

The diagonal spread strategy is bullish or bearish depending on the difference between the strike prices and the price of the underlying security, relative to the strike prices and their expiration months.

DIFFERENTIAL
Compensation to a dealer for the completion of an odd-lot transaction for a customer. Term is specific to odd-lot transactions on exchanges where the differential—commonly ⅛ point, although there are exceptions—is added to purchases and subtracted from sales.

Term also is used generally of any trading situation where the dealer widens his quote because the customer is buying or selling a relatively small amount of the security. For example, a government security dealer widens his quote from 95.16 bid—95.20 offered to 95.10 bid—95.24 offered because a customer only wishes to buy $10,000 face amount of the bonds.

DIGITS DELETED
Exchange tape designation when tape has been delayed. Normally, all digits and variations are displayed. With digits deleted only the variations are displayed.

For example, normal transactions might read:

45-⅞........46-⅛........46-¼

With digits deleted, tape would display:

5-⅞........6-1⅛........¼

The viewer is expected to supply the missing digits.

DIRECTOR

Person elected to serve on board of corporation or trust. In the latter case, the more common expression is trustee.

Power of board of directors is given in corporation's charter.

In recent years, "affiliated persons" has become the general term for directors, elected corporate officers, and holders of 10% or more of outstanding shares of a corporation.

DIRECT PARTICIPATION PROGRAM

General term used by National Association of Securities Dealers (NASD) for partnership agreements that provide a flow-through of tax consequences to the participants. Subchapter S corporations, which provide tax consequences similar to partnerships, are usually included in this concept.

REITS, pension, and profit-sharing plans, individual retirement accounts, annuities, and investment companies are usually excluded from the definition of direct-participation programs.

DIRECT PLACEMENT

Used of an issuer's sale of a new security to one or more institutional clients without the assistance of a broker-dealer.

Occasionally used of private placement where broker-dealer acts as an agent. This later usage is more commonly called a private placement.

DISCOUNT

1   As noun: the dollar (or point) difference between the price of a security and its redemption value. For example, a bond with a face value of $1,000 is selling at a $50 discount if its current market value is $950.
2   As adjective: used to describe a security selling at a discount or offered for sale at a discount. For example, Treasury bills are discount securities.
3   As verb: the act of factoring the long-term effects of news into one's estimate of the present value of a security. For example, the stock has gone down in value because the market is discounting the news of a threatened labor strike.

Also used as a past participle. For example, the news is discounted.

DISCOUNT BOND
A bond, originally sold at or near par, which is currently selling below its par value.

Also called a discounted bond.

See also DEEP DISCOUNT BOND.

DISCOUNT BROKER
Exchange members who will provide execution-only services for clients and, as a result, charge lower, or discounted, commissions.

The principal difference between discount brokers and full-service brokers is that the latter will give investment advice and portfolio suggestions. Discount brokers enter orders for clients who wish to buy or sell. They also provide margin accounts and, occasionally, custodial service. They do not provide advice or other research services.

Discount brokers cater to a clientele of customers who make their own investment decisions and who do not expect the broker to supply investment opinions.

Also called discount houses.

DISCOUNT RATE
Interest rate charged by the Federal Reserve when member banks borrow from the Fed against eligible securities as collateral. The discount rate, which the Fed changes from time to time to implement its monetary policies, becomes the floor beneath which the member banks will not loan money. For example, if the discount rate is 12%, a bank would lose money if it reloaned the funds at 12% or below.

See also DISCOUNT WINDOW.

DISCOUNT WINDOW
Term for the loan facility provided by the Federal Reserve Bank whereby member banks can borrow against the collateral value of eligible securities.

See also DISCOUNT RATE,.

DISCOUNT YIELD
Measurement of return that computes interest on face value of security rather than on dollar amount invested. Used in figuring yield on U.S. Treasury bills. The formula is:

$$\text{Yield} = \frac{\text{Discount}}{\text{Face amount}} \times \frac{360 \text{ days}}{\text{Days until maturity}}$$

For example, if a client buys a $10,000 Treasury bill for $9,500 when 180 days remain to maturity, the discount yield is calculated as follows:

$$\text{Yield} = \frac{500}{10000} \times \frac{360}{180}$$
$$\text{Yield} = 0.05 \times 2$$
$$\text{Yield} = 10\%$$

Also called discount basis.

See also EQUIVALENT BOND YIELD (to compare with regular method of computing current yield).

DISCRETIONARY ACCOUNT

Brokerage account that permits a designated employee of the member firm to make investment decisions on behalf of a client. The investment decisions include buying and selling, the selection of the securities, and the time and price of the trade.

Authorization for such accounts must be given in writing by the customer and must be accepted by an officer of the member firm.

Member firm customers may verbally give discretion about time and price for specified trades. This limited discretion does not require written authorization.

DISCRETIONARY ORDER

An order to buy or sell that an employee of a member firm entered because she has limited power of attorney over a client's account.

Industry rules require that such orders be marked discretionary, be entered in accord with the customer's investment objectives, and be approved promptly by a designated person in the member firm.

DISINTERMEDIATION

Term describing the action of an investor who has left funds on deposit with a portfolio intermediary (e.g., a bank, savings and loan, or insurance company), removes those funds, and makes a direct investment in other securities. For example, a bank depositor who receives 5-¼% on a pass-book deposit, withdraws funds to purchase treasury securities paying 11%.

Disintermediation occurs when rates on direct security investments are substantially higher than the rates paid by portfolio intermediaries.

DIST

On exchange ticker tapes, DIST designates an exchange distribution. See also EXCHANGE DISTRIBUTION.

DISTRIBUTION
General term used to designate the sale of a large block of stock. The distribution may be primary, as in an underwriting, or secondary, as in an exchange distribution.

DISTRIBUTION AREA
Term describing a relatively narrow price range for a security over a relatively long time. For example, a stock trades between 36 and 38 for a six-week period. Called a distribution area because the implication is that sellers are disappointed but buyers are willing to purchase the security at those prices. In practice, it is difficult to tell whether the primary cause for the sideways price movement comes from sellers, who are distributing, or from buyers, who through their limit orders are accumulating.

DISTRIBUTION STOCK
Stock sold publicly by persons affiliated with the issuer pursuant to an effective shelf registration.

DISTRIBUTOR
Term for the underwriter of mutual fund shares.
Also called wholesaler.
See also UNDERWRITER.

DISTRICT BUSINESS CONDUCT COMMITTEE
Committee appointed by the members within 1 of the 13 districts of the National Association of Securities Dealers (NASD). The DBBC is empowered to hear trade practice complaints against a member or a person associated with a member under the Code of Procedure.
See also CODE OF PROCEDURE.

DIVERSIFICATION
Process whereby an investor, to reduce the risk of selection, spreads investment dollars over many securities or uses a single investment with a portfolio invested in many securities.

DIVERSIFIED
Term used of management investment companies—both closed and open-ended—if at least 75% of its assets are represented by four forms: cash, government securities, securities of other investment companies, and other securities. Purpose: so no more than 5% of the management company's total assets are invested in the securities of any one issuer and they hold no more than 10% of the voting securities of any issuing corporation.

DIVIDEND

1 A distribution of cash from net profits or of securities made at the discretion of the board of directors to the equity shareholders of a corporation. Cash dividends are taxable to the recipient. Generally, stock dividends are not taxable at the time of receipt.

2 A distribution of cash from net income made by a regulated investment company. Under Subchapter M of the IRS Code, the tax treatment of such distributions is dependent on the original source: long- or short-term capital gains, interest income, or security dividends.

DIVIDEND EXCLUSION

Amount of dividends not subject to federal taxation.

1 For individuals, current law excludes the first $100 of dividends—$200 on a joint return—from federal taxation.

2 For domestic corporations, current law excludes 85% of the dividends received from an equity issue of another domestic corporation. Not every domestic issuer qualifies, so tax advice is required.

3 For dividend reinvestment programs, current law permits the exclusion of $750—$1,500 on joint returns—of dividends received from utility stocks if the dividends are reinvested in qualifying new issues of stock of the same corporation.

DIVIDEND PAYOUT RATIO

A method of comparing payout ratio of companies within the same industry or companies in general. Comparison is relative and, of itself, has no further investment decision value. Companies with high dividend payout ratios usually are not considered growth companies.

The formula is:

$$\frac{\text{Annual common stock dividend}}{\text{Earnings available for common stock}}$$

DOING BUSINESS AS

Used of an individual who does business under a different commercial name. For example, John Jones d/b/a/Gotham Appliance and Repair.

Also abbreviated as D/B/A or d/b/a.

DOLLAR BONDS

1 Long-term municipal revenue bonds usually quoted in dollars (i.e., in points), rather than in yield to maturity.

2 Bonds of foreign issuers sold in the United States and denominated in U.S. dollars.
3 Bonds, denominated in U.S. dollars, they are issued, bought, and sold in foreign countries.
Also called Eurobonds, although such bonds are traded in Mexico and Japan.

DOLLAR COST AVERAGING
Method of formula investing based on the periodic investment, in the same security, of equal dollar amounts. The result in every case will be an average cost that is less than the average of the prices paid. Method, however, does not guarantee a profit. There will be a profit only if sale price exceeds average cost per share.

Method is applicable to most management investment company securities and to the sharebuilder plans sponsored by many brokerage firms.

DO NOT REDUCE
Instruction that may be added to good till cancelled (GTC) limit buy orders and sell stop orders—also to sell stop limit orders—telling specialist that on ex-dividend day the customer does not want the order reduced by the amount of a cash dividend.

DNR instruction does not affect the handling of stock dividends. Special rules apply.

DON'T KNOW
Industry term for a questioned trade (one where there is some discrepancy in the transaction records) on the comparison sheet for daily trades between broker-dealers.

See also QT.

DOUBLE-BARRELED
Used of municipal revenue bonds if the payment of interest and the repayment of principal is further guaranteed by another municipality that will make the payments from general taxes. For example, a housing authority issues revenue bonds. The bonds are double-barreled if a city or state pledges to pay interest and principal if rents from the housing project are insufficient. Do not confuse with overlapping debt (i.e., a bond with two issuers).

DOUBLE BOTTOM
Description of a stock's price movement if it reaches, on two different occasions, the same low price. For example, on two occasions in the past year or so, a stock dropped to 36. Technical analysts see the

double-bottom price as a support level. Hence, a subsequent drop below this price is a sign of a continued decline in price.

Term also can be expanded, such as triple bottom, and so on.

See also DOUBLE TOP.

DOUBLE-DECLINING-BALANCE METHOD
Depreciation method that accelerates depreciation in earlier years and lowers it in subsequent years. Starts with percentage of straight-line depreciation, doubles it, and applies same percentage in subsequent years. For example, if straight-line depreciation is 10%, DDB is 20%. Both methods meet at scrap value, although DDB will usually get to scrap value earlier, thus it has a tax advantage in earlier years.

DOUBLE TOP
Description of a stock's price movement if it reaches, on two different occasions, the same high price. For example, on two occasions in the past year or so, a stock rose to 42. Technical analysts see the double-top price as a resistance level. Hence, a subsequent rise above this price is a sign of a continued rise in price.

Term can also be expanded such as triple top, and so on.

See also DOUBLE BOTTOM.

DOW JONES AVERAGE
Measurement of market price movement based on 65 stocks: 30 industrials, 20 transportation, and 15 utility issues. Relatively few persons follow the composite average; instead, they follow the industrial average, DJIA, and the relative movement of the other two averages.

DOW JONES INDUSTRIAL AVERAGE
A measurement of general market price movement for 30 widely held NYSE-listed stocks. Called an average because no adjustment is made for the number of shares outstanding in the component stocks. Average is found by adding the prices of the 30 stocks and dividing by an adjusted denominator. Over the years, because of stock splits, stock dividends, and substitutions of stocks, the denominator has been changed from 30 to 1.30. The 30 component stocks and the current denominator can be found in The Wall Street Journal in the footnotes to the chart of the average.

DOWNTICK
Sale of a listed security at a price that is lower than the price of the previous regular-way transaction. For example, the last regular-

way transaction was at 29. If the next regular way transaction is at 28-⅞ or below, it is said to be a downtick.

See also REGULAR WAY TRANSACTION AND ZERO-MINUS TICK.

DOW THEORY

Interpretation of primary market trend. Dow Theory holds that there is no primary market trend (i.e., a trend that will last—either upward or downward—for a year or more) unless there is substantial correlation between the movements of the industrial, transportation, and utility averages.

DR

Commonly used designation, Dr, of a debit in a client's account with a brokerage firm. For example, a client's statement reads $2,500 Dr, which signifies that the client owes the brokerage firm $2,500.

From the Latin debetur, abbreviated Dr, meaning it is owed.

DRAFT

A negotiable instrument that will, if endorsed, transfer money from the account of the payer to the account of the payee. Significant difference from a check: a check is a debit on the books of the issuer as soon as it is issued; a draft is not a debit until it is presented for payment.

DUE BILL

Document attached by selling broker to delivered securities that gives title to the buyer's broker for a specified number of shares or dollars.

A due bill is attached if seller sold securities with a dividend, interest, or other distribution but delivery occurred too late to make buyer the holder of record. The due bill, in effect, rectifies this failure to deliver on time to make the buyer the holder of record. For example, buyer purchases 100 XYZ with a dividend. Record date is May 15; delivery is made by the seller's broker on May 16. Buyer's broker will accept securities only if a due bill for the dividend is attached.

Also called due bill check.

DUTCH AUCTION

General concept: Bidders do not bid up for a purchase; instead, seller offers down until a satisfactory price is reached.

In practice, an offering that is accepted at a price sufficient to sell all of the items for sale. For example, if 30,000 items are offered, and bidders bid 30 for 10,000 and 29 for 15,000 and 28 for 5,000, the issue will be sold at 28 because the total bids are for 30,000 and that satisfies the needs of the seller.

You will occasionally hear the term Dutch auction used of the weekly T-bill auction; the term is used inaccurately.

E

EARNINGS BEFORE TAXES
Commonly used expression for earnings of a corporation after payment of bond interest but before payment of federal and other taxes.

EARNINGS PER SHARE
Net income of a corporation after taxes and required payments to preferred shareholders.

Called primary earnings per share if corporation also has convertible securities or other common stock equivalents outstanding. Fully diluted EPS also will reflect effect of conversion or exercise of stock options. For example, a company has primary earnings of $4.00 per share and fully diluted earnings of $3.50. This means, right now all common shareholders have an EPS of $4.00; but if all the "calls" on the stock were exercised, the earnings would be $3.50. Calls do not include listed stock options; these are contracts between a writer and a holder and do not involve the issuing corporation.

EASTERN ACCOUNT
Commonly used underwriting account for municipal securities. Basic concept: syndicate as a group assumes financial responsibility for success of the venture. Thus, gains or losses for participants in the account are not dependent on what they sell, but on their participation in the account. For example, in a divided account, member A has a 10% participation. Member A sells 15% of the bonds, but the entire syndicate only sells 80% of the bonds it bought. Member A would be responsible for 10% of the remaining bonds despite overselling his percent participation.

Also called divided account.

EDGE ACT
Federal law, passed in 1919, permitting commercial banks to conduct international business across state lines. As a general rule, domestic banks may only conduct business in the state where they are chartered.

Often, you will hear securities related to such interstate banking activities called Edge Act securities.

EFFECTIVE DATE
Date when a registered offering may begin to be made. Usually it is the 20th day following the filing of a registration statement with the SEC, unless the SEC has issued a deficiency letter requiring the issuer to make certain adjustments in the registration statement.

SEC, either on its own initiative or upon request by the issuer, may set an earlier effective date.

EFFECTIVE SALE
Common expression for the price of the round-lot transaction on an exchange that determines the execution of an odd-lot order. For example, if a client enters a market order to buy 50 shares of a listed security, and the next round-lot transaction is at 33, that sale will be effective. The odd-lot buyer will pay 33 plus the differential of ⅛ point payable on odd-lot transactions.

ELECT
1 Round-lot transaction that causes either a round-lot or an odd-lot stop order or a stop-limit order to become a market or limit order. For example, a customer has entered a sell stop order at 55; a transaction occurs at 54⅞; the stop order to sell at 55 is elected and is now a market order to sell.
  See also ODD LOT and ROUND LOT.
2 Transaction at a price that a member, usually a specialist, has guaranteed to another customer. For example, a specialist has stopped an order at 55. A transaction at 55 elects the stop, and the specialist must execute at the guaranteed price.

ELIGIBLE SECURITY
Widely used term, which may refer to:
1 Securities traded by Federal Open Market Committee.
2 Securities that Federal Reserve will accept for loans at discount window.
3 Securities that have loan value under Regulation T, whether in the general, special bond, or special subscription accounts.
4 Securities that a carrying broker may deposit at the Options Clearing Corporation as collateral for short option positions.
5 Securities that exchange members may trade in the OTC market although they are listed on the exchange.

EMANCIPATION

Legal term for the passage of a person from a status of servitude to freedom. Commonly used applications:

1 A person, not yet of legal age, who is permitted to enter into binding contracts. For example, the court permits a minor to sell a piece of property.

2 A person, although a minor, who is permitted to act as an adult because of special economic reasons. For example, mother and father die in an accident; they have three children ages 17, 11, 9. The 17-year-old is permitted by the court to act as guardian for the 11- and 9-year-old children. The 17-year-old child has been emancipated by the court.

EMPLOYEE STOCK OWNERSHIP PLAN

A plan by which employees systematically buy out present owners of a corporation. Shares thus purchased are held in a trust.

Abbreviated ESOP.

ENDORSE

1 To guarantee. Examples: to endorse a conventional over-the-counter option; to endorse a certificate as signed by the registered owner.

2 To sign a certificate, as registered owner, so title may be transferred. Examples: to endorse a check; to endorse a stock or bond.

EQUIPMENT TRUST CERTIFICATE

Bond, always issued in serial maturity form, that pledges the equipment used to conduct a business. Common carriers (e.g., railroads, air lines, container ships) are the most frequent issuers. Usually, such bonds are not callable.

See also NEW YORK PLAN; PHILADELPHIA PLAN.

EQUITY

1 Security representing residual ownership in a corporation. If there is no preference in payment of dividends, it is called common stock; if preference is shown among owners, it is called preferred stock.

2 Liquidating value of a client's margin account. For example, if client owns securities worth $30,000 and the client's debit is $12,000, the equity in the account is $18,000.

EQUITY REIT

A real estate investment trust (REIT) that uses stockholder equity to buy and lease commercial and residential property. Generally considered a conservative security.

EQUITY SECURITY

A certificate that designates a proportional ownership in a corporation: principally common and preferred stock.

Rights, warrants, convertibles, and long call options are considered the equivalents of equity securities in many situations. For example, in determining whether a sale at a loss is a wash sale for taxation purposes.

EQUIVALENT BOND YIELD

Used to compare the discount yield on money market securities to the coupon yield on government bonds. For example, a Treasury bill with a 90-day maturity is sold at a discount yield of 12%. The purchase price is $97,000, the discount is $3,000. The equivalent bond yield is:

$$\frac{\$3,000}{\$97,000} \times \frac{365}{90} = 12.54\%$$

The number 365 is used because interest on government bonds is computed on a 365-day year rather than the 360-day year used for T-bills.

EQUIVALENT TAXABLE YIELD

Comparison of the nontaxable yield on a municipal bond to the taxable yield on a corporate bond at a client's tax bracket. For example, a client in the 40% tax bracket is offered a municipal bond with a yield of 12%. What is the corporate bond yield after tax that equals the nontaxable yield on the municipal is calculated thus:

$$\frac{\text{Municipal yield}}{1 - \text{tax bracket}} = \frac{12}{1 - .40} = \frac{12}{.60} = 20\%$$

ERISA

Acronym for Employee Retirement Income Security Act, passed in 1974, that gives governmental jurisdiction over the establishment, operation, and funding of most nongovernmental pension and benefit plans.

ESCHEAT

A state law regarding the disposal of abandoned property (e.g., bank balances, unpaid insurance policies). These properties are governed by escheat (pronounced es-sheet) laws. Normally, such assets revert to the state, but rightful owners subsequently can claim the property.

ESCROW

Assets placed with an independent third party to insure that all parties to a contact fulfill its terms. For example, a client purchases a contractual mutual fund at a sales charge of $500. The sales charge is wholly or partially refundable under certain circumstances. The $500 will be placed in escrow until the client either fulfills the conditions of the contract or rescinds it.

Also called escrow account.

ESCROW RECEIPT

A paper often used by writers of call option contracts who have underlying securities on deposit with an exchange-approved bank. The bank issues an escrow receipt to broker, thereby guaranteeing delivery of shares to broker if call is exercised against writer.

EURODOLLAR

Common term for dollars held by banks in European countries. Such dollars, originally received by European merchants for goods sold to American companies, will be used to pay for intercountry trades or for petroleum purchases; in this case, they become petrodollars. If such dollars are used to pay for trade with the United States, they become regular dollars on deposit with banks in the United States. Many European debt securities are issued with payment promised in Eurodollars.

See also EURODOLLAR BONDS.

EURODOLLAR BONDS

Bonds issued by European or American corporations. Bonds have interest and principal payments in dollars. As a general rule, such bonds are not registered with the SEC and cannot immediately be sold in the United States.

EURODOLLAR CD

Short-term time deposits issued by European banks. The deposits are made in Eurodollars, and interest and principal repayment are in Eurodollars.

See also LIBOR.

EVALUATOR

Independent third party who assigns a resale value to an asset for which a limited market exists.

See also EVALUATOR'S FEE.

EVALUATOR'S FEE

Fee charged by an evaluator. Many portfolios must be evaluated periodically, either by law or to establish redemption price. For example, a unit investment trust contains letter bonds for which no ready market exists; the units, however, are redeemable. The evaluator establishes an estimate of the resale value of the bonds and charges a fee for this service.

EXCESS MARGIN

Dollar value of client's equity above initial Regulation-T margin (Reg-T excess) or maintenance requirement (maintenance excess). For example, a client has securities worth $50,000 in a margin account with a debit balance of $20,000. Client has equity of $30,000; this is $5,000 greater than the current $25,000 Reg-T initial margin and $17,500 greater than maintenance requirement of $12,500.

See also SPECIAL MISCELLANEOUS ACCOUNT.

EXCESS RESERVES

Banking term that signifies that the total reserves of a bank on deposit with the Federal Reserve plus the cash on hand exceeds the statutory reserve requirement based on the bank's deposits. For example, if a bank has a statutory requirement of $1,000,000, its reserves with the Fed are $800,000, and it has cash in its vault of $250,000 (a total of $1,050,000), the bank has an excess reserve of $50,000. Excess reserves may be withdrawn, lent to other banks, or lent to customers.

See also FEDERAL FUNDS.

EXCHANGE DISTRIBUTION

Nonpublicized sale of a large block of stock through an exchange. Offer is made through one or two member firms. When sufficient buy orders are accumulated, trade is made on the floor within existing market. Completed transaction is then announced on exchange tape. Seller pays all transaction costs.

Tape symbol: DIST.

EXDIVIDEND

Security contract that does not entitle buyer to the next dividend on the security. Trade is exdividend because settlement date is after the record date that determines the holders who will receive the dividend.

See also EXDIVIDEND DATE.

EXDIVIDEND DATE

Date on or after which buyer will not receive the next dividend on a security. On regular way transactions, exdividend date is the fourth business day before the record date.

See also REGULAR-WAY TRANSACTION.

EXECUTION

Popular term for a transaction between a buyer and a seller. Also called a trade.

EXEMPT SECURITIES

1   Securities exempted from the registration requirements of the Securities Act of 1933. For example, government and municipal securities.
2   Securities exempted from certain provisions of the Securities Exchange Act of 1934 in terms of margin, registration of dealers who make a market in them, and certain reporting requirements. For example, a class of equity securities of a corporation that now has less than 300 holders is exempted from quarterly and annual reporting.

Also called Exempted Securities.

EXERCISE

Most common usage: holder of a put or call elects the option of selling (put) or buying (call) the underlying security according to the terms of the option contract.

EXERCISE LIMIT

Maximum number of contracts of the same class of option that may be exercised within five consecutive business days. Usual exercise limit for equity-type options is 2,000 contracts.

EXERCISE NOTICE

Advisory form submitted to Options Clearing Corporation by broker stating that it demands fulfillment of terms of a long option contract. OCC will then assign performance to a broker representing a writer of contract.

Incorrectly used of client; it is broker who enters exercise notice upon request of client.

EXERCISE PRICE

Dollar value per share at which holder of long option may elect to exercise.

See also STRIKING PRICE.

EXIMBANK
Popular name for the Export-Import Bank of the United States, which was established in 1934 as an independent federal agency. It facilitates exports and imports by borrowing from the U.S. Treasury to finance them. It provides direct credits to foreign borrowers, export insurance for U.S. businesses, and export credit guarantees.

EX-LEGAL
Term from municipal trading: a security that does not have attached the legal opinion of bond counsel. Trades can be made but buyer must be informed that delivery will be ex-legal. Most currently issued municipal bonds have legal opinion printed directly on bond certificate.

EXPENSE RATIO
Ratio, usually expressed in cents per $100 of investment, that compares mutual fund expenses for management fee and other overhead expenses to average net asset value of outstanding shares. Normally given in annual report of fund. For example, an expense ratio of 43 cents means that an investor pays 43 cents per year per $100 of investment in the fund for the services of the fund. Expenses are withheld by fund from current income and are not an out-of-pocket cost to investor.

EXPIRATION
An option or privilege ceases to have value. Examples: an equity-type option expires on the Saturday after the third Friday of a particular month; a security is convertible until April 15, 1992; and so on.

EXPIRATION CYCLE
Cycle of three-month intervals for which option contracts ordinarily will be traded. There are three cycles January (JAJO), February (FMAN), and March (MJSD). Usually three of four months in cycle are traded at same time. When the current month expires (e.g., January), the last month in the cycle will begin to trade on the next business day. Thus, the October contract will be added to the currently traded April and July contracts.

EXPIRATION DATE
Saturday after the third Friday of the contract month for equity-type options. Option expires worthless at 10:59 p.m., Chicago time, unless it is previously exercised by the holder.

EX-RIGHTS

Status of the underlying security on the day after the rights and their accompanying prospectus are distributed to present security holders. On or after that date, the security and the rights trade separately and the buyer of the security from a previous holder will not get the rights.

EXTRAORDINARY

Used with income or charges on corporation income statements. In every case, term signifies a one-time event. For example, the write-off of a loss, or the sale of property.

F

F

Used uppercase to mean foreign. Appears in newspaper report of corporate sales and earnings following name of company. Signifies that primary securities market is outside the U.S. or Canada.

FACE AMOUNT CERTIFICATE

Debt instrument that obliges issuer to pay a stated amount, the face value, on a fixed date more than 24 months after issuance. May be purchased lump sum or by installments. Rate of interest is fixed, although additional interest may be paid if issuer's income from investment warrants it.

Also called face amount certificate company.

FACE VALUE

Value of a bond stated on the bond certificate. It is also the redemption value at maturity, although, if issuer calls bond before maturity, there may be a premium added to face value as redemption price.

Also called par value. This usage of par value is limited to bonds.

FAIL POSITION

Industry term describing a broker-dealer's inability to deliver securities to the buyer's broker because his customer did not deliver the securities sold. Or, looked at from a buying broker's viewpoint, the inability of a selling broker to deliver securities purchased.

In practice, a broker-dealer will have a net fail position. It will be a fail-to-receive position if other brokers did not deliver securities to satisfy his clients; it will be a fail-to-deliver position if he was not able to satisfy the delivery needs of brokers to whom his clients sold.

FAIL TO DELIVER
Past-due contract between brokers where the seller has not presented the security to the buyer for payment.

Normally used as a noun; also used as a verb: "The broker failed to deliver."

FAIL TO RECEIVE
Past-due contract between brokers where the buyer has not made payment because seller's broker has not yet made delivery.

Normally used as a noun; also used as a verb: "The broker failed to receive."

FAIR MARKET VALUE
Price at which a buyer and seller are willing to exchange an asset. Generally synonymous with current market value determined by the competitive forces of supply and demand operating in a free and open marketplace. Endeavors to rig the price to favor the buyer or seller are manipulative and violate federal laws.

NASD also defines it in terms of swaps against syndicate offerings: the price that a dealer normally would pay for the security in the ordinary course of business if there were no swap involved.

FAMILY OF FUNDS
Mutual funds, each with a different investment objective, that are managed by the same investment manager. Generally, funds in the same family are exchangeable on a dollar-for-dollar basis, although usually there is a fee for administrative expenses, and there may be an additional sales charge if a client switches from a fund with a lower sales charge to a fund with a higher sales charge.

IRS considers the exchange a sale followed by a purchase, thus there may be a tax consequence on the shares swapped.

FANNIE MAE
Nickname for the Federal National Mortgage Association. Also used of the debt securities of the FNMA; For example, "I bought some Fannie Maes."

See also FEDERAL NATIONAL MORTGAGE ASSOCIATION.

FARTHER OUT, FARTHER IN
Use of maturity dates (or expiration dates) on options. The concept: one's obligations or opportunities are extended or retracted.

See also DIAGONAL SPREAD.

FAST MARKET

Term designating a rapid volume of activity in a class of listed option. Floor officials initiate special exchange procedures to manage order flow efficiently. New orders may be delayed, and if a fast market cannot be controlled, it may be necessary to use a rotation to establish an orderly market.

FAVORITE FIFTY

Term describes the 50 largest equity holdings of major institutional investors. Often used in the past to describe major institutional holdings that resisted downside moves in bear markets.

Also called first-tier investments.

FEDERAL DEPOSIT INSURANCE CORPORATION

Membership corporation sponsored by the federal government to insure repayment of savings and time deposits if a member bank becomes insolvent. Current coverage is $100,000 per separate account at each insured bank.

FEDERAL FARM CREDIT BANKS

Formerly, the Federal Land Banks, the Federal Intermediate Credit Banks, and the Banks for Cooperatives issued their own securities. The Federal Farm Credit Banks was organized to consolidate and reduce financing costs for these banks.

Since 1980, the securities issued have been called the Federal Farm Credit Banks Consolidated System-wide Bonds.

FEDERAL FUNDS

Excess reserves of member banks of the Federal Reserve system. These excess funds can be loaned to other member banks, usually on an overnight basis, at the federal funds rate.

Term also used of any immediately usable funds that can be used to pay for government securities transactions. In this sense, the term includes cleared credit balances in client accounts, in special miscellaneous accounts (SMAs) in margin accounts, checks drawn by a member bank of the Fed on its account with the Fed, and—with the increased popularity of money market funds—transfers from these funds to the client's cash or margin account.

FEDERAL FUNDS RATE

Negotiated interest rate charged by a bank that loans excess reserves to a bank that needs to increase its reserves.

Probably the most sensitive indicator of monetary conditions because it is an overnight rate and, unlike the prime and discount rates, is a market rather than a posted rate.

FEDERAL HOME LOAN BANK

The FHLB serves savings banks, savings and loan associations, and cooperative banks in much the same way the Federal Reserve serves commercial member banks. The FHLB regulates these banks and lends money against acceptable collateral.

FEDERAL HOME LOAN MORTGAGE CORPORATION

Abbreviation FHLMC. Nickname: Freddie Mac. Government-sponsored corporation owned by FHLMC. Purpose is to purchase qualifying conventional residential mortgages from FHLMC members, which it then packages under its own name and assurances and resells to the public.

FEDERAL HOUSING ADMINISTRATION

FHA, operating under the Department of Housing and Urban Development (HUD), insures mortgage loans, principally on residential housing.

FEDERAL INTERMEDIATE CREDIT BANKS

Government-sponsored corporation that makes loans to banks and other credit institutions engaged in agricultural financing projects.
See also FEDERAL FARM CREDIT BANKS.

FEDERAL LAND BANKS

Supervised by Farm Credit Administration, the FLB are owned by farmers through land bank associations. FLB makes agricultural purpose loans to farmers and ranchers secured by first mortgages on real estate.
See also FEDERAL FARM CREDIT BANKS.

FEDERAL NATIONAL MORTGAGE ASSOCIATION

Nickname: Fannie Mae. Government-sponsored, publicly owned corporation was created to give liquidity in the secondary market for FHA-insured and for some conventional mortgages. Mortgages are purchased from approved holders using the proceeds from the sale of FNMA debentures and notes.

FEDERAL OPEN MARKET COMMITTEE

Committee of Federal Reserve governors and of presidents of six Federal Reserve Banks. Purpose: to make short-term monetary decisions to achieve long-term objective of Fed as regulator of money and credit supply.

Chief tool is the sale of government securities to decrease money supply, or purchase of government securities to expand money supply.

FEDERAL RESERVE BOARD

A statutory board of seven members, appointed by the President and with the advice and consent of the Senate for terms of 14 years, to regulate banking and credit activities in line with the goals of the Federal Reserve Act of 1913.

Principal tools: setting reserve requirements, open market activities, establishing the discount rate, controlling credit in the margin purchase of securities.

Commonly abbreviated Fed or FRB.

See also FEDERAL RESERVE SYSTEM.

FEDERAL RESERVE SYSTEM

Commonly means the Federal Reserve Bank, the 14 district banks, and the member banks of the Federal Reserve. Basically, a membership corporation, sponsored by the Federal Reserve Act of 1913.

The FRS has 2 functions: to act as a central bank and fiscal agent of the United States and to regulate credit in the American economy.

Also abbreviated FRB or Fed.

See also FEDERAL OPEN MARKET COMMITTEE.

FED WIRE

Computerized network linking the Fed with its district banks, member banks, and primary dealers in government securities. The network is used to transfer funds between banks and to transfer ownership of treasury and some agency securities by means of book-entry notation.

FICTITIOUS CREDIT

A credit in a client's account that represents the proceeds of a short sale and the margin required by Regulation T. It is called fictitious because the client may not withdraw the credit since both the proceeds and the margin protect the broker and the lender of the borrowed securities.

Opposite: a free credit balance (i.e., funds on deposit with a broker that may be withdrawn whenever the client chooses).

FIDELITY BOND

Insurance policy that protects broker-dealers from loss caused by misplacement of funds or securities, check forgery, fraudulent trading practices, or securities forgery. Policy covers such activities by employees, officers, or partners. Exchange and NASD rules set the amount of insurance that is required.

Also called fidelity bond insurance or blanket fidelity bond.

FIDUCIARY

Person entrusted with the control of assets for the benefit of others. Most states have laws governing the conduct of fiduciaries.

Fiduciaries are generally court-appointed: executors of wills, administrators of estates, receivers-in-bankruptcy, and committees for incompetents. Trustees also are considered fiduciaries. The document of appointment usually limits the power of fiduciaries and sets guidelines for their activities.

Custodians under Uniform Gifts to Minors Acts are fiduciaries in the sense they may not alienate assets for their own benefit. They are not, however, directly governed by a written court-approved document governing the conduct of such accounts.

FILL

Commonly used industry term for the execution of an order to buy or sell a security.

Execution of less than the amount designated in the order is a partial fill.

FILL OR KILL

A limit order to buy or sell that the client instructs, as follows: If this order cannot be executed immediately at its limit price, cancel the entire order. FOK orders, although they may be buy or sell orders, are usually buy orders.

FOK orders, in most cases, are for a significant quantity of the security—one that would otherwise cause a significant price change if a market order to buy-sell were entered.

If the order is not executed, the client will want to reassess his strategy.

FINANCIAL ACCOUNTING STANDARDS BOARD

An independent body of certified public accountants that studies bookkeeping practices and publishes opinions about these practices. Generally, corporations abide by these standards in the preparation of financial reports.

FINANCIAL FUTURE

Futures contract for interest-sensitive securities: T-bills, T-notes, T-bonds, CDs, and GNMA pass-throughs.

Trading is governed by the Commodities Futures Trading Commission (CFTC) and requires special registration.

Trend of financial futures trading is often an indicator of interest rates, but interpretation of trend requires sophisticated assessment of the basis, which is the difference between cash and futures price.

FINANCIAL PRINCIPAL

A National Association of Securities Dealers' examination for a person qualified to prepare and approve member firm's financial statements and computation of net capital requirements.

FINDER'S FEE

Remuneration to a person who refers business to another. For example, "The finder's fee for the referral of Company A to Company B in their merger was $500,000."

FIRM COMMITMENT

The underwriter, either through negotiation or competition, agrees to buy the securities to be issued. The underwriter, therefore, owns the securities. If the securities are sold at the public offering price, the underwriter usually makes a profit. If the securities are not sold at the public offering price, the underwriter may have a diminished profit or a loss.

In no case can the underwriter make a profit from a sale above the public offering price (unless the securities are exempt) because federal law requires that a bona fide public offering be made.

Also called firm commitment underwriting.

See also FREERIDING; WITHHOLDING; BOUGHT DEAL.

FIRM ORDER

1. A buy or sell order on behalf of a broker-dealer's proprietary account.
2. A buy or sell order given to a broker-dealer. Normally, set terms and conditions are established for a fixed time. The order can be executed within that time without further confirmation from the customer.

FIRM QUOTE

Commonly accepted term for a bid-offer at which a market maker is willing to buy or sell a generally accepted round lot of a security.

Ethics of the industry require that any quote not firm be identified as either a nominal or a subject quote.

FIRST CALL DATE

Used in municipal and corporate bond offering sheets to designate earliest future date when the issuer of a debt security may exercise the privilege of redeeming all or part of an issue at the price set forth in the indenture. For example, AJAX 11s of '02 FC '85, which means the AJAX 11% bonds that mature in 2002 have their first call date in 1985.

FIRST IN, FIRST OUT
Accounting method of assigning cost to inventory used to produce salable goods.

Opposite: last in, first out—LIFO.

Accounting method is choice of corporation, and IRS approval is required to change more than once.

Important note: on sale of securities, IRS presumes FIFO unless owner designates that some other method of valuation was used.

FISCAL AGENT
Manager of securities sales for the U.S. government or one of its agencies. Responsible for obtaining capital by distributing its debt instruments. For example, the Federal Reserve is the fiscal agent of the U.S. government.

FISCAL YEAR
Any consecutive 12-month period of financial accountability for a corporation or other governmental agency. Often abbreviated FY with a date. For example, FY May 31. The firm's fiscal year goes from June 1 to May 31 of the following year.

FIT
As a noun: signifies ability of an investor to purchase securities that meet the portfolio needs of the investor in terms of credit rating, price, yield, and so on. For example, "We've got a fit with the AJAX 14s priced to yield 15.50."

FITCH
Shortened term for Fitch Investors Services. Fitch provides corporate bond ratings that give investors an insight into the degree of credit risk entailed in investing in the bond of the corporation.

See also FITCH SHEETS.

FITCH SHEETS
A chronological record of successive trade prices for listed securities maintained by Fitch Investors Services. For example, "I found the price in the Fitch Sheets."

FIVE HUNDRED DOLLAR RULE
Under Regulation T, a broker-dealer need not invoke buy-in, sell-out procedures against an account if the cash deficiency is less than $500. For example, a client buys securities worth $10,000 plus commissions. Client's check is for $10,000, but the client is out of

town and cannot be reached. The broker need not liquidate a portion of the account to recoup the $287.50 commission that was not included in the check.

FIVE PERCENT RULE

One of NASD Rules of Fair Practice that is used to define fair and reasonable in the determination of markups, markdowns, and commissions. It is an ethical rather than a mathematical criterion and permits exceptions based upon other relevant factors that pertain to the transaction.

Also called five percent guideline.

See also PROCEEDS SALE and RISKLESS TRANSACTION.

FIXED ANNUITY

Investment contract sold by an insurance company for an immediate or installment payment of premiums. When annuitized, the insurance company guarantees periodic fixed payments to the annuitant, either for life or for alternate periods—according to the election made by the annuitant. By guaranteeing payments, the insurance company assumes both the mortality and the investment risks of the annuitant.

FIXED ASSETS

Accounting term for assets of a corporation that are not readily salable and which represent the depreciated value of property, equipment, and other tangible assets.

FIXED-CHARGE COVERAGE

Comparison of corporation's income before interest and taxes with annual interest payments on funded debt. For example, income before interest and taxes is $10 million and bond interest is $2 million per year. The fixed-charge coverage is 5.

Fixed-charge coverage is a measurement of the safety of a bond and enters into rating by bond-rating services. It is, however, a relative number because a large coverage may indicate that a company is underleveraged and has not fully used its borrowing potential.

Also called times fixed charges.

FIXED LIABILITY

Commonly used for longer-term debts of a corporation maturing in more than one year.

Also called funded debt.

FIXED TRUST

Term used of those unit investment trusts that have a fixed portfolio of securities. To be distinguished from participating trusts, the normal organizational form of a plan company that sells units in a contractual mutual fund.

Fixed trusts usually invest in a type of security. For example, in corporate bonds, government bonds, and municipal bonds to provide steady income to unit holders.

FLAG

Term from technical analysis to designate a pattern of stock price movements that, in general, resembles a triangle with the apex to the viewer's right.

Usually indicates an indecisive subsequent move in the stock's price. Often used by technical analysts to buy an option straddle so a profit may be obtained from either an upward or downward move in the price of the security.

Also called a pennant, triangle, or coil.

FLASH

If the volume on an exchange is so great that current displays show transactions occurring more than five minutes ago, it is customary to interrupt the tape display to flash a current price for a widely traded security.

For example:

ABC   XYZ   FLASH LMN
    52   31   24

The LMN price represents an interruption and is a current price. Also called flash prices.

FLAT

1 A bond that is sold without accrued interest.
   See also FLAT BOND.
2 A market maker's inventory that is neither long nor short (i.e., the market maker has a net zero position).
3 An underwriter's position if all of the securities are sold from the account.

FLAT BOND

Description of a bond that trades without accrued interest.

Bonds in default trade flat. Income bonds, if no interest has been declared, trade flat.

Most common application of flat bond: if a bond trades on a date that makes the settlement date the same as the coupon payment date, the bond will trade flat. Reason: the accrued interest will be 180 days; therefore, the seller will retain the current coupon to recoup the interest due. The buyer begins to accrue interest on the settlement date but has no accrued interest to pay the former owner.

FLAT MARKET

A market that is typified by a horizontal price movement because of little or no market activity in the security.

Do not confuse with stabilization, consolidation, or distribution. Each of these terms often is associated with active trading during a sideways price movement having an indecisive future movement. A flat market implies a sideways movement because there is little or no activity in the security.

FLAT SCALE

Municipal bond expression: there is little difference between short-term and long-term yields over the maturity range of a new serial maturity issue.

FLOAT

1   The number of shares in the hands of the public; thus, it gives insight into the number of shares available for trading. For example, "ABC has a small float."
2   Float also is the time lag in the check-clearing process. Float may be advantageous to the checkwriter, or disadvantageous to the check depositor, depending on the number of days it takes for a check written to appear as a debit, or a check deposited to appear as a credit.

FLOATER

Slang expression for floating rate notes (i.e., of debt securities whose semiannual rate of interest is indexed to a money market interest rate).

FLOATING AN ISSUE

Industry jargon for the issuance and public distribution of a new issue of securities. For example, "LMN is floating an issue of convertible debentures."

FLOATING DEBT

Term primarily used in municipal security analysis for debts that will mature within five years.

Also called bonded debt.

FLOATING RATE NOTE

A note, usually with a 5- to 7-year maturity, whose stated rate of semiannual interest is indexed to some preestablished money market rate. The money market rate may be an average of T-bill rates or some other sensitive market rate.

Because rate is variable, the holders of FRNs have substantially reduced interest rate risk.

FLOATING SUPPLY

Term most commonly used of the dollar value of municipal bonds offered in the Blue List. For example, the floating supply is about $2.5 billion.

Also used of individual securities to designate quantity of an issue in the hands of persons willing to sell at current levels. For example, "We estimate that the floating supply is no more than 50,000 shares."

FLOOR

Used of exchanges to designate the place where auction transactions in listed securities occur.

See also UPSTAIRS MARKET.

FLOOR BROKER

Popular name for commission house broker. Term designates a member of an exchange who, as an employee of a member firm, executes buy and sell orders received from the customers of the member firm.

FLOOR OFFICIAL

Exchange term for a member or an employee of the exchange who is authorized to settle disputes in the auction procedure. Thus, if a dispute arises about priority or precedence in the settling of an auction, or if there is a question about the existence of a fair and orderly market, the normal procedure is to call upon a floor official for an on-the-spot judgment. In practice, the judgment of the floor official is accepted.

FLOOR TICKET

A summary of the order ticket entered by the registered representative when a customer enters an order to buy or sell securities. The floor ticket contains the essential information needed to complete the transaction. Term is generally used of the ticket sent to exchanges, although it can also be used of OTC order instructions.

Industry rules specify the kind of information that must be contained on floor tickets.

FLOOR TRADER

Member of an exchange who is registered as a competitive trader. Such members trade for their own accounts and are governed by rules that approximate the rules that govern specialists.

FLOWER BONDS

Certain designated issues of U.S. Treasury bonds that are acceptable at par in the payment of estate taxes if the bonds were owned by the decedent at the time of death. The last of currently outstanding flower bonds will mature in 1998.

Also called estate tax anticipation bonds.

FLOW OF FUNDS

Used in conjunction with bond resolution of municipal revenue issues. Flow of funds statement usually establishes this priority: (1) operation and maintenance, (2) bond debt service, (3) expansion of the facility, (4) a sinking fund for the retirement of debt before the original maturity. Bond resolution will give precise flow of funds application; it differs from issue to issue.

Also called flow of funds statement.

FOCUS REPORT

Acronym for Financial and Operational Combined Uniform Single report. Broker-dealers must make such reports to SROs (self-regulatory organizations) on a monthly and quarterly basis. Reports detail capital, earnings, trade flow, and other pertinent information.

FORBES 500

Directory of the 500 largest publicly owned corporations, compiled by Forbes magazine. Directory compares and ranks each of these companies by sales, assets, profits, and market value of shares.

FORCED CONVERSION

Term used to describe this situation: a convertible security is selling above its call price because of the market value of the underlying common shares. Issuer calls the convertible security at the call price. Owner of the convertible is forced to convert to common shares, to sell the convertible, or to accept a loss of potential value by accepting the call price.

FORM 3

Document filed with the Securities and Exchange Commission by officers, directors, and holders of 10% or more of equity securities of a company registered with the SEC. Document states beneficial ownership of stock or other security that may be converted into equity security: rights, warrants, options, or convertibles. The form is available from the SEC.

FORM 4

Document filed with the Securities and Exchange Commission by officers, directors, and holders of 10% or more of equity securities of a company registered with SEC to reflect net changes in security ownership. Document must be filed within 10 days after the end of month in which the changes occur. The form can be obtained from the SEC.

FORM 8K

Public report that must be filed with the Securities and Exchange Commission by a reporting corporation. Report must be filed in month following any material event that affects the company's financial situation. Criterion: would this event materially affect the buying or selling of the corporation's securities? The format of the report is established by the SEC.

FORM 10K

Report that must be filed annually with the Securities and Exchange Commission by reporting corporations. This includes all listed corporations and corporations with 500 or more shareholders and with assets of $1 million or more. The SEC outlines information that must be included in report. Summary of 10K report must be included in the annual report that is to be sent to registered shareholders.

FORM 10Q

Report that must be filed quarterly with the Securities and Exchange Commission by reporting corporations. Summary of the report must be sent to stockholders.

Investment companies do not file quarterly reports; instead, they send semiannual reports to shareholders.

FORMULA INVESTING

Investment strategies based either on time or on profit and loss experience. All are based on preestablished rules that minimize emotional prejudices.

Principal applications: dollar cost averaging, a method of risk reduction based on the periodic investment of equal dollar amounts; constant dollar plan, a method of so allocating profits in a bond-stock portfolio that the profits in one portfolio are reinvested in the other so there will be—according to a prestated time frame—a basic balance between equity and fixed-income investments.

FORTUNE 500

Directory of the 500 largest U.S. industrial corporations, compiled by Fortune magazine. The directory compares sales, net income, and stockholders' equity. Frequently the second 500 are given in a subsequent issue of Fortune. The same criteria are used. Financial and utility corporations are not included in the directory.

FORWARD CONTRACT

Completed transaction in a commodity, security, or financial instrument at a negotiated rate with a future settlement date. For example, a forward contract for 100,000 ounces of silver at $6.54 per ounce with a delivery date on March 15.

Because the forward contract is completed, it may be used as a cover for a sale of a futures contract.

Forward contracts are available for most commodities, precious metals, and government securities and agencies.

FORWARD PRICING

Term used to describe SEC regulation of bid-offer prices for mutual funds. Under forward pricing, all incoming orders to buy and sell become effective on the next net asset valuation of fund shares.

Sell orders are executed on the net asset valuation (minus any redemption charge). In practice, funds do not charge for redemptions.

Buy orders are executed at the public offering price. No-load funds have the same buy and redemption prices.

FOR YOUR INFORMATION

Often used as a prefix to a quote. It means that market maker is unwilling to trade at that price but is supplying the quote as a courtesy. Price can be used for valuation, but is not a firm quote.

FVO, for valuation only, is often used as a substitute for FYI.

FOURTH MARKET

Term commonly used for a computerized subscription service. Subscribers can enter orders, either to buy or to sell. Computer then searches for the other side of the trade. Service is used by institutional investors, who trade directly with each other and do not use a brokerage firm.

See also INSTINET.

FRACTIONAL DISCRETION ORDER

Order to buy or sell that gives the executing broker discretion, within a prestated limit, for the execution of the order. For example: "Buy 2,000 ABC at 45, discretion one half point" (i.e., maximum price 45½).

FREE BOX
Industry slang for a bank vault or other secure location used to store fully paid customer securities.

Many broker-dealers use the Depository Trust Company (DTC) as a free box for their customer-owned securities.

FREE CREDIT BALANCE
Cash held by a broker in a customer's account that may be withdrawn by the customer at any time.

Free credit balance should not be confused with the credit that results from a short sale. This latter credit is held in escrow to secure the loan of securities made to the client when the short sale was made.

Entries in the special miscellaneous accounts (SMAs) of margin customers are not considered free credit balances.

FREE CROWD
Term often used of the active crowd for bond trading on the New York Stock Exchange.

See also ACTIVE BOND CROWD and CAN CROWD.

FREED UP
Term signifying that members of an underwriting syndicate are no longer bound to sell the security at the price agreed upon in the agreement among underwriters. For example, "The manager was unable to stabilize the offering, so the account was freed up."

Also called free to trade.

FREERIDING
1 NASD rule violation that results if a member of an underwriting account withholds a portion of a public offering and resells it at a profit.
2 Used of customers who buy, then sell at a profit, without depositing money to show ability and intent to pay. Regulation T requires that such customer accounts be frozen for 90 days. Freeriding is prohibited in margin accounts.
See also FROZEN ACCOUNT.

FREE RIGHT OF EXCHANGE
Term used if a security holder may change the security from bearer to registered format, or vice versa, without charge.

See also REGISTERED SECURITY.

FRONT-ENDING AN ORDER

Term describing block orders where a broker-dealer agrees to buy a portion of a block with the provision that he will execute the remainder of the order as agent. For example, "We front-ended the order for 100,000 shares by taking 25,000."

FRONT-END LOAD

Contractual purchase plan used by many mutual funds. In exchange for some privileges, customer agrees that a large portion of first year's contributions will be used to offset total sales charges over the life of the contract.

See also LOAD SPREAD OPTION.

FRONT-RUNNING

Industry slang for someone who, with prior knowledge of an impending block transaction in a security, buys or sells options in that security.

FROZEN ACCOUNT

Regulation T requires cash account customers to pay promptly and not make a habit of selling securities before they are paid for. Customers who violate this rule have their account frozen for 90 days. During this period, such customers must pay in full for purchases before the buy order is entered, and sell orders will not be entered unless the broker has the certificates in hand.

See also FREERIDING 2.

FULL DISCLOSURE

General principle of ethical sales: the seller must fairly represent the item being sold. In U.S. securities law, this principle is incorporated in the Securities Act of 1933 that regulates the public sale of corporate securities. The concept of disclosure also is applied in the Securities Exchange Act of 1934 to secondary markets for most corporate securities.

FULL FAITH AND CREDIT

Expression signifying that an issuer's reputation and taxing power are pledged in the payment of interest and the repayment of principal for a specified debt security. U.S. government securities and general obligation bonds of states and municipalities are backed by the full faith and credit of the issuer.

FULLY DILUTED EARNINGS PER SHARE

Computation of corporate earnings applicable to each share of common stock that would be outstanding if all convertible and exchangeable securities were tendered for common shares at the beginning of the accounting period.

If such conversion had not been made, and earnings were divided among the previously outstanding shares, the term "primary earnings per share" is used.

FULLY DISTRIBUTED

Term used when a public offering of securities is successfully sold to institutional and retail customers. A public offering is not fully distributed if large portions of the offering are sold to traders and dealers.

FUNDAMENTAL ANALYSIS

Quantitative approach to forecasting based on a corporation's balance sheet and income statement. The strengths and weaknesses, as shown by arithmetic formulas and by other measurement of economic and industry trends, can indicate future price movements in the security.

See also TECHNICAL ANALYSIS.

FUNDED DEBT

Commonly, those debts of a corporation that will mature in more than one year.

On corporation balance sheets, funded debt is usually identified as long-term liabilities.

FUNGIBLE

Any bearer instrument that is freely transferable and equal in all respects to any other instrument of the same class of the same issuer. Perfect example: a dollar bill that you lend is paid back by another dollar bill.

As a general rule, common stock of the same issuer is fungible. Other securities, with different maturities, call dates, or par value are not fungible.

FUTURES CONTRACT

Completed, but transferable, agreement to make or take delivery of the object of the contract at a specified time at a specified price. The most common futures contracts center on commodities and financial instruments.

A futures contract should not be confused with an option contract. An option contract is not completed and leaves with the buyer of the option the choice of requiring or not requiring the completion of the contract.

FUTURES MARKET

General name for marketplaces where contracts for the future delivery of commodities and certain financial instruments are traded according to preestablished conditions.

The principal futures marketplaces are: Chicago Board of Trade, Chicago Mercantile Exchange, COMEX (New York), Kansas City Board of Trade, and New York Futures Exchange. There also are futures markets in London and Canada. Spot (cash) markets for commodities exist throughout the world.

G

GAP

Term used of a stock's price trend if the range for one trading session does not overlap a portion of the subsequent trading session. For example, range on Monday 40 low to 40-½ high; range on Tuesday 41 low to 41-½ high. There was a gap in the trading pattern.

A gap often is a sign of a reversal because the market is overbought or oversold.

GARAGE

Nickname for the annex floor to the north of the main trading floor of the New York Stock Exchange.

GENERAL ACCOUNT

Federal Reserve term for a client's margin account. All equity transactions in which a broker maintains a creditor relationship with the customer must be made in the general account. Some transactions, however, may be made in special margin accounts (e.g., subscriptions, bonds, convertibles, and arbitrages).

See also EQUITY.

GENERAL OBLIGATION BOND

A municipal security whose interest and principal payments are backed by the full faith, credit, and taxing power of the issuer. Usually included in this category are limited tax bonds to be repaid from real estate taxes and special assessment bonds to be repaid by user fees.

Popularly abbreviated GO.

GIFT TAX

Federal or state tax levied upon the person who gives an asset to another and who does not receive full consideration in exchange.

Under the law, there is an annual exclusion of $10,000 per recipient. The gift tax is applicable to the dollar value above the exclusion. There is no gift tax on gifts between spouses.

GILT-EDGED
Term applied to the security of a corporation that has proved, over time, its ability to pay continuous dividends or interest. It refers more often to high-quality bonds than to stocks.

GINNIE MAE PASS-THROUGH
A security that represents a proportional interest in a pool of mortgages. The security is called a pass-through because homeowners send monthly mortgage payments to a bank, which passes through the security holder's share of the payment after deducting a service charge.

Timely payment of interest and principal is guaranteed by the Government National Mortgage Association (GNMA or Ginnie Mae). Original principal amount is stated on the security certificate, but remaining unpaid principal is reduced monthly.

Technical name for these securities is GNMA Modified Pass-Through, because the coupon rate or production rate on the certificates is modified by the deduction of ½% from the loan rate of the mortgage pool. This deduction pays for the sponsoring bank's services. The principal is passed through without deduction.

See also HALF-LIFE.

GIVE UP
Term used when an exchange member, acting as an agent for another member, designates that party as the person with whom the contra broker has traded. For example, Member A trades with Member B and "gives up the name of" Member C as the person with whom Broker B has traded.

The term also is used if a customer of one firm, while traveling, enters an order to buy or sell with another firm, with the instruction that his regular broker handle the clearing details of the transaction.

GLASS STEAGALL ACT
Federal law that prohibits commercial banks from owning broker-dealer affiliates. Bank holding companies, however, may own such affiliates. Law forbids commercial banks from owning, underwriting, or trading corporate securities for proprietary accounts. Law also forbids banks from underwriting most municipal revenue bonds.

GO AROUND
When the Federal Open Market Committee canvasses primary bank and nonbank dealers for their bids and offers, the process is called a go around.

GO-GO FUND
Popular name for investment companies that specialize in highly speculative ventures.

GOING AWAY
Term used by municipal bond syndicates to designate one or more serial maturities of the issue that have been purchased in large amounts by an institutional account (going away) or by another dealer to use as inventory for future sales (going away for stock).

GOOD DELIVERY
Industry term for a certificate that meets certain standards and thus is negotiable among brokers. These standards apply to proper denomination, endorsement, signature guarantee, and other qualifications. If a certificate is in good deliverable form and is presented by the selling broker, it must be accepted by the buying broker.

GOOD FAITH DEPOSIT
1 Deposit required by member firms when a customer, unknown to the firm, enters an order to buy or sell. Usually a good faith deposit is 25%.
2 Deposit, usually 1 to 5% of the principal amount of the issue, made by competing municipal underwriters with the issuer. Losing syndicates have the deposit returned. The winning syndicate leaves the deposit with the issuer and it becomes part of the final settlement for the issue.

GOOD MONEY
Common expression for federal funds. Federal funds are called good money because they can be used immediately without going through bank clearance.

GOOD TILL CANCELLED ORDER
An order to buy or sell, usually at a limit or stop price, that remains in effect until cancelled by the customer. Although the order and its terms remain in effect indefinitely, industry practice is to require periodic verification from the customer that he wishes the order to remain in force.

GOVERNMENT NATIONAL MORTGAGE ASSOCIATION

Government-owned corporation, operating within the Department of Housing and Urban Development (HUD); facilitates financing in the primary mortgage market by:

1 Purchasing mortgages from private lenders to encourage construction.
2 Guaranteeing the timely payment of principal and interest on certain pools of mortgages.

Nickname is Ginnie Mae. The name often is used of the securities of the GNMA.

GRANDFATHER CLAUSE

A provision generally written into new rules that permits persons previously engaged in certain specific functions and procedures to continue to qualify without undergoing new tests or other qualification procedures.

Also called grandfathering.

GRATUTITY FUND

Special fund that provides death benefits for the next of kin of deceased members of the exchanges. Fund is made up of contributions from the members. NYSE fund payment varies from $20,000 to $100,000 depending on the tenure of the decedent. The ASE fund payment is $75,000.

GREEN SHOE

Provision in an underwriting agreement that permits the syndicate to purchase additional shares at the same price as the original offering. In this way, the underwriting group can cover shares sold short without financial risk.

Also called the green shoe clause.

GROSS NATIONAL PRODUCT

Dollar value of the final goods and services produced in the U.S. economy. The GNP is considered the principal coincident indicator of the state of the American economy. Looked at from the point of view of users, the GNP is equal to the national income.

On a quarterly basis the Bureau of Economic Analysis (Department of Commerce) compiles and reports two GNPs: the normal, which is the total for the quarter, and the real GNP, the total after the effects of inflation are removed.

GROSS SELECTION

Depends on the context. Most common usage: a preliminary selection before the final selection is made.

GROSS SPREAD
Dollar difference between the public offering price of a new issue of securities and the proceeds to the issuer. The gross spread is further subdivided into the manager's fee, the dealer's (or underwriter's) discount, and the selling concession.

GROUP NET
Buy order given to manager of a municipal securities syndicate. Purchaser, who is a nonmember, agrees to pay the public offering price and to leave the entire spread in the account for the benefit of the syndicate. Group net orders are priority orders and are confirmed before typical retail orders.

Also called group net order.

See also MEMBER TAKEDOWN.

GROUP SALES
Term refers to the sale of SEC-registered offerings by the manager of the syndicate to institutional investors. The shares come from the "pot" established by the syndicate. Credit for the sale is proportional to the takedown of the individual members of the syndicate.

GROWTH STOCK
Equity security of a company that is expected to increase in market value at a relatively rapid rate. Growth usually is a function of rapidly increasing earnings, although special situations may cause a stock to be considered a growth stock.

Growth stocks usually are marked by a relatively high price-earnings ratio and a low dividend payout ratio.

GUARANTEED BOND
A bond, or preferred stock, for which the payment of principal and the interest, in the case of a bond, or the dividend, in the case of a preferred stock, is guaranteed by someone other than the issuer. Guaranteed securities are common in the issues made by a subsidiary. In this case, the parent corporation guarantees the security issued by the subsidiary.

Also called guaranteed stock.

GUARANTEED INCOME CONTRACT
Investment contract sold by insurance companies to pension and to profit-sharing plans, usually for 3 to 10 years. In return for a large capital investment, the insurance company guarantees a specified rate of return on the invested capital. The insurance company assumes

all market, rate, and credit risks on the securities held in trust to collateralize the obligation.

GUARANTEE LETTER

Letter issued by a commercial bank on behalf of a customer who has written a put option. The letter, which specifies both the dollars and the put contract involved, promises to pay a specified sum when, and if, an assignment notice is presented.

GUN JUMPING

Industry slang for:
1 The illegal act of soliciting buy orders before an SEC registration is effective.
2 Buying a security based on information that is not yet public.

H

HAIRCUT

Industry term for the valuation of securities used to compute the broker-dealer's net capital. The haircut varies with the class of security, its market risk, and time to maturity. The haircut may vary from 0% to 30% (which is common for equity securities) to 100% for fail positions that have little chance of being settled in the member firm's favor.

HALF-LIFE

Term used of GNMA pass-throughs. It is the time after issuance when it is estimated that one half of the principal amount on a pool of mortgages shall have been repaid. Based on FHA experience of prepayment and default, GNMA pass-throughs are presumed to have a half-life of 12 years. In practice, the half-life of a specific pool may be longer or shorter than 12 years.

HARD DOLLARS

Actual dollars paid for the research or other services provided by a firm to a client. The expression is used in contrast to soft dollars. For example, a computer analysis of a client's portfolio may cost $3,000 hard dollars; or $10,000 soft dollars, if the client directs portfolio transactions through the firm that provided the computer service.

HEAD AND SHOULDERS

Bar chart pattern of a stock's price movement marked by a shoulder line, neck line, and head line conforming, in general, to a person's upper torso. As the price movement approaches the shoulder line on the right, technicians consider the trend as bearish—a head and shoulders top. The reverse pattern is upside down, with the head at bottom. Such a pattern is considered bullish—and called a head and shoulders bottom.

HEDGE

Used both as a verb and a noun to indicate reduced risk.

A hedge involves an offsetting securities position that limits loss. A hedge that eliminates the possibility of future gain or loss is a perfect hedge.

Example of a perfect hedge: a client holds appreciated stock and sells short against the box.

Example of an imperfect hedge: buy a stock and sell a call. Client is hedged against loss by the amount of the premium received.

See also BOX.

HEDGE CLAUSE

Statement that appears in a research report, market letter, or other security valuation in which the writer disclaims responsibility for the accuracy of information that the writer took from what are considered to be reliable information sources. The intent is to remove liability for the accuracy of the information, although the writer is not absolved from negligence in the use of the information.

HEDGED TENDER

Situation envisions a seller (a tenderer) who anticipates that less than the full amount of stock tendered will be accepted by the buyer. The tenderer sells short a portion of the amount tendered so she is protected if the full amount of her tender is not accepted.

HEDGE FUND

Slang term for a limited partnership that speculates in securities. Limited partners have limited risk, but their rewards are shared by the general partners.

Term also is used of funds that use hedging techniques. For example, calls, puts, margin, and shorting to increase return.

HEMLINE THEORY

Stock market theory that the trend in the hemline of women's dresses is accompanied by a corresponding trend in the prices for stocks. For example, if hemlines are trending down, stock prices are trending down; if up, stock prices are trending up. Obviously, there is an upper limit on this theory.

HIGHBALLING

Fraudulent swap technique. A client's holdings are purchased by the dealer above current market value so he does not have a loss. However, the client swaps for a new holding above its market value. The dealer accepts the "loss" on the purchase so he can build in a present gain on the sale.

HIGH-GRADE BOND

A bond with a rating of AAA or AA.

HISTORICAL YIELD

Originally, the yield on a mutual fund that took the annual dividend and divided it by the average public offering price. With the abrogation of the SEC's Statement of Policy in 1980, funds have been free to compute yield by any reasonable method. Most funds now take annual yield and divide it by a reasonable average. Money market funds typically use yield to average life.

HIT THE BID

Expression used when a seller is willing to accept the bid made by a buyer. For example, if the quote is 18 to a quarter, a seller who hits the bid sells at 18.

HOLDER OF RECORD

The person whose name appears on a company's register of security holders at the close of business on the record date assigned by the company. The disbursing agent for the company will send the dividend or interest to that person on the payment date determined by the company.

HOLDING COMPANY

Under federal law, this is any corporation, partnership, trust, association, or organized group of persons that owns or controls 10% or more of the outstanding voting securities of a public utility company.

Term also is used of any company organized to own and manage other companies.

HOLDING PERIOD

The time that an investor owns a capital asset. On purchases followed by a sale, the IRS computes a long-term holding as follows: take the date following the purchase date; long-term holding begins on that calendar date one year later. For example, a purchase is made on February 28 in a non-leap year. The next day is March 1. One year later, the holding is long-term. There is a different computation of holding period on gifts and bequests.

HORIZONTAL PRICE MOVEMENT

A term describing a succession of transaction prices in a security that are relatively the same. For example, a security that has a price range of between $8 and $10 per share over 1 or 2 months has a horizontal price movement.

Many persons use sideways price movement to describe the same series of prices. Key concept: The price does not vary substantially over time. As such, a horizontal price movement is indecisive and does not indicate a trend in the price of the security.

HORIZONTAL SPREAD

Technically, a horizontal spread is the purchase and sale of an equal number of contracts of options of the same class with the same striking price, but with different expiration months. For example:

> Buy 5 ABC April 60 calls
> Sell 5 ABC Jan   60 calls

Also called a calendar spread.

HOT ISSUE

NASD term for an SEC-registered public offering with an over-the-counter bid that is higher than the fixed public offering price on the day the security is offered for sale. For example, a syndicate offers an issue at $31 per share. At the end of the trading day, the OTC bid is $32 per share. This is a hot issue and special rules apply to the syndicate's distribution of the security.

See also FREERIDING and WITHHOLDING.

HOT STOCK

1 Securities that are stolen.
2 Securities that rise rapidly in price on the initial sale date.
   See also HOT ISSUE.

HOUSE MAINTENANCE REQUIREMENTS

The lowest dollar levels to which the equity in a customer's margin account may decline before more equity must be supplied, or collateral will be liquidated. The requirement is set by the broker-dealer and is somewhat higher than the levels mandated by the self-regulatory organizations in their minimum maintenance requirements.

See also MAINTENANCE REQUIREMENT for examples.

HOUSE RULES
A broker-dealer's internal policies and procedures pertaining primarily to the opening and handling of customers' accounts and customers' activities in those accounts. House rules are often more strict than industry rules.

HOUSING AND URBAN DEVELOPMENT
Department of the federal government that fosters, through loan guarantees and other measures of public policy, lower-income and middle-income housing in the United States.

HOUSING STARTS
One of the 12 leading indicators of movement in the U.S. economy. A change in the number of housing starts can severely affect a number of industries: banking, construction, forest and wood products, and other industries that supply materials for housing.

HYBRID ANNUITY
An insurance company investment contract that combines features of both a fixed and a variable annuity in varying percentages, as elected by its subscribers.

HYPOTHECATION
Term refers to the pledging of securities or other assets as collateral for a loan while still keeping ownership. For example, if a client buys securities on margin, the securities are held by the broker (i.e., they are hypothecated, as a pledge that the client will repay the loan).

HYPOTHECATION AGREEMENT
Written agreement between customer and broker-dealer that details the rules under which the account is opened and carried. Principal parts of the agreement: securities purchased on margin are held by the broker-dealer; these securities may be repledged by the broker-dealer to finance the account; the broker-dealer may sell the pledged securities if needed, to protect its financial interest in the account.

Also called customer agreement or margin agreement.

I

ILLIQUID
Used of a security that does not enjoy an active secondary market; thus, the holder may find it difficult to sell the security and thereby go back to cash.

IMBALANCE OF ORDERS

Market situation in which there is such an excess of either buy or sell orders that no orderly market is possible. If this happens before the opening, the opening of the market will be delayed; if it occurs during the market day, the specialist will suspend trading until sufficient contra orders are obtained to resolve the imbalance.

IMMEDIATE FAMILY

Under the National Association of Securities Dealers' rules on Freeriding and Withholding, certain sales are prohibited to brokerage employees and each's immediate family. This latter term includes parents, mother- or father-in-law, brothers or sisters, and brothers- or sisters-in-law, children, and any relative to whose support the prohibited employee contributes.

IMMEDIATE-OR-CANCEL ORDER

Customer limit order to buy or sell a security, usually in significant quantity, with this qualification: any portion of the order that is not filled at the limit price is to be cancelled.

IMMEDIATE PAYMENT ANNUITY

A single payment annuity contract with the election of annuity payments to begin immediately. The payments, usually monthly, are for the life of the subscriber, or for a specified number of years, according to the election made.

INACTIVE BOND CROWD

New York Stock Exchange term for those listed bonds that trade infrequently. Limit orders to buy or sell such bonds are stored in steel cabinets to the side of the bond trading floor. Brokers with orders to buy or sell such bonds can seek a contra broker's order in the cabinet, with the trade completed in the bond trading area.

IN-AND-OUT TRADER

A day trader, who generally keeps no overnight position in a security or commodity and who endeavors to profit from intra-day price fluctuations.

INCENTIVE STOCK OPTION

Economic Recovery Tax Act (ERTA) of 1981 provides this form of executive compensation. Under ISO of ERTA, executive pays no tax when option is exercised. Difference between exercise price and sale price, if stock is held more than one year, is a long-term capital gain.

INCOME BOND

Bond that promises to pay interest only if earned or to the extent it is earned. Income bonds are normally exchanged for outstanding bonds of a bankrupt company that is being reorganized.

Also called adjustment bond.

INCOME INVESTMENT COMPANY

Popular classification of a management investment company whose primary investment objective is to provide maximum income to fundholders.

INCOME SHARES

A class of securities issued by dual-purpose investment companies, the other class of shares being capital shares. All income from both classes of shares accrues to the income shareholders; all capital gains accrue to the capital shareholders.

Because there is a minimum income guarantee, the income shares become the equivalent of cumulative preferred shares.

INDENTURE

The written deed of trust between an issuer and its bondholders. The indenture details the terms, conditions, and repayment provisions for the debt. Under the Trust Indenture Act, the indenture must also provide for the appointment of a trustee to oversee the agreement.

INDEX

A broad-based measurement of general market trend. The measurement is called an index because security prices are weighted to reflect the number of shares outstanding and the index, as a result, gives an insight into value change rather than only price change. Principal examples: the NYSE and ASE indices, the Standard & Poor's Index, and the NASDAQ OTC Index.

INDEX FUND

A fund with a portfolio of securities that includes many of the same securities composing a popular index and in the same proportional quantity as the index. Thus, over time, the fund should mirror the performance of the index.

INDICATION

A price range within which a security may trade. Indications are often given if normal trading cannot begin, or if it was halted because of an imbalance of orders on one side of the market.

INDICATIONS OF INTEREST

Indication by a client that he may be interested in the purchase of a security currently in registration with the SEC. This is not a firm commitment by either the client or the underwriter, and such indications must be reconfirmed by the client when the registration is effective.

INDIVIDUAL RETIREMENT ACCOUNT

Personal retirement program for employed persons. Under present law (1982) an employed person may deposit up to $2,000 of earned income annually. The deposit is (1) a deduction from income and (2) tax sheltered until withdrawn at age 59-½ or later. Withdrawal must begin no later than the calendar year in which person becomes 70-½. Deposits must be made under a qualified plan.

See also IRA ROLLOVER.

INDIVIDUAL SEGREGATION

Method used by some brokers to identify fully paid client securities left with the broker. The segregation may be effected by registering the security in the client's name, or by attaching an identification with the client's name to certificates registered in the name of the broker.

INDUSTRIAL DEVELOPMENT BOND

Municipal revenue bond whose debt service is paid from net lease payments made by an industrial corporation to the municipality. For the interest income to be exempt from federal taxation for the bondholder, the corporation must use the facilities to improve civic services or for pollution control activities.

Also called industrial revenue bond.

INITIAL MARGIN

Term from Regulation T of the Federal Reserve to designate the percentage that must be supplied by a customer who places himself at risk in a margin account. At the present time, the initial margin is 50% of the purchase price or 50% of the proceeds of a short sale. Regulations G and U apply similar standards if a person purchases securities with money borrowed from a bank (U) or from another lender (G).

INSIDE INFORMATION

Legal and industry term for material information that (1) would influence the purchase or sale of a company's security and (2) has not been publicized in a widely used medium. For example, a company suffered a dramatic loss and this fact has not yet been announced publicly.

INSIDE MARKET

Inside market quotes are the bid or asked prices at which one dealer will buy from or sell to another. In contrast, retail market quotes are the prices at which customers may buy or sell to the dealer.

Also called wholesale or inter-dealer market.

INSIDER

Slang for a person who (1) controls a corporation, (2) owns 10% or more of a company's stock, or (3) has inside information. The term is used most often of the directors and the elected officers of a corporation.

See also INSIDE INFORMATION.

INSTALLMENT SALE

A securities transaction in which the contract price is set, but the proceeds are paid, over time, in installments. As a general rule, gains or losses on such transactions are considered to be prorated for tax purposes.

INSTINET

Computerized trade execution service, Institutional Networks Corporation, registered with the SEC as a stock exchange. Exchange permits subscribers to search the system for the opposite side of a trade, without the cost of brokerage fees. Used by many mutual funds and other institutional investors. Trades are reported on the composite tape if the security is listed.

See also FOURTH MARKET.

INSTITUTIONAL INVESTOR

Industry term for an investor who, because of the size or frequency of transactions, is eligible for preferential commissions and other special transaction services. The term is often used of banks, mutual funds, insurance companies, and large corporate investment accounts, although definition will vary from one brokerage firm to another.

INTER-BANK RATE

Interest rate at which banks are willing to buy and sell excess reserves among themselves. Similar to federal funds rate, although both banks and nonbanks participate in the federal funds market.

INTERMARKET TRADING SYSTEM
Electronic system that links the floors of the American, Boston, Midwest, Pacific, Philadelphia, and New York stock exchanges. The system provides a comparison of bids and offers on the exchanges. A buyer or seller, therefore, can choose the best market. The actual transaction is completed outside the system by telephone or telex.
See also CONSOLIDATED TAPE.

INTERMEDIARY
A person or organization helping an investor to make, or to implement, investment decisions (i.e., persons who permit the investor to buy into a portfolio of securities). For example, an insurance company, a bank, or a mutual fund are called portfolio intermediaries. Persons who assist an investor with the execution of orders to buy or sell, or who provide investment advice, are called marketing intermediaries.

INTERMEDIATE TERM
A relative expression for a period somewhere between a short and a long time.
1   When used of fundamental security analysis: intermediate is between 6 months and 1 year. For example, "We expect the stock to rise in the intermediate term."
2   When used of debt securities: intermediate term signifies that 1 to 10 years remain to maturity.

INTERMEDIATION
The placement of investment dollars with a portfolio intermediary; the intermediary, in turn, invests the dollars in securities, mortgages, or other investments. The investor accepts the investment judgment of the intermediary.
The opposite term is disintermediation. In this situation, the investor withdraws dollars left with the portfolio intermediary to make direct security investments.

INTERNATIONAL MONETARY MARKET
A division of the Chicago Mercantile Exchange that provides a marketplace for futures contracts in foreign currencies, silver coins, and U.S. Treasury bills and notes.

INTERPOLATION
Mathematical procedure for the approximation of either price or

yield when the actual bond's maturity falls between listed maturity dates. For example, if the bond yield table gives the price for 11 years and 11 years and six months, and your bond is 11 years and three months, take a price that is halfway between the two prices. The same principle applies to yield differences.

INTERPOSITIONING

A potentially unethical practice whereby a broker employs a second broker to complete a transaction between a customer and a market maker. The customer, therefore, pays for two agency transactions. The customer pays more or receives less than he would have if the original broker had dealt directly with the market maker.

INTERSTATE COMMERCE COMMISSION

Federal agency that has jurisdiction over transportation companies that do an interstate business. Agency also regulates offerings of equipment trust certificates.

INTER VIVOS TRUST

Trust, either temporary or permanent, established by one living person for the benefit of another. Term is used in contrast to a testamentary trust; that is, a trust that will be operative only when the person who established the trust dies.

IN THE MONEY

Expression used of any option series if the strike (exercise) price and market price are such that the option holder could exercise at a profit, independent of the premium and other transaction costs. For example, if a call is held at a strike price of 30 and the stock is at 32, the call is in the money.

Also said of long put options if the price of the underlying stock drops below the exercise price of the option.

See also INTRINSIC VALUE.

IN THE TANK

Slang: a security or an entire securities market that is quickly losing value. For example, "ABC is going in the tank."

INTRINSIC VALUE

Arithmetic statement of the dollar difference between the strike (exercise) price of an option and the market price of the stock, if the option can be exercised at a profit. For example, the strike price of a put is 40 and the stock is at 37. The intrinsic value is 3. If an option is at or out of the money, it has no intrinsic value.

INVENTORY
1   The dollar value of raw materials, goods in progress, or completed goods that a corporation owns.
2   The net security position, either long or short, that a dealer or specialist has in a security.

INVENTORY TURNOVER
A measurement of a corporation's efficient use of assets in terms of turnover of saleable goods.

The best formula: cost of goods sold divided by average inventory for the year. Year-end inventory can also be used. For example, a corporation's cost of goods sold is $12 million and its average inventory is $2 million. Its inventory turnover is 6 (times a year).

INVERTED SCALE
An offering of serial bonds in which short-term yields exceed long-term yields.

INVERTED YIELD CURVE
Term describing the graph of yields on similar debt securities if short-term yields are higher than long-term yields. For example, "The yield curve on AA utility issues is inverted."

See also YIELD CURVE.

INVESTMENT ADVISER
Person or organization who sells investment advice for a fee. Banks, brokers, and general circulation periodicals are exempted from registration with SEC; otherwise, investment advisers with 15 or more customers must register and abide by the provisions of the Investment Advisers Act. Most states have specific laws for investment advisers and often require a registration examination.

INVESTMENT ADVISERS ACT OF 1940
Act that requires those who sell investment advice for a fee to register with the SEC. In general, the act applies to those who sell advice to 15 or more persons on an interstate basis. There are numerous exceptions; the most important are banks, brokers, and general-circulation newspapers. State laws often differ widely from federal law for investment advisers. Legal advice is needed if one intends to sell investment advice for a fee.

INVESTMENT BANKER

General term for a broker-dealer who assists corporations with the distribution of securities or with other money management or public relations services.

Investment bankers do not take time and demand deposits and, as a general rule, do not make short-term loans to corporations, as do commercial banks. In many other respects, however, commercial and investment banks compete for government and municipal securities business.

Also called an underwriter.

INVESTMENT COMPANY ACT OF 1940

Public legislation that regulates the issuance of investment company securities. The law is administered by the SEC. The act sets standards for the organization, operation, and pricing of investment company securities, their public sale and reporting requirements, and, in many cases, for the allocation of portfolio investments.

INVESTMENT GRADE

Designation given by a national rating service if it includes a bond in one of its top four categories from AAA (top) to BBB (bottom) of the investment grade category. Standard & Poor's and Fitch use these symbols. Moody's uses Aaa to Baa for the same designation. Bonds rated below investment grade are increasingly speculative.

See also JUNK BOND and PRUDENT MAN RULE.

INVESTMENT HISTORY

Term applicable to the NASD rule on Freeriding and Withholding if a sale of a hot issue is made to decision makers of institutional-type accounts. As a general rule, sales of hot issues may be made if the amount is small and is in line with the history of investment in the account. Usually, this history embraces a reasonable time (e.g., 3 years) and a reasonable number (e.g., 10) of securities transactions. The rule does not list specific measurements.

INVESTMENT LETTER

Written agreement between a seller and a buyer on the occasion of a private placement of securities. In this letter from the buyer to the seller, the buyer agrees that the purchase is being made for investment purposes and not for resale. Two years is a typical holding period to prove that investment was the objective.

See also LETTER STOCK.

INVESTMENT TAX CREDIT

A 10% tax credit permitted to the purchaser of certain tangible assets in the year that the purchase is made. The typical credit is 10% of the cost. The purpose of the law is to encourage the purchase of certain assets that enhance employment or public service. Tax advice is needed because the tax credit varies and can be recaptured as taxable income if a premature sale of the asset is made.

IRA ROLLOVER

Provision of the tax law that permits a person who terminates employment and who receives a lump-sum distribution of pension benefits to reinvest in an individual retirement account (IRA) within a period of 60 days. Funds thus rolled over continue to be tax sheltered until withdrawn.

ISSUE

1   The act of distributing securities to investors.
2   Any class of securities. For example, the Treasury bonds that will mature in 2002, the ABC common shares, the XYZ 4-¼% preferred stock.

ISSUED AND OUTSTANDING

Term used for the number of a corporation's authorized shares that are held by investors, including corporate officers.

The term does not include unissued shares and those treasury shares repurchased by the company.

ISSUER

A corporation, trust, association, municipality, or government that is legally empowered to distribute its own securities.

J

JAJO

Abbreviation for January, April, July, October. JAJO stands for the successive expiration months of successively offered option contracts. Normal practice is to have three of the four months offered in series at any single time.

Alternatives: FMAN and MJSD. Listed options are normally offered in one or the other series so option expiration dates are spread throughout the year.

JOINT ACCOUNT

1 A brokerage account that involves two or more clients.

See also JOINT TENANTS WITH RIGHT OF SURVIVORSHIP and TENANTS IN COMMON.

2 An investment banking account, or syndicate.

See also EASTERN ACCOUNT and WESTERN ACCOUNT.

JOINT ACCOUNT AGREEMENT

Form that must be signed by all parties to a joint account. Although the details of such joint accounts may differ, one thing is common: any party to the account may make purchase or sale transactions. This protects the broker. Assets, whether held in the account or transferred out, are in joint name and are for the benefit of all account owners.

JOINTLY AND SEVERALLY

Expression used in Eastern accounts for municipal underwritings. Such accounts are undivided and the entire account is responsible for the entire offering. Thus, an account member with 3% of the participation who sold 3% of the offering would still be responsible proportionately for any unsold bonds in the offering.

See also SEVERALLY BUT NOT JOINTLY (for divided accounts) and EASTERN ACCOUNT.

JOINT TENANTS WITH RIGHT OF SURVIVORSHIP

Two or more persons who maintain a collective account with a broker, but there is no specific fractional financial interest. Upon the death of one party, his ownership passes immediately to the other party. There is no probate, but there could be estate taxes if the decedent's portion, except in the case of a spouse, exceeds estate tax exemptions.

JUNK BOND

Industry expression for bonds with a credit rating of BB or lower. Such bonds have speculative overtones.

JURISDICTION

The right of a regulatory body to hear a case, and the corresponding power to render a judgment. For example, "This case involved a claim of fraud and thus the NASD decided that it did not have jurisdiction; instead, it recommended that the clients seek their remedies at law."

K

KANSAS CITY BOARD OF TRADE
A commodities exchange located in Kansas City, Missouri. Its brokers specialize in agricultural commodities and futures contract trading.

KEOGH PLAN
A retirement investment program for self-employed persons. Contributions are limited to the lower of 15% or $15,000 each year. Contributions are deductible from gross income.

Self-employed persons must cover full-time employees with the same percentage coverage that they give themselves. Legal advice is needed for full details of Keogh plans.

On January 1, 1984, the law becomes more complex. It gives a 20% contribution, but it subtracts contributions from earned income.

KICKER
A special feature or added benefit of a security. Term is generally used as a noun. For example, "This bond has a floating rate, and—as a kicker—you can put it to the issuer at par in five years."

KNOW YOUR CUSTOMER
Industry obligation, imposed by New York Stock Exchange's Rule 405 but equally implied by other industry rules, that requires a brokerage firm and its registered representatives to know the important facts about the customers with whom they do business. The rule requires due diligence because what may be unimportant for one customer may be very important for another.

L

LAPSED OPTION
An option that has expired unexercised and therefore is worthless.

LAST IN, FIRST OUT
Method of inventory valuation. Under LIFO, the last items received into inventory are considered to be the first items sold. In an inflationary period, this would cause the cost of goods sold to be higher than the cost of goods sold if first in, first out (FIFO) valuation were used.

By increasing the cost of goods sold, LIFO valuation will decrease working capital, profits, and taxes.

LAST SALE

Industry usage for the most recent transaction in a specific security. The term is used of stock exchange transactions. The last sale is important for the application of the uptick rule for short sales, and often limits buying and selling transactions of specialists and floor traders.

Common usage reserves the term closing sale for the last trade of the day.

LATE TAPE

Term used if the exchange tape is significantly behind schedule in the reporting of completed transactions. As a rule of thumb, if the tape is five or more minutes late, initial digits of the transaction price will be deleted. For example, a transaction at 45-½, when the tape is late, would appear 5-½.

LAY OFF

Used in conjunction with a standby underwriting if the manager of the syndicate allocates unused rights to the syndicate members.

LEG

Describes one or the other side of a transaction that partially offsets an existing position without closing out the position. For example, a client buys a call at 50. To turn this into a call spread, the client could add a leg by selling a call at 60.

You will also see the term to "take off a leg" if one side of a spread is closed, leaving the other side as either long or short.

LEGAL

Term is capitalized but is not an acronym. It refers to a centralized computer data bank of NYSE customer complaints, enforcement information, and the findings of exchange examiners in their audit of the records and activities of a member firm.

LEGAL AGE

Age at which, under the law of the state of residence, a minor reaches majority. This is an important concept for persons with multiple residences or who are under the Uniform Gift to Minors Act.

LEGAL INVESTMENT

A security that is considered to be eligible for selection by a fiduciary for the portfolio which the fiduciary manages. As a general rule, securities within the top four ratings of a national rating service are considered to be legal investments.

LEGAL LIST

Various states restrict the investments of fiduciaries to specific securities on a list prepared by the state. As a general rule, the securities are specified high-quality debt and equity securities.

See also PRUDENT MAN RULE.

LEGAL OPINION

A statement of counsel given to an issuer of municipal securities that specifies that (1) interest income is exempt from federal taxation, (2) enabling legislation permits the issue, (3) no restrictive covenant on prior issues is violated by this issue. Although the legal opinion is subject to future adjudication, no syndicate will accept an issue for sale without a legal opinion.

LEGAL TRANSFER

Industry term for a security that is so registered that documents, other than a stock-bond power, are required to effect its transfer from a seller to a buyer. Buying brokers will not accept securities requiring legal transfer; it is the selling broker's obligation to complete the legalities so the certificate is transferrable.

Securities registered under the Uniform Gift to Minors Act are not considered legal transfers, but securities registered to a corporation or to a deceased person are.

LENDER OF LAST RESORT

Member banks of the Federal Reserve may borrow against eligible securities; the monies thus borrowed may be loaned or used to fulfill reserve requirements. In this way, the Fed is the lender of last resort. The ability of members to borrow is not without restrictions, however, and for this reason the discount window and the moral suasion of the Fed come together in this concept of lending.

See also DISCOUNT WINDOW.

LENDING AT A PREMIUM

If a short seller must pay the lender of the borrowed securities a fee, the security is lending at a premium. For example, the lender requires a premium of $1 per day per 100 shares for the loan of the securities. The premium is over and above the requirement that the loaned securities be (1) marked to the market, and (2) reimbursed for any dividends-interest payable.

LENDING AT A RATE

When a person sells short there is a credit in his account. If the short seller demands payment for the money that is held in escrow to protect the lender of the securities, the securities sold short are said to be lending at a rate.

LESSEE MEMBER

A real person who has leased the use of membership on an exchange from a member for a fixed time for a fixed fee. For example, when exchange memberships were selling at $250,000, a person leased a membership for $40,000 per year. The lessor member was getting 16% on invested capital; the lessee was leveraging a $40,000 investment, with a chance for a return on the other $210,000, to get the total return on the $210,000 and the income from the use of the seat.

LETTER BONDS

Bonds sold privately with ability for transfer or resale subject to terms of an investment letter.

LETTER OF INTENT

1 A written promise by a mutual fund shareholder to invest, during a 13-month period, a specified sum of money to qualify for a reduced percentage sales charge.
2 A preliminary contract between two parties negotiating a merger or an acquisition.

LETTER SECURITY

The name given to an unregistered security that is purchased privately from the issuer. The term arises because the issuer, in the private sale, asked the purchaser to state in a letter that the purchase was made as an investment and not for purposes of immediate resale.
See also INVESTMENT LETTER.

LEVEL DEBT SERVICE

Requirement of a municipality's charter that the annual debt service (i.e., the combined total of interest and principal payments) be approximately equal each year. The purpose is to provide for effective budgeting of the tax revenues of the municipality.

LEVEL I SERVICE OF NASDAQ

Subscription service that provides, on an electronic screen, the highest bid and lowest offer of NASDAQ-traded securities. The market maker is not identified.
This service, which often is marketed through the QUOTRON or

the BUNKER-RAMO corporations, is used by brokerage firms to give up-to-date information to account executives and clients.

See also NASDAQ.

LEVEL II SERVICE OF NASDAQ

Subscription service that provides, on an electronic screen, the market makers and their bids and offers for NASDAQ-traded securities.

This service, available to institutional investors and to the traders of NASD members, is used to give competitive information on NASDAQ-traded securities.

See also NASDAQ.

LEVEL III SERVICE OF NASDAQ

Subscription service that provides, on an electronic screen, the market makers and their bids and offers for NASDAQ-traded securities.

It also permits subscribers, who are registered market makers, to compete by entering their own bids and offers for the securities in which they are registered. In effect, therefore, Level III is an electronic marketplace.

See also NASDAQ.

LEVERAGE

In finance, the term leverage is applied to:

1 The control of a large amount of money by a small amount of money. For example, a warrant or a long call controls a large amount of money with a small amount.
2 The use of borrowed money at a fixed rate of interest to achieve a greater rate of return. For example, a client buys on margin or a company borrows money.

See also TRADING ON THE EQUITY and BOND RATIO.

LEVERAGED

A business or financial enterprise that uses borrowed money at a fixed rate of interest in an endeavor to achieve a greater rate of return on the total invested capital. For example, "An investor leveraged his equity by buying the security in a margin account."

LEVERAGED BUYOUT

The purchase of a controlling interest in a company through the use of borrowed money. Often the lender, in addition to normal interest rates, acquires some portion of the equity securities in the acquired company.

For example, "Company A took over Company B through a leveraged buyout."

LEVERAGED COMPANY

A business enterprise whose total capital comprises both equity and debt. Industrial corporations with more than one third of their capital in the form of long-term debt are said to be highly leveraged.

Leverage is an endeavor to increase the return on equity by accepting an increased risk of bankruptcy; that is, an inability to meet the interest and principal payments on the debt.

LEVERAGED INVESTMENT COMPANY

1 An open-end investment company whose charter permits bank loans as part of the invested capital of the fund.
2 A dual purpose fund with both income and capital shares. Because all dividends go to the income shares, and all capital gains to the capital shares, the investors in both classes of shares, in effect, leverage each other.
See also LEVERAGE.

LEVERAGED LEASE

A lease contract for equipment that is substantially financed by a nonrecourse loan. The lessee has the use of the equipment without the outlay of capital. The lessor retains the residual value of the depreciated asset when the contract expires and the immediate advantage of the investment tax credit and depreciation writeoffs.

See also DEPRECIATION; INVESTMENT TAX CREDIT; and NONRECOURSE LOAN.

LIABILITY

In finance, any claim for money against the assets of a company. Thus, all debts—whether short-term or long-term—are liabilities. However, securities, whether common or preferred, have no claim on the assets of a company.

LIBOR

Acronym for London Interbank Offered Rate. It is the rate at which deposits of U.S. dollars are traded in London. LIBOR is often used as the base for the determination of the changes in the interest rate on Eurodollar notes that have a floating rate.

LIEN

A claim against property made to a creditor. For example, a margin account customer gives the broker a lien against assets in the account, or a bond gives the bondholder a lien against the company's plant.

LIFTING A LEG

Expression used when an investor with a hedged investment removes one or the other part of the hedge. For example, a client with a long call and a long put (i.e., a straddle) makes a closing sale of the long call. This leaves the client with a long put outstanding. The client has lifted a leg.

See also LEG.

LIMITED DISCRETION

Written authorization given by a client to a registered representative. The authorization permits the representative to close existing option positions and, within the last days prior to expiration, to exercise option positions without prior consultation or approval from the client.

LIMITED PARTNER

A member of a partnership who has no vote in the management of the partnership. Limited partners are also called silent partners. Their potential loss is limited to their capital contribution, and usually they receive a fixed dollar return that is payable in full before the general partner shares in any profits.

LIMITED TAX BOND

A form of general obligation municipal bond used by cities and other local municipalities. The bond and its interest are paid from real estate taxed at a specified rate on the assessed valuation of property.

See also AD VALOREM and MILL.

LIMITED TRADING AUTHORIZATION

Brokerage account in which the client permits an account executive, through a written agreement with the brokerage firm, to make discretionary buy and sell transactions in the client's account. The authorization is limited in the sense that the account executive may sell and reinvest the proceeds of the sale but may not remove assets from the account.

Also called discretionary account.

LIMIT ORDER

A type of buy or sell order used by some customers in the secondary market for securities. The customer establishes a limit price (i.e., a maximum buying price or a minimum selling price). Brokers will endeavor to get a better price for the customer if this is possible, but the broker may not violate the limit price set by the client.

LIMIT ORDER INFORMATION SYSTEM

An electronic communication system that reveals the specialists' books on participating stock exchanges. The system reveals the locale, quantities, and prices. The system provides competition and protects against disadvantageous executions if a better execution is available elsewhere.

LIMIT PRICE

A price qualifier set by the customer on his order to buy or sell. If it is a buy limit order, the customer requires that the purchase be made at or below the limit price. If it is a sell limit order, the customer requires that the sale be made at or above the limit price.

LINE OF CREDIT

Arrangement that enables a prospective borrower to obtain a maximum sum of money during a predetermined time period. For example, "The ABC Bank gave its client a $1 million line of credit for 6 months."

See also SPECIAL MISCELLANEOUS ACCOUNT.

LIQUID ASSET

Cash and marketable securities are generally considered liquid assets. The expression is commonly used in the analysis of corporate financial statements, but is also used of brokerage clients to determine the suitability of certain relatively illiquid investments for their portfolios. For example, "This investment is not suitable unless the client has $50,000 in other liquid assets."

LIQUIDATION

1 The process whereby securities or other assets are sold to produce cash.
2 The term also is used in the securities industry to describe an involuntary sale of securities in a client's account. For example, "When the client failed to meet the call, the broker met it with a liquidation."

LIQUIDITY

1 The quality of an asset that permits it to be converted quickly into cash without a significant loss of value.
2 On an issue-by-issue basis, liquidity refers to the ability of the marketplace to absorb a reasonable amount of buying and selling without excessive price volatility.

See also MARKETABILITY.

LIQUIDITY DIVERSIFICATION

Technique used by portfolio managers whereby bond portfolios are diversified by maturities. This reduces interest rate risk because the cash flow from frequently maturing securities can be reinvested at advantageous rates.

LIQUIDITY RATIO

An infrequently used ratio that compares cash and marketable securities owned by a company to its current liabilities. It is the most strict of the measurements of corporate liquidity.

See also ACID-TEST RATIO and CURRENT RATIO.

LISTED OPTION

A class of put or call option that has been admitted to trading on a registered exchange. The decision to trade the class of option is made by the exchange.

The term listed option is popularly used; technically, it is an exchange-traded option.

LISTED STOCK

The stock of an issuer who has applied for and received the privilege of having the stock traded on a registered stock exchange. As a general rule, the exchange will delist the stock if it fails to maintain the continuing qualifications for listing.

LOAD FUND

Industry term for either the percentage sales charge (load) or the open-end investment company shares (load fund) if there is a sales charge when such shares are purchased.

See also NO LOAD.

LOAD SPREAD OPTION

Misnomer for annual sales charge allocation on some contractual mutual funds. It is not an option of the customer. Under this method, the total sales charge may not exceed 9% of the contract. However, during contract's first four years, up to 20% of any year's contributions to the fund may be credited against the sales charge, if total charges in the first four years are not over 64% of one year's contributions by the planholder.

See also CONTRACTUAL PLAN.

LOAN VALUE

The maximum percentage credit, based on the current market value of an eligible security, that a broker may extend to a margin account customer if the customer (1) makes a commitment through an initial purchase or (2) deposits fully paid securities into a margin account.

Regulation T of the Federal Reserve Board sets the loan value on listed equity and convertible securities and on some NASDAQ-traded securities. The exchanges or the brokers establish the loan value on other types of securities.

LOCKED IN
Industry slang for an investor who is unwilling or unable to sell because a sale will actualize a paper gain or loss.

LOCKED MARKET
A temporary situation in a highly competitive market signifying that the bid and offer prices are the same. Once the offsetting buys and sells are completed, the market will unlock.

LONG BOND
1 An investor's position in a debt security: the security is owned and title can be transferred by sale or gift.
2 A debt security with a maturity date that is more than 10 years away. In this latter sense, the expression is generally used in the plural. For example, "The portfolio is almost entirely in long bonds."

LONG COUPON
1 A new issue of bonds or notes on which the first coupon payment will be greater than the usual six-month coupon period. For example, a bond dated April 1 with the first coupon to be paid on December 1. Normally, subsequent coupons will be at six-month intervals.
2 Interest-bearing bonds with maturities in excess of 10 years.

LONG HEDGE
Strategy used to lock in a future yield on fixed-income securities if a drop in interest rates is anticipated. Two strategies: (1) Buy a futures contract on the security. Risk: the investor can lose more than the good faith deposit on the purchase if interest rates rise dramatically. (2) Buy a call option on the security. Risk: the purchase of the call automatically makes the investor's breakeven point the execution price plus the premium paid. Thus, the call may not be profitable unless a drop in interest rates is dramatic.

LONG LEG
This term identifies the position owned by a client who holds an offsetting position in a security. For example, a client puts on a call spread in a class of option. The long call is the long leg.
See also LEG.

LONG POSITION
Financial term signifying ownership, the right to transfer ownership, and financial risk if the asset (e.g., bond, stock, option, or other security or commodity) declines in value.

Term is also used of securities owned by a client that are in the possession of client's agent. For example, "The client's securities are long with his broker."

Long can also mean that a broker-dealer owns more stocks or bonds than she has contracted to deliver (e.g., a broker-dealer has a net long position in ABC).

LONG TERM
1 Noun: As defined by the Internal Revenue Service, a holding period for securities in excess of 12 months that qualifies subsequent sale of those securities for long-term gain or loss treatment.
2 Adjective: Refers to bonds whose maturity is greater than 1 year.

LONG-TERM DEBT
1 A debt instrument with more than 10 years to maturity.
2 In financial statement analysis, long-term debt is variously used. It always means more than 1 year to maturity in balance sheet bookkeeping, but analysts may change their usage of long-term to cover bonds of 5 or 7 years, or longer terms.

LONG-TERM GAIN
A profit on a capital transaction that is eligible for preferential tax treatment. On a purchase followed by a sale, a long-term gain can result if the asset was held more than 12 months.

Special rules apply if the asset was received through a gift or bequest.

LONG-TERM LOSS
A loss sustained on the sale of a capital asset that was held more than 12 months.

See also SHORT SALE RULE.

M

M
1 Following a number, M stands for 1,000 times the number; For example, 10M = 10,000.

2   On the pink sheets, published daily by the National Quotation
    Bureau, M before the name of a stock signifies that the security
    is eligible for margin purchases.
3   In parentheses, (M) is often used to designate that a security is
    traded on the Midwest Stock Exchange.
4   Followed by a number, M stands for the nation's money supply
    as variously measured by the Federal Reserve. For example, M1
    M1A, M2, and so on.

MAINTENANCE CALL

A notice to a margin account customer sent by the carrying broker.
The notice states that the client's equity is insufficient to meet industry
or brokerage rules. The call is for a specific amount of money and
must be met promptly by a deposit of funds or securities. If the call
is not met, the broker will liquidate sufficient securities in the account
to remove the maintenance deficiency.

Also called maintenance margin call.

MAINTENANCE REQUIREMENT

1   As an absolute dollar amount, industry rules require that a
    client's equity be $2,000 or more in a margin account with a debit
    balance.
2   As a relative dollar amount, industry rules require that a client's
    equity be a stated percentage of long or short market values.
    Most brokerage firms require that the client's equity be 30% on
    listed stocks, convertibles, and corporate bonds held in margin
    accounts. There are special maintenance requirements on other
    securities.

MALONEY ACT

Section 15.A of the Securities Exchange Act of 1934. The
amendment, sponsored by the late Senator Maloney, permits the
registration of self-policing associations of securities dealers.

The National Association of Securities Dealers (NASD) is registered
with the SEC under this provision of the 1934 Act.

Also called the Maloney Amendment.

MANAGEMENT COMPANY

An investment company that provides day-to-day management of
a portfolio of securities and that permits the investment manager to
sell the portfolio securities and reinvest the proceeds in other
securities.

Management companies may be either closed or open-end. This

latter form, popularly called a mutual fund, is by far the most popular form of investment company.

MANIPULATION

The act of depressing or raising securities prices artificially so that prices do not represent true value. This is done by creating an appearance of active buying or selling, either alone or in concert with others. Manipulation violates federal securities laws and is subject to criminal and civil penalties.

MARGIN

1 The client's equity in a securities account that has an outstanding loan of money (a long margin account) or a loan of securities (a short margin account).
2 The client's good-faith deposit when the client buys or sells a futures contract. In this sense, margin ensures performance at the prescribed future time.
   Substantial additional margin can be required on a daily basis if the futures contract goes against the purchaser or seller.

MARGIN ACCOUNT

A brokerage account in which a client may maintain a creditor-debtor relationship with the broker. The client may owe money loaned for the purchase of securities, or securities loaned for sales made short. Regulation T of the Federal Reserve System regulates the conduct of margin accounts, although industry rules may further limit the maintenance of credit in such accounts.

MARGIN AGREEMENT

A document signed by a margin account customer that details the conduct of accounts in which the broker loans money or stock to a customer.

Commonly called the customer agreement or the hypothecation agreement.

See also HYPOTHECATION AGREEMENT.

MARGIN CALL

A broker's notice to a customer following a purchase or a short sale for funds sufficient to satisfy the initial margin requirements of Regulation T. The dollar amount of the margin call will be the requirement on the activity, as specified by Regulation T, minus any available funds in the account.

Technically, a margin call may result from an activity in either a margin or a cash account.

MARGIN DEPARTMENT

Common name for the group within a broker-dealer's operations area that monitors client accounts so there is a record of client holdings, short sales, debits and credits, and the compliance of such accounts with Reg-T, exchange, and member-firm requirement for the extension or maintenance of credit.

Also called the credit department or the cash-margin department.

MARGIN OF PROFIT

In financial statement analysis, margin of profit answers this question: How much of the income received from a sales dollar remains after the cost of goods sold (and administrative expenses, if these are not originally included) are subtracted from income from sales? For example, if sales income is $100 and cost of goods sold is $80, my margin of profit is $20, or 20% of sales.

See also OPERATING RATIO.

MARGIN REQUIREMENT

Percentage of the purchase price or of the proceeds of a short sale that a client must account for if he puts himself—and thus his broker—at risk by a commitment. Although Regulation T determines this percentage requirement if a client purchases or sells short listed securities, industry rules often specify higher margin requirements.

MARGIN SECURITY

Although the technical definition is more extensive, a margin security is one that may be purchased or sold short in a margin account and that permits the client to maintain a debtor-creditor relationship with his broker.

MARKDOWN

1 The difference between a dealer's bid and asked price. It is the dealer's spread looked at from the viewpoint of a seller.
2 A sudden drop in a dealer's quote to reflect a drop in market values. Investors generally call this a sale price.
3 A reevaluation of the syndicate price by a municipal bond account if the market is unreceptive.

MARKETABILITY

Although marketability is synonymous with liquidity on the sell side, on the buy side the term implies that buyers can purchase reasonable amounts of a security without severely raising its market price. Thus, a security has good marketability if it can be easily resold or readily purchased in an active secondary market.

MARKET IF TOUCHED ORDER

A commonly used order in commodity markets, often called MIT. It is the opposite of a stop order for securities. For example, a sell stop order for securities is triggered if, in a falling market, the stop price is reached. An MIT order for commodities would be triggered if, in a rising market, the price were reached.

MARKET INDEX

Market averages and indices are general measurements of market movement.

Averages emphasize price movement.

Indices, because they include weighting of prices in terms of outstanding shares, emphasize changes in value for outstanding shares.

In practice, the marketplace assesses all of the factors, and as a result, there is substantial similarity between price and value trends.

MARKET LETTER

A form of sales literature issued by a broker-dealer for distribution to customers. It centers on economic, political, or supply-demand factors that may affect securities prices. For example, "If money is in short supply and investors are bearish, do not expect your security to go up." Market letter must be approved by a designated person within the issuing firm, must be retained in the records of the firm, and must conform to the general norms for all sales literature.

MARKET MAKER

A dealer who is habitually willing to buy or sell a round lot of a security at his stated bid or offer.

MARKET ORDER

If one starts with the concept that the market for a security is the highest bid and the lowest offer, a market order is an order to buy or sell a specific number of shares at the best available price once the order is received in the marketplace.

See also GOOD TILL CANCELLED ORDER, LIMIT ORDER, and STOP ORDER.

MARKET PRICE

For exchange-traded securities, the last reported sale price.

In the over-the-counter market, a consensus of market-maker quotations can be used.

If a rarely traded security is involved, expecially for the evaluation of an estate on the day of death, the opinion of analysts and traders in the same or similar securities is often used.

MARKET TONE
A market is said to have good market tone if dealers and market makers are willing to trade actively on narrow spreads between bid and asked prices.

MARKING
A manipulative action by a trader or investor involving the execution of an option contract at the close that does not represent the fair value of the contract and that results in a net improved equity position in the client's account.

MARK TO THE MARKET
A request by a party to an unsettled contract who has become unsecured because of a change in the market value of the underlying instrument.

The most common marks are:
1   A request for more margin if a stock sold short goes up in value.
2   A request for more margin if a short call that is uncovered, or a short put that is uncovered, goes against the writer.
3   A when-issued security declines in value before settlement date.

MARKUP
1   The dollar difference between the bid and asked price for a security. Also called the spread. In this sense, markup is the dealer's potential profit if he can consistently buy and resell at his quoted prices.
2   Markup is a term used if there is a sudden rise in prices and a dealer or an underwriter of municipal securities increases the asked price to reflect this increased demand for the security.

MARRIED PUT
Expression used if a client buys a security and, on the same day, buys a put and elects to hedge the stock with the put. If this election is made, the put premium, if the put expires, is not a capital loss; instead, the premium paid for the married put is added to the purchase price of the underlying stock to get the client's basis for the stock. Tax advice is needed for the method needed to marry the stock and the long put.

MATCHED AND LOST
Report sent back from an exchange floor if a client's market order is not executed at the price reported on the tape. Although exchange

regulations give priority to the first bidder at a price, the same rules give precedence to other bidders with large orders once the first bidder is filled. It is possible, therefore, for a buyer or seller who misses the first transaction, because of time priority, to miss subsequent transactions at that price because of order size.

MATCHED BOOK
Broker-dealer term that describes an equal borrowing and loan situation. The broker-dealer can make a profit if the borrowings are made at one rate of interest and the loans at a higher rate. Repurchase agreements (repos) and reverse repurchase agreements are used to achieve a matched book and thus finance the dealer's security inventory.

MATCHED ORDERS
Purchases and sales of the same security by the same beneficial owner at the same time and price. The purpose is to give the impression of extensive trading in the security. Matched orders, which are usually made through different brokers, are violations of the Securities Exchange Act of 1934.

MATCHED SALE PURCHASE TRANSACTIONS
Used by the Federal Open Market Committee to fine-tune member bank reserves and their ability to extend credit. The procedure involves the sale of government securities and a contingent provision to repurchase the securities at the same price in the future. The Federal Reserve pays interest for the money thus acquired at competitive rates.

MATRIX TRADING
Traditionally there are yield spread differences between fixed-income securities of the same class with different ratings, or between fixed-income securities of different classes. When these spreads diverge from traditional ranges, astute traders can profit by buying and selling the right securities if the ranges subsequently return to traditional patterns.
Matrix trading is a form of bond swapping.

MATURITY DATE
The specified day on which the issuer of a debt security is obligated to repay the principal amount, or face value, of a security. It is rare for an equity security to have a maturity date, although dual purpose mutual funds assign a maturity date for income shares.
Also called maturity.

MEDIUM-TERM BOND

The expression is practical rather than legal. Bonds, or notes, with maturities from 2 to 10 years in the future are usually called medium-term or intermediate-term bonds.

If a medium- or intermediate-term bond is called a note, it usually implies that the security is not callable by the issuer.

MEMBER TAKEDOWN

Term means that a syndicate member will buy bonds from the account at the takedown or member's discount price and sell them to the customer at the public offering price.

The term is used of retail sales of primary municipal offerings. Member takedown sales have the lowest priority when subject orders are directed to the syndicate manager. An underwriting spread on municipal offerings is divided into the manager's fee and the takedown, which includes additional takedown and the concession.

Often written with a hyphen between member and takedown.

See also DESIGNATED NET, GROUP NET, and TAKE DOWN.

MERCHANT BANK

A British term for the rough equivalent of commercial bank in the United States: a bank that takes demand and time deposits. There is, however, a difference: merchant banks in England may underwrite new issues of corporate securities. The underwriting of corporate securities is not permitted under the banking laws of the United States.

MERGER

Popular name for the union of two corporations. Merger generally implies a friendly union and states nothing about the name of the resulting company. Acquisition also is used of the union of two corporations. Acquisitions may be friendly or unfriendly and generally result in the loss of corporate identity for the acquired company.

MEZZANINE BRACKET

Popular name for those underwriters who, while not the major underwriters of an issue, generally subscribe for the next largest portion of the issue.

MIDWEST STOCK EXCHANGE

A registered national exchange, located in Chicago. In addition to providing trading facilities for the securities listed there, the MSE also provides a marketplace for many securities traded on the NYSE.

MILL

One 1,000th part of a dollar ($.001), or $\frac{1}{10}$th of a cent. Municipalities usually state property taxes in mills and multiples thereof based on the assessed valuation of the taxable property. For example, if the assessed valuation of property is $1 million and the tax is 8 mills per dollar of valuation, the total tax would be: $1,000,000 times .008, or $8,000.

Sometimes spelled mil.

MINI MANIPULATION

Manipulative transactions in an option stock so its price movements are sufficient to cause a premium change in an option position previously established. Mini manipulation is difficult to detect, but it can be easily seen that a small movement in the underlying stock would be multiplied many times if the manipulator has a large position in an underlying option.

MINIMUM MAINTENANCE

The minimum equity, or margin, required either by exchange or National Association of Securities Dealers (NASD) rules, or by brokerage firm requirements.

1 There is a $2,000 maintenance in all accounts with a debit balance or a short position.
2 The exchanges and the NASD require a 25% maintenance on long margin accounts, and as a general rule, 30% on short margin accounts.
3 Many member firms have special maintenance requirements on debt securities, option accounts, or on securities selling below a specified dollar value per share.

MINIMUM VARIATION

As a general rule, securities trading is in points, with a minimum price variation. In securities that trade in terms of points alone, the minimum variation is $\frac{1}{8}$th of a point, although government notes and bonds normally trade in minimum variations of $\frac{1}{32}$d. If securities normally trade on a yield basis, the minimum variation is 1 basis point (i.e., a variation of .01% of yield). Of course, any security may trade at the last transaction price. In this case, there is no variation.

MINOR

Someone who has not reached the age of majority in his or her state or residence. Brokerage accounts for minors are undesirable because losses can be recouped when the minor reaches majority. Court-appointed guardians and custodians under Uniform Gift to

Minors Accounts can make legally binding investment decisions on behalf of a minor, and such accounts are permitted.

MINORITY INTEREST
1   Any group of corporate owners that, collectively, own less than 50% of the voting shares of a corporation.
2   A corporation that owns, usually as an investment, less than 50% of another corporation.
3   A person, either real or legal, who lends long-term funds to another corporation is also said to have a minority interest.

MINUS
Used as a word or as a symbol (−).
1   Sales to underwriters or other dealers are often made minus a concession or reallowance.
2   A sale in the marketplace that is lower than the previous price is called a minus tick.
3   If the closing sale in a security is lower than the previous day's close, the stock table will list the change (e.g., as − ¼).
4   The discount at which a closed-end fund is selling below the net asset value of the fund.

MINUS TICK
Industry jargon for any transaction price that is lower than the previous transaction price. For example, if the previous sale was 20 and the next sale is 19-⅞, the sale at 19-⅞ is said to be on a minus tick.
See also ZERO-MINUS TICK.

MISSING THE MARKET
Term describing the fact that an agent failed to execute a transaction at a price that was available, and that the subsequent transaction was disadvantageous to the customer. In this case, the agent must make up the amount lost by the client. The term implies negligence on the part of the agent but not fraud. Thus, the action is nonfeasance, but not malfeasance.

MIXED ACCOUNT
A client's margin account containing both long and short security positions.

MM
1   Commonly used abbreviation for million. For example, 10MM equals 10,000,000. Also abbreviated MYN.
2   Also used for market maker.

MO

Used in newspaper reports of a company's earnings if the principal marketplace for the security is the Montreal Stock Exchange.

MOBILE HOME CERTIFICATE

A variety of Ginnie Mae (GNMA) security that represents mortgages on mobile homes. Although these securities generally have shorter maturities than other Ginnie Mae securities, they have the same guarantees for the repayment of principal and for the timely payment of interest.

MONETARIST

An economic theory holding that economic recession and boom is primarily a function of the control of the money supply rather than a function of governmental fiscal policy. For example, in a recession, a monetarist would moderate the recession by controlling the money supply; a Keynesian economist would increase governmental spending. Supply-side economics is a variation of monetarist economics.

MONETARY POLICY

1 General term that describes the actions of the Federal Reserve as it controls the supply of money and credit in the U.S. economy.
2 Term, usually qualified by an adjective, to describe the direction of the Fed's policies. For example, the Fed's monetary policy is expansive.

MONEY MARKET

1 An abstraction for the dealers and their communication network who trade short-term, relatively riskless, securities.
2 The securities traded in the money market. The principal securities are: U.S. Treasury bills, bankers' acceptances, commercial paper, and negotiable certificates of deposit.
   Repurchase agreements and reverse repurchase agreements, although they are not securities, are considered part of the money market.

MONEY MARKET FUND

Popular name for open-end investment shares that invest in short-term money market securities in an endeavor to provide investors with (1) relatively risk-free investments that (2) give a daily payment of competitive short-term interest rates.

MONEY SPREAD

Common term for a vertical spread. For example, a client buys a call at 40 and sells a call at 50, with both calls expiring in the same month. This client is moderating the risk of a long call at the lower price by using the premium on the short call to defray part of the cost of the long call. The opposite would be true if the client bought a call at 50 and sold a call at 40.

MOODY'S

Popular name for Moody's Investors Service, a registered investment adviser. Moody's investment ratings for bonds, preferred stock, and, to a limited extent, common stock are considered norms for investment decisions by fiduciaries.

MOODY'S INVESTMENT GRADE

A rating given by Moody's Investors Service to specific municipal short-term debt issues. The rating is further subdivided:

MIG 1—Best quality.

MIG 2—High quality.

MIG 3—Favorable quality.

MIG 4—Adequate quality.

The 4 ratings are investment grade or bank quality.

MORAL OBLIGATION BOND

Term popularly given by the securities industry to those municipal bonds authorized by one session of a state's legislature in such a way that subsequent sessions are not legally bound to follow the directives first given. Buyers, therefore, have an implied moral obligation of future legislatures to pay interest and principal, but there is no legal obligation to do so.

MORAL SUASION

Term popularly used of the Federal Reserve's ability to persuade compliance with its general monetary policy outside of its statutory ability to do so. For example, a call from the Fed chairman to a member bank asking it to participate in the sale of securities, or to lower its bid in the T-bill auction, would be exemplify moral suasion.

MORTGAGE BANKER

General name for the middleman between the originator of a mortgage (e.g., a bank or credit union) and the investor who assumes the mortgage risk by purchasing the mortgage. This gives liquidity to the original lender and passes the mortgage risk, with its reward, to the investor.

MORTGAGE BOND

A longer-term debt security that promises to pay interest and to repay principal, and that pledges real property, either land or plant or both, as collateral for the loan. Mortgage bonds are always designated as such, and the indenture will specify whether the mortgage is 1st or 2d and will state the restrictions on the further issuance of bonds.

MORTGAGE POOL

Term used to designate a group of mortgages on the same class of property, the same interest rate, and substantially identical maturity dates. For example, a mortgage pool might contain mortgages with a total face value of $2,100,503.56 at a rate of 16% that will mature in 29 years and 6 months.

MORTGAGE REIT

Term designating a real estate investment trust (REIT) that uses the capital provided by the trustholders as a leveraged investment. The trust, in turn, borrows money from a commercial bank and relends it. The trust hopes to profit from the spread between the interest paid to the bank and the interest paid by the borrower. Mortgage REITS can be highly profitable in times of stable interest rates but are highly speculative if interest rates rise.

MULTIPLIER

Term applied to the reciprocal of the Fed's reserve requirement on deposits. For example, at a 20% reserve requirement (⅕th), the reciprocal is 5/1. Thus, a deposit of $100,000 in a bank requires a reserve of $20,000; the remaining $80,000 could be a base for loans of $400,000. Theoretically, $100,000 in cash could expand into $500,000 in loans. In practice, banks are more conservative, but the multiplier does apply to a limited extent.

Also called multiplier effect.

MUNICIPAL BOND

A debt security that is issued by a state, city, or other political subdivision chartered by the state. All municipal bonds have these elements in common: (1) there is enabling legislation to permit their issuance and (2) the interest income is exempt from federal taxes.

MUNICIPAL BOND INSURANCE ASSOCIATION

An insuror, jointly owned by a consortium of insurance companies, that insures the timely payment of interest and the repayment of principal by municipal bond issuers. The insurance fee is paid by the issuer. Bonds so insured have the highest rating (AAA) and thus the issuer can sell the bonds at lower interest rates. In practice, the lower interest rate fully offsets the premium paid to the insuror.

MUNICIPAL INVESTMENT TRUST

A municipal investment trust, or MIT, is a form of unit investment trust that provides a diversified investment in a portfolio of municipal securities. Purpose: to give the holder monthly income exempt from federal taxation.

MUNICIPAL NOTE

In general, notes are shorter-term municipal debt obligations. Almost always, debts of 2 years or less are described as notes. The term note also is used of debt obligations with 2 or more years to maturity. In practice, therefore, a note is a security that the issuer describes as a note. Normally, notes are noncallable.

MUNICIPAL SECURITIES RULEMAKING BOARD

Registered with the SEC under the 1975 amendments of the '34 Act, the MSRB proposes rules and provides arbitration facilities to broker-dealers and bank dealers in municipal securities. Members of the MSRB continue to report to their original self-regulatory organization, as established under federal law, but they agree to conform to the rules established by the MSRB and approved by the SEC.

MUTILATED SECURITY

Any certificate for a security that has: (1) the name of the issuer or the issue obscured; (2) a portion of the security missing, perforated, or so cut that the security cannot be properly identified, or transferred, or that will prevent the purchaser from exercising the rights of an owner. It is the obligation of seller to rectify a mutilation by asking the transfer agent to guarantee all rights of ownership to a buyer.

MUTUAL FUND

Popular name for the shares of open-end management investment companies. Such shares represent ownership of a diversified portfolio of securities, which are professionally managed and which are redeemable at their net asset value. The prospectus of the mutual fund will detail the features of the fund.

The term also is used of any investment company security, but this usage is not common.

MUTUAL FUND CUSTODIAN

A commercial bank or trust company that holds in safekeeping the monies and securities owned by a mutual fund. The custodian generally, but not always, acts as the transfer agent and disbursing agent of the fund. To act as custodian, the bank must qualify under the provisions set forth in the Investment Company Act of 1940.

N

N
1 Used in the newspaper tables of company earnings to designate that the principal market for the company's securities is the New York Stock Exchange.
2 Used, lowercase, in the stock transaction tables in the newspaper to designate that a stock is newly listed on an exchange.
3 Used, lowercase, in the U.S. government securities bid-offer tables to designate a note rather than a bond.

NAKED OPTION
Industry jargon for:
1 The writer of a call who does not own the underlying security, a convertible security, or a long call at a strike (execution) price equal to or lower than the strike price of the call that was written and that does not expire before the call that was written.
2 The writer of a put who is not short the underlying security, or who does not own a long put with a strike price equal to or higher than the strike price of the put that was written and that does not expire before the put that was written.

NAKED POSITION
Any security position, either long or short, that is not partially or completely hedged from market risk as prices fluctuate. For example, the writer of a call option is naked if he does not own the underlying security; he is partially hedged if he owns the underlying security, in that he cannot lose if the stock goes up, but he can lose if the stock goes down.

NARROWING THE SPREAD
Action by a broker-dealer or a specialist whereby he bids higher or offers lower than the previous bid or offer, thus narrowing the spread between bids and offers.

Also called closing a market.

NASDAQ
Acronym for National Association of Securities Dealers Automated Quotations. It is a subscription computerized service, owned by the

NASD. It displays, on an electronic screen, current quotes made by registered market makers in specific OTC securities.

See also LEVEL III, LEVEL II, and LEVEL I SERVICES.

NASD FORM FR-1

A blanket certification form used by foreign broker-dealers and banks who want to subscribe to a hot issue in distribution but are not members of the syndicate. The form, when signed, attests to their understanding of the National Association of Securities Dealers' (NASD) rules on the allocation of hot issues and promises to abide by them.

NATIONAL ASSOCIATION OF SECURITIES DEALERS

The NASD is a nonstock membership organization, registered with the SEC under the provisions of the Securities Exchange Act of 1934. Membership is limited to broker-dealers in securities, or securities underwriters, who have an office in the United States, who are not commercial banks, and who promise to abide by the rules and regulations of the association.

NATIONAL CRIME INFORMATION CENTER

Computer information service, operated under authorization of the SEC, to which the theft or misplacement of securities must be reported. As such, the NCIC can be used to check the validity of ownership of securities offered for sale. For example, a person comes to a broker-dealer and wants to sell 2,000 shares of IBM. A check of the security and its certificate number through NCIC will determine if that certificate has been reported as stolen or misplaced.

NATIONAL MARKET ADVISORY BOARD

A board of 15 persons appointed for terms of 2 to 5 years by the SEC. The board, mandated by the 1975 revisions of the 1934 Act, advises the SEC about the establishment, operation, and regulation of securities markets, especially on the subject of a "national market" for securities.

NATIONAL QUOTATION BUREAU

A subsidiary of the Commerce Clearing House that gathers bids and offers from market makers in over-the-counter (OTC) securities and disseminates them to subscribers. The service gives OTC equity security quotes on pink sheets and corporate bond quotes on yellow sheets. The pink and yellow sheets also identify the market makers. The service is printed each business day.

See also PINK SHEETS and YELLOW SHEETS.

NATIONAL SECURITIES CLEARING CORPORATION
Formed by the merger of the NASD, NYSE, and ASE clearing facilities, this organization receives trade information, validates it, and facilitates the delivery and receipt of money and securities for its members.

NC
Abbreviation for noncallable. Often used on bond offering sheets to designate bonds that are noncallable.
See also NONCALLABLE.

NEAR MONEY
Popular designation for a bond or other debt security that is close to its redemption date.

NEGATIVE CARRY
Term used if the percentage of return on a security is less than the interest charge paid for the money borrowed to buy the security. For example, a bond with a 12% return that was purchased with funds borrowed at 13% would have a negative carry.

NEGATIVE YIELD CURVE
Term used of fixed-income securities if interest rates for shorter-term securities are greater than rates for longer-term securities of the same class and rating. Term derives from the graph which depicts yields on the y-axis against times to maturity on the x-axis.
Also called yield curve with a descending slope.

NEGOTIABLE
1 Any instrument that is readily transferable.
2 A security in registered format that has an assignment and power of substitution signed by the registered owner, either on the certificate or on an accompanying stock or bond power.
3 A price that is not firm and thus is subject to further clarification and discussion.

NEGOTIABLE CERTIFICATE OF DEPOSIT
A time deposit at a fixed rate of coupon interest. The issuer must redeem at maturity at the face value plus the stated interest rate. Holders can, however, resell the instrument in the secondary market at prevailing rates. To be negotiable, such certificates of deposit (CDs) must have face values of $100,000 or more, with $1 million and multiples thereof being most common. Maturities of less than one

year are common, but there is no time limit and CDs of three to five years are also issued.

NEGOTIATED BID

Term used of an underwriting if the issuer and a single underwriting syndicate agree upon a price through discussion and mutual understanding. Most common stock underwritings are negotiated.

Negotiated bid is used in distinction to competitive bid. In a competitive bid, competing syndicates propose their price to the issuer. The issue is awarded to the syndicate with the highest bid. Competitive bids are common in municipal bond underwritings.

NET

1 As noun: dollar difference between proceeds of a sale compared to a purchaser's adjusted cost of acquisition. A negative number is a loss; positive, a gain.
2 As verb: the act of netting. Netting may be by individual transaction or by completed transactions for a specified time. For example, taxpayers must net all completed securities transactions for their tax year.

You will also see "net down" used to describe this process.

NET ASSETS

Bookkeeping term: the dollar difference between a corporation's assets and liabilities. Used in this sense, net assets also are called net worth or stockholders' equity.

NET ASSET VALUE

Used by investment companies to identify net tangible asset value per share. It is calculated by subtracting liabilities from the portfolio value of a fund's securities and other items of value and dividing by the number of outstanding shares. In most cases, the net asset value is the bid price for these shares.

Net asset value is popularly used in newspaper mutual fund tables to designate the bid price per share for the fund.

NET CAPITAL REQUIREMENT

Popular term for SEC Rule 15c3–1 that mandates the ratio of net capital; that is, cash and other assets readily turned into cash, and aggregate indebtedness, which is customer-related indebtedness that must be maintained by a broker-dealer.

The rule is complex, and various measurement standards can be used. In general, however, it can be said that aggregate indebtedness may not exceed net capital of a broker-dealer by more than 1500%.

NET CHANGE

Used in newspaper stock, bond, and mutual fund financial reports to designate the point difference between today's price and the price on the previous trading day for that security.

As a general rule, the net change represents the difference between closing prices on listed securities and the difference between bid prices on OTC securities.

NET CURRENT ASSETS

The dollar difference, if a positive number, between the current assets of a corporation and its current liabilities.

If current assets are divided by current liabilities, the resulting quotient is called the curent ratio. Thus, if a corporation has curent assets of $5 and current liabilities of $2, its net current assets are $3 and its current ratio is 2-½ to 1.

Also called net working capital.

NET LIQUID ASSETS

The dollar difference, if any, between a corporation's cash and readily marketable securities and its current liabilities. Thus, a corporation with $5 in cash and $5 in marketable securities and current liabilities of $7 has $3 in net liquid assets.

Net liquid assets is the strictest measurement of a corporation's ability of meet current debt obligations.

NET PROCEEDS

The actual dollars that a client receives from a completed sale of a security.

The net proceeds are the contract price minus the cost of the transaction plus any adjustments that must be made. For example, a client sells a security for $40, but there is a brokerage charge of $1, so the net proceeds are $39. However, if a client sold a call at $30 for a premium of $2 and the call were exercised, the client's net proceeds would be $32.

The term is important because it is the basis for tax gain-loss computations.

NET QUICK ASSETS

A more strict measurement of corporate liquidity; it starts by removing inventory from current assets. The remaining current assets are then compared to current liabilities. If current liabilities are subtracted from this number, the remainder is net quick assets. If this is divided by current liabilities, the quotient is the acid-test ratio.

For example, if current assets minus inventory are $8 and the current liabilities are $5, the net quick assets are $3 and the acid-test ratio is 1.6 to 1.

NET SALES
Primary entry on the income statement of a corporation. Net sales represent the dollar value received for products and services minus any adjustments that must be made for refunds or returns.

NET TANGIBLE ASSETS PER SHARE
Most common formula: take total assets of a corporation and subtract any intangible asset on the balance sheet to get total tangible assets. Then, subtract all liabilities and the par value of preferred stock. Divide the remainder by the number of common shares outstanding to get net tangible assets per common share.

NET TRANSACTION
Term used of a securities transaction where no additional fee is levied on either the buyer or the seller. For example, an underwriter offers shares of a new issue at $31 net. The buyer will pay $31 and there will be no added charges.

NETWORK A
A subscription service provided by the Consolidated Tape Association. Network A gives successive round-lot transaction reports, as they are received, for New York Stock Exchange-listed securities regardless of the marketplace on which the transaction occurred. In practice, therefore, tape displays of NYSE-listed stocks may represent transactions on the NYSE, on any of the exchanges, or on the third or fourth markets.

NETWORK B
A subscription service provided by the Consolidated Tape Association. Network B gives successive round-lot transaction reports, as they are received, for American Stock Exchange-listed securities regardless of the marketplace on which the transaction occurred. In practice, therefore, tape displays for ASE-listed stocks may represent transactions on the ASE, on any other exchange, or on the third or fourth markets.

NET WORTH
The dollar value by which assets exceed liabilities.
Also called stockholders' equity when used on corporate balance sheets.

NEW ACCOUNT REPORT
Document required to be prepared, maintained, and updated by all broker-dealers who conduct business with customers. The new account form must contain essential information about the customer: the background, financial circumstances, and investment objectives of the customer.

NEW ISSUE
Popular term for any security offered for sale by the issuer. Technically, a new issue offers authorized but previously unissued shares. In practice, the term also encompasses the resale of treasury shares.

NEW MONEY
Used if an issuer offers new bonds with a greater par value than the par value of bonds to be retired through a call or maturity. For example, a company issues bonds worth $12 million to refund bonds with a par value of $10 million.

NEW MONEY PREFERRED
Legal term for preferred stocks issued after October 1, 1942. New money preferred shares provide corporate holders with an 85% tax exclusion for cash dividends.

Old money preferred shares provide only a 60% exclusion of cash dividends to corporate holders.

NEW YORK FUTURES EXCHANGE
The New York Futures Exchange is a wholly owned subsidiary of the New York Stock Exchange. The NYFE (pronounced knife) provides for the trading of futures contracts in Treasury bills, notes, and bonds, and in GNMA debentures.

NEW YORK MERCANTILE EXCHANGE
A commodities exchange, located in New York City, on which futures contracts in certain metals, currencies, petroleum, and agricultural products are traded.

NEW YORK PLAN
An infrequently used method for issuing equipment trust certificates, which are serial debt obligations that a common carrier, such as an airline or railroad, issues to buy equipment. Basically, the issuing company acquires title to the equipment under a

conditional bill of sale. As the serial maturities are retired, the issuer gradually assumes full title to the equipment.

See also PHILADELPHIA PLAN.

NEW YORK STOCK EXCHANGE

The best known, largest, and oldest securities market in the U.S., founded in 1792. Generally, the shares traded on the NYSE are those of larger companies. Prices of stocks traded are determined by public demand and supply. NYSE does not own, buy, sell, or establish the prices of stocks.

About 23 locations (posts) on the floor of the Exchange are assigned for trading in and for giving quotes on a specific security. (A quote is the highest bid price to buy or the lowest offer to sell.) At each post 100 or more securities are traded. The NYSE has over 1,300 individual members who are governed by a Board of Governors.

See also SPECIALIST.

NEW YORK STOCK EXCHANGE INDEX

A market measurement of the value change of an average share of common stock listed on the New York Stock Exchange.

The index is measured hourly and at the end of the trading day. The NYSE index is a composite measurement. It is divided into four categories: industrials, transportation, utilities, and finance companies. The index gives a value measurement because it takes into account the number of outstanding shares for the individual stocks. Average price change measurements also are provided to the news services.

Also called the NYSE composite index.

NIFTY FIFTY

A term used of the top 50 stocks favored by institutional investors. The term was popular in the 1970s when, despite bear markets, these institutional favorites maintained their value.

You will also see the term first tier or top tier to designate these securities.

NINE-BOND RULE

Popular term for the NYSE Rule 396 requiring that orders for nine listed bonds, or less, be sent to the floor to seek a market. In practice, it means the order must be left on the floor for an hour, or until the NYSE closes for the day—if such time is smaller. Customers may request rule be waived, but the accepting member firm may, in this case, only execute agency orders for the bonds. Usually, the nine-bond rule works to the advantage of small investors in bonds.

NO-ACTION LETTER

Often it is difficult to determine whether an activity is prohibited under the securities laws of the United States. In such a case, the party contemplating the action may write to the SEC for a specific opinion. A no-action letter from the SEC means that it will undertake neither civil nor criminal action if the activity occurs as indicated. No-action letters are specific to the inquirer and are applicable only to the circumstances outlined in the inquiry.

NO LOAD

Popular designation of those open-end investment companies that do not levy a sales charge. NL is commonly used in mutual fund columns in the financial section of newspapers.

In practice, no load means that both the bid and offer price of the fund are the same (i.e., the net asset value of the underlying shares).

NOLO CONTENDERE

Legal term, from the Latin: "I do not wish to contend (or contest) the action. . . ." Technically, it implies partial but not full guilt, and thus is usually the preliminary step to an out-of-court settlement.

NOMINAL EXERCISE PRICE

The dollar value for a GNMA option contract found by multiplying the strike price times the unpaid principal balance on a GNMA certificate with an 8% stated rate of interest. For example, at a strike price of 65 and an unpaid principal balance of $98,000 on a certificate with an 8% coupon, the nominal exercise price is $63,700.

See also AGGREGATE EXERCISE PRICE.

NOMINAL QUOTATION

A bid and offer given by a broker as an estimate of the value of a security. The broker, however, is unwilling to trade at the prices given. NASD and other industry rules require that nominal quotations be clearly identified as such.

NOMINAL YIELD

The yield, stated as a percentage, on a fixed-income security that divides the annual payout in dollars by the par value of the security. Thus, the nominal yield on a bond that pays $110 per year in interest and that has a par value of $1,000 is 11%.

Also called the coupon yield, although this term is inappropriate for preferred stock.

NONCALLABLE

A security, either equity or debt, that does not give the issuer the option of redeeming the security before the maturity date, in the case of bonds, or during the lifetime of the issue, in the case of preferred stock.

Most securities, even if callable, are noncallable for a period of years after issuance.

The absence of callability or the details of the call privilege are always stated at the time of issuance.

NONCLEARING MEMBER

A National Association of Securities Dealers member or an exchange member who does not maintain his or her own operations function; instead, the person uses the facilities of another member to make comparisons and to arrange for final settlement of contracts. The nonclearing member pays a contractual fee to the clearing member for these services.

NONCOMPETITIVE BIDS

Term used in conjunction with auctions for U.S. Treasury securities. Persons who wish to buy $500,000 or less of Treasury bills or $1 million or less of Treasury notes and bonds may enter noncompetitive bids. Such bidders always receive an execution, and the price they will pay is the average of the prices paid by those competitive bidders whose bids are accepted by the Treasury.

Also called noncompetitive tenders.

NONPURPOSE LOAN

A loan, collateralized by securities, where the proceeds of the loan will not be used to purchase or carry or trade securities subject to the Federal Reserve's credit regulations and limitations. Lenders, to insure compliance with the Fed's regulations, will normally require a signed statement from the borrower if securities are used as collateral for the loan.

NONQUALIFYING ANNUITY

An annuity—either fixed, variable or hybrid—that is not purchased in an IRS-approved pension plan. Because it is nonqualifying, it is purchased with aftertax dollars. Nonqualification, however, does not take away the tax sheltering of the growth of the original investment dollars, subject to the provisions of the Internal Revenue Code.

NONQUALIFYING STOCK OPTION

An option, granted by the issuing corporation, to purchase a fixed number of shares at a fixed price on or before a specified date. Such options are often granted to corporate executives. Because it is nonqualifying, the difference between the option price and the fair market value is considered as earned income in the tax year when the option is exercised. Thus, this difference is subject to withholding and income taxes.

NONRECOURSE LOAN

Used of direct participation programs. A limited partner borrows funds to partially finance his participation in the partnership and pledges as collateral his ownership in the venture. The lender, therefore, can attach the ownership but not other assets of the partnership. The advantage to the borrower is the leverage it provides.

Recourse loans that pledge the assets of the partnership itself can only be made by the general partner on behalf of all the partners.

NONRECURRING CHARGE

One-time income or expense entries on the income statement of a corporation.

Also called extraordinary items, with the implication that there will be no similar entry in the future. For example, the sale of an asset, such as property, or the write-off of a loss are typical one-time nonrecurring income and charges.

NONREFUNDABLE

Provision of a bond indenture in which the issuer promises not to retire a bond issue by funds from a second bond issue. The provision may be permanent, or limited to a refunding at a future date, or to a refunding only if a new issue can be made at a fixed interest rate difference from the present issue. For example, an issuer of 14% bonds promises no refunding unless a subsequent issue can be made at 11% or less.

NO-PAR VALUE

An equity security which has no minimum dollar value assigned to each share. Instead, a stated value is assigned and used in the makeup of the corporate balance sheet.

Also called no-par stock.

NORMAL INVESTMENT PRACTICE

A norm used to justify the allocation of hot issue securities to the personal accounts of decision makers of institutional accounts. For example, if the senior trust officer of a bank has, over the past two years made 10 purchases from the underwriter, with an average of

$2,000 per issue, it would not be unethical to allocate $2,000 of a hot issue to her account. The exclusive purchase of hot issues does not justify a normal investment practice.

Also called history of investment in the account.

NORMAL TRADING UNIT
The accepted minimum trading quantity for a purchase or sale. For equity securities, 100 shares is normal, although 10- or 25-share units exist, and some institutional traders now make markets with 500-share units.

Purchases and sales below the unit of trading are called odd lots.

Bond market units may vary, but it is not uncommon for units to be 25 bonds for municipals, 100 bonds for governments, and 250 bonds for corporates.

Also called normal unit of trading, also a round lot.

NOTE
A debt security with a relatively limited maturity, as opposed to a long-term bond. The expression "note" is commonly used of government securities with maturities of from 2 to 10 years.

Privately placed corporate debt securities and noncallable shorter-term debt securities are commonly called notes.

Municipal notes may be very short term or they may have maturities up to 2, 3, or even 4 years.

In practice, a note is a debt security so-called by the issuer. No specific time limitations can be given as a universal rule.

NOT HELD
Abbreviation for not held: an instruction that may be added to a market order to buy or sell. It permits a floor broker, but not a specialist, to use time or price discretion for the effective execution of the order. Used principally for large orders.

Older practice was to use DRT (i.e., disregard tape).

Both NH and DRT mean that the customer will not hold the floor broker responsible if a better execution might have been possible.

NOT RATED
1 Used of bonds and preferred stocks that are not rated by one of the national services. The designation is factual and implies neither the lack nor presence of credit risk.
2 Used in tombstones of debt issues, particularly municipals, to designate that a serial maturity is not being reoffered for sale.
3 Used as an abbreviation for nonrefundable.
   See also NONREFUNDABLE.

NOVATION

The substitution of one debt for another by the payment of a dollar difference. Many synonyms could be used: restructuring, postponing, and the like.

Here is a frequent example of novation: a GNMA forward contract is cancelled, another contract is substituted, and either the buyer or the seller makes a cash settlement to the other, depending on market conditions and the conditions of the new contract.

Novation is not considered to be a capital transaction by the Internal Revenue Service; therefore, gains are ordinary income gains and losses are ordinary income losses.

NOW ACCOUNT

Acronym for negotiable order of withdrawal. Term for a savings bank account that permits checking privileges. The depositor can earn interest on savings until such time as checks are presented for payment. In practice, therefore, NOW accounts are a combined savings and checking account.

NUMBERS ONLY

Synonym for a nominal quotation. For example, in response to a request for a quote, a dealer responds 18–19, numbers only. The response does not obligate the dealer to make a transaction.

O

O

Used in newspaper reports of a corporation's earnings to designate that the principal market for the corporation's securities is over the counter (OTC).

OARS

Acronym for Opening Automated Report Service. Computerized service subscribed to by specialists on the New York and the American stock exchanges to facilitate opening and reopening of the market for individual securities.

ODD LOT

Specific name for exchange transactions that are for less than the unit of trading. For example, a trade for 90 shares if the unit of trading is 100 shares.

Technically, over-the-counter (OTC) transactions are negotiated; thus, there are no odd-lot transactions. In practice, OTC transactions below the units of trading are also called odd-lot transactions; but there is no standard odd-lot differential charged for purchases or sales. The trader, however, will change the bid for smaller sales, or change the offer for smaller purchases.

ODD-LOT THEORY

Hypothesis, on a theory of Garfield Drew, that one may predict a general market trend opposed to the trend of odd-lot transactions. Thus, if odd-lotters are buying, sell; if selling, buy.

The theory is without statistical validity and has no predictive value. For example, in the past 10 years, with big market drops in terms of total return versus inflation, odd-lot holders have been sellers on balance—the right thing to do. The theory is historical and has no present value.

OFF BOARD

Although the term may be used of any over-the-counter transaction, the most prevalent usage is of a transaction in a listed security that is completed either in the OTC market or is completed within the member firm itself. For example, if a member firm receives a sell order for a listed security that is transacted OTC, or that it buys for its own account, the transaction is off board.

OFFER

The price at which someone is willing to sell a security. In practice, the amount the offerer is willing to sell is a round-lot of the security. On exchange transactions, the offer price is commonly combined with a size; that is, the number of shares so offered.

Also called offer price.

Asked price is a common synonym for offer price.

OFFERING DATE

The date on which a security is first offered for sale to the public. See also DATED DATE.

OFFERING PRICE

The lowest price at which someone is willing to sell a round lot of a security.

Also called the asked price.

See also OFFER.

OFFERING SCALE

The prices, expressed in points and decimal parts of a point or as eighths, or expressed as a yield to maturity, at which the underwriters will sell the individual serial maturities of a bond issue.

The expression is commonly used in municipal underwriting. For example, the 10s of 1992 are offered at par, while the 11s of 2002 are offered at 11.50 (i.e., at a discount to yield 11.50% to maturity).

Also called the scale.

OFFER WANTED

Offer wanted (OW) is often entered in the pink or yellow sheets by a dealer who wants another dealer to make an offer for the security.

See also PINK SHEETS and YELLOW SHEETS.

OFF-FLOOR ORDER

General New York Stock Exchange term for an order that originates off the floor of the exchange. As a rule, off-floor orders take precedence over orders that originate on the floor. For example, a typical order from a member firm customer is an off-floor order, while an order from a competitive floor trader, who is on the floor at the time, is not.

OFFICE OF SUPERVISORY JURISDICTION

A National Association of Securities Dealers' term for an office, or a group of offices, supervised by a parent office of a member. The concept involves two ideas: the office of supervisory jurisdiction (1) must have a written set of procedures that is to be followed and (2) must be responsible for the ethical conduct of registered representatives within the OSJ. Every member of the NASD must have at least one office of supervisory jurisdiction.

OFFICIAL NOTICE OF SALE

An announcement by a municipal issuer that it is soliciting competitive bids for a forthcoming issue of municipal securities. The notice gives important facts about the issue: par value, conditions of the issue, and name of a municipal official who can be contacted for other information about the issue. Such notices appear in the Daily Bond Buyer under the heading, Official Notice of Sale.

OFFICIAL STATEMENT

A comprehensive document often published by municipal issuers. Similar to the prospectus of a registered offering of securities: it gives pertinent facts about the issue. Official statements commonly are published for revenue bond issues; less frequently for general obligation issues.

Industry rules require the official statement, if published, or a summary thereof prepared by the principal underwriter, be sent to purchasers of new municipal issues.

OFFSET

General term for a transaction that:

1. Eliminates a commitment in a futures or forward contract by means of an equal and opposite transaction in an identical commodity or security. For example, a long contract for $1 million GNMA 9% of September 1983 can be offset by the sale of a forward contract for the same amount, coupon, and date.
2. Hedges, partially or fully, a present position in a security or commodity. For example, a client with a long-term paper profit in a security sells an equal number of shares short against the box.

See also HEDGE and BOX.

OFFSHORE

As an adjective: to qualify a financial organization that is domiciled outside the United States and thus not regulated by U.S. securities laws. For example, a mutual fund, domiciled in the Bahamas, is an offshore fund. The fact that an organization is offshore does not mean that its securities may be legally sold within the United States. The designation is factual only. To legally sell securities within the United States, they must conform with U.S. laws.

OLD MONEY PREFERRED

A designation given to preferred shares of domestic corporations. Preferred shares of domestic corporations issued before October 1, 1942, are—if held by another domestic corporation—eligible for a 60% exclusion of dividends from taxable income. Preferreds issued after that date are called new money preferreds and are eligible for an 85% exclusion if the holder is another domestic corporation.

Also called old money.

ONE CANCELS THE OTHER

Concept: A client enters an order for two transactions; if order A is transacted, order B must be cancelled.

Most member firms dealing with the public will not accept such an order.

Also called an alternative order.

ON-FLOOR ORDER

General designation for an order originating on the floor or from the property owned by the exchange. This designation is to make sure that persons who are members cannot use their inside information of floor conditions to take advantage of buyers or sellers who do not have access to this information.

ONGOING BUYER OR ONGOING SELLER

Term to describe a buyer or seller who wishes to accumulate, if a buyer, or distribute, if a seller, by making many purchases or sales of a given security. Ongoing buying or selling, if done with limit or scale orders will normally result in a better average price than a one-time order to buy or sell a large quantity of a security.

OPD

Tape symbol designating a transaction that is:
1   Either the first transaction of the day in a stock whose opening was delayed beyond 10:30 EST.
2   Or, if used before 10:30, designates a transaction that represents a significant change from the previous day's close. Normally, this is 1 or more points for stocks selling below $20, or 2 or more points for stocks selling above $20.

OPEN

As adjective:
1   Used of syndicate members who will accept indications of interest, or of market makers who will accept bids or offers.
2   Used of security orders to buy or sell that are not yet executed or, more commonly, of good-till-cancelled orders.

OPEN-END MANAGEMENT COMPANY

A management investment company that issues new shares if people wish to buy them, and whose shares are redeemable whenever the present holders wish to tender them back to the management company.

Popularly called a mutual fund.

OPEN-END MORTGAGE

A bond, with property as collateral, whose indenture permits further bond issues based on the same property. In the event of default, creditors for all issues made under an open-end mortgage have equal claim on the value of the asset.

OPENING PURCHASE

A transaction that establishes or increases a customer's long position in an option series. For example, a customer, with no position in the ABC Jan 50 calls, buys five calls as an opening purchase.

OPENING SALE

A transaction that establishes or increases a customer's short position in an option series. For example, a customer, with no position in the LMN Apr 50 calls, writes five calls as an opening sale.

The expression opening sale is factual; it is used independently of the customer's position in the underlying security or option. Thus, an opening sale may be either covered or uncovered.

OPEN INTEREST

The aggregate number of exercisable contracts, for either an option series or a commodity future, that are curently existing on the records of a clearing corporation. An open interest of one means that there is a buyer and seller with the same contract specification. For example, a writer of an LMN Apr 50 call and a holder of an LMN Apr 50 call that has neither been exercised nor expired.

OPEN-MARKET OPERATIONS

Term used specifically of sales or purchases by the Federal Reserve of securities in the secondary market. Such purchases or sales expand or contract the money supply.

Term also is used generically of the Fed's ability to make such transactions and thereby change monetary policy.

OPEN ON THE PRINT

Term used by a block positioner who takes the opposite side of the trade from an institutional client. The transaction will appear as completed on the consolidated tape, but the block positioner wants its sales force to know that they are to seek buyers or sellers to offset the resulting risk position. For example, a block positioner is short 10,000 shares because, on a sale of 100,000 to an institutional client, the block positioner sold its inventory of 90,000 and went short 10,000 shares. The sales force will look for sellers of 10,000 shares so the firm can cover its short position.

OPEN ORDER

Technically, any unexecuted order to buy or sell a security. In practice, open order is used as a synonym for a good-till-cancelled order.

OPEN REPO

A repurchase agreement (repo or RP) without a specific date for the repurchase. Such repos are continued on a day-to-day basis. Either party may terminate the agreement at any time, and interest rates are negotiated as market conditions dictate.

OPERATING RATIO

Commonly accepted formula: divide operating income by cost of goods sold. Thus, if a corporation receives $100,000 from sales and it costs $80,000 to produce and to sell the goods, its operating ratio is 80%.

The operating ratio, subtracted from 100%, gives the margin of profit ratio. Thus, a company with an operating ratio of 75% has a margin of profit ratio of 25%.

OPERATIONS

General term for that function of a broker-dealer responsible for execution, clearance, and settlement of customer transactions and the record keeping of customer accounts.

ALso called operations department.

Industry slang normally refers to transacting, clearing, delivery and settlement as the "street side," with customer record keeping as the "customer side" of individual transactions.

OPPORTUNITY COST

Expression that compares current yields on a fixed number of dollars. For example, a customer can invest $10,000 at 10% with little risk of loss. Instead, the customer invests at 5% because the second investment, which gives only 5%, presents an opportunity for substantial gain. The customer takes a known decrease in yield for the unknown opportunity to make substantial profits. The known decrease in yield is the opportunity cost.

OPRA

Acronym for Options Price Reporting Authority. It is a subscription service that publicizes option transactions and quotations on a ticker tape or a CRT device.

OPTION

A privilege enabling the holder to take some market action in a fixed quantity of a security, at a fixed price within a specified time.

Calls, a privilege to buy, and puts, a privilege to sell, are the most common types of options. Corporations also grant options to buy stock to selected corporate executives.

Technically, rights, warrants, and convertibles also are options to buy.

OPTION AGREEMENT

An agreement by a customer of a member firm who opens an option account. The agreement normally contains three parts: (1) a verification by the customer of the financial information about the customer, (2) the receipt of the Option Clearing Corporation prospectus, and (3) an agreement to abide by exercise and position limits and the other rules and regulations of options trading.

Also called option information form.

OPTION HOLDER

A person who has purchased a put or call option and has not sold the option, nor exercised it while the option is still in effect.

OPTION PREMIUM

The dollar price, with further variations in 8ths or 16ths, per share paid by the holder of an option to the writer for the privilege given by the option. For example, a call on 100 shares for 3 months at $50 per share sells at a premium of $3. The purchaser of the option must pay the writer $300 for the privilege of holding the option.

OPTIONS CLEARING CORPORATION

Corporation equally owned by the exchanges that handle option transactions. The OCC (1) issues and guarantees option transactions, (2) compares transactions and processes the money transactions, (3) maintains records, (4) assigns option exercises to the writers of options.

Of particular importance is the prospectus of the OCC, which outlines risks, establishes rules for the conduct of accounts, and sets the norms for ethical conduct in the handling of options accounts.

OPTION SERIES

A put or a call that has a specified exercise price and a specified expiration month. For example, a Monsanto January 50 call is an option series, as is an Eastman Kodak April 70 put.

Purchases and sales of listed options are always made by series: an investor cannot buy or sell a type or class of option—only a series of option—because the transaction requires another investor on the other side of the trade to make the offsetting sale or purchase.

OPTION SPREAD

A simultaneous long and short position in a class of option. Thus a client who buys (holds) an XYZ Jan 50 call and who writes (sells) an XYZ Jan 60 call is said to have a call spread.

Option spreads may be call spreads, put spreads, bearish (profitable if the market goes down), or bullish (profitable if the market goes up).

OPTIONS PRINCIPAL MEMBER

An individual who has purchased from an exchange or from another member the right to buy and sell listed options on the floor of that exchange.

OPTION WRITER

The seller of a put or a call. In exchange for the premium paid by the purchaser of the option, the writer grants the privilege to the buyer to demand performance: to buy from the writer in the case of a call, or to sell to the writer in the case of a put, in accord with the provisions of the option contract.

OR BETTER

Order ticket designation for limit orders. The designation is used for limit buy orders above the prevailing best offer, or for limit sell orders that are below the prevailing best bid.

Technically, all limit orders are "or better"; thus, OB is ordinarily an in-house designation to inform order clerks that the customer's order was meant to be a buy above the current market, or a sell below the current market.

ORDER BOOK OFFICIAL

Employees of the Pacific or Philadelphia stock exchanges who accept orders for options that are not capable of immediate execution. If and when such orders can be transacted, the OBO makes the trade, on an agency basis, and notifies the member firm that entered the order.

Employees with similar functions on the Chicago Board Options Exchange are called board brokers.

ORDER TICKET

The form, completed by a registered representative, that contains the customer's instructions to buy or sell plus the other qualifications imposed by the customer on the transaction. Federal law requires that customer instructions be entered on an order ticket and that the order tickets be maintained for a specified time.

ORIGINAL ISSUE DISCOUNT

Technical designation given to an issue of bonds by the Internal Revenue Service. Once designated as OID, a bondholder must periodically adjust upward the cost of acquisition so that, if such a bond is held to maturity, there will be neither capital gain nor loss. The difference between purchase cost and adjusted cost is considered income. Professional tax advice is always needed because there is a difference in the tax treatment of government and corporate OIDs and municipal OIDs.

ORIGINAL MATURITY

Time difference between issue date and maturity date at the time a bond is issued. Thus, a bond issued in October 1982 that will be due in October 2002 has an original maturity of 20 years. Once issued, the original maturity shortens. It is customary to refer to the time remaining to maturity as the current maturity; thus, in October 1984, the bonds referred to above will be 18-year bonds.

ORIGINATOR
Term commonly used of a bank or a savings and loan that was the original mortgagor of a pool of loans. When the pool of mortgages is resold (e.g., in the form of Ginnie Mae passthroughs), the bank is called the originator of the pool.

OTC MARGIN STOCK
Any stock, traded exclusively in the over-the-counter market, whose issuer meets certain, qualifying criteria and, therefore, broker-dealers are permitted to extend credit on the purchase or short sale of such securities by Regulation T of the Federal Reserve.

OTC OPTION
This is a call or put whose strike price, expiration, and premium are negotiated.
Also called a conventional option.

OUT FOR A BID
Municipal bond marketing term: a dealer lets bonds to an agent so he can solicit their sale. The broker, who will receive a fee if the bonds are sold, is thus in a position to offer the bonds to prospective clients.

OUT OF THE MONEY
Industry term for any option whose exercise would result in a negative cash flow. Thus, a call at 50 would result in a negative cash flow if the underlying stock were at 49-⅞ or below, and a put at 50 would result in a negative cash flow if the underlying stock were at 50⅛ or above.
Out of the money is always computed independently of premiums received and dividends that could be obtained by an exercise.

OUTRIGHT PURCHASES OR SALES
Expression that refers to net purchases or sales by the Federal Open Market Committee. Thus, the expression excludes buys or sells that may be partially offset by repurchase or reverse repurchase agreements.

OVERALLOTING

Practice of investment bankers, if so permitted by the underwriting agreement, to sell more shares than are available for distribution. Shares so overalloted are being sold short by the syndicate in the hope that overeager buyers will resell the shares to the syndicate and thus the net short position will be covered at a profit. Normally, the percentage of shares, or of bonds, that may be overalloted is limited in the agreement among underwriters.

OVERBANKED

Slang for underwritings where the initial allotment to syndicate members exceeds the number of securities to be offered. Obviously, by the time the details of the underwriting are completed, participation will equal 100% of the offering. Some potential members will drop out; others will decrease their allotment; or, if too many members drop out, others will increase their allotments. Overbanking is common as the details of the underwriting are worked out.

OVERBOOKED

Slang for an underwriting where the indications of client interest exceed the number of securities available.

Although the term is technically applicable to registered offerings, it also is used of exempt offerings that are not subject to registration. In the latter case, however, the expression oversubscribed is more common.

OVERBOUGHT

Expression used by technical analysts if (1) they expected the price of a security to rise, but (2) it rose too fast and thus is prone to an imminent correction. In the jargon of technical analysts, it is a "gap"; that is, trading opens substantially above the close of the previous day, which is usually associated with an overbought condition.

OVERLAPPING DEBT

Term used of municipal securities if (1) there are co-issuers of a security, or (2) if a higher-ranking municipality and a lower-ranking municipality share responsibility for an issue.

Thus, if two townships were to issue a common security, or if a township and a village in the township were to issue a security, we would have an example of overlapping debt.

Do not confuse overlapping debt with the term double barreled, which states that a revenue bond is backed by a tax-collecting municipality if revenues are not sufficient for bond debt service.

OVERNIGHT POSITION
Industry term used by broker-dealers to describe their inventory in a security at the end of the trading day. For example, a broker-dealer is said to have an overnight positon in ABC of 500 shares if, at the end of the trading day, the dealer has purchased the shares but not yet sold them. This dealer has a long overnight positon. However, another broker-dealer who had sold short 300 shares of ABC and had not yet repurchased them has a short overnight position.

OVERNIGHT REPO
The most common form of repurchase agreement. In an overnight repo, the seller agrees to repurchase a security at an increment over the original purchase price. The agreement may require that the purchase be made at 100.00 and the repurchase at 100.04. Thus, .04% of a $1 million par value would be an overnight interest of $400. Annualized, $400 as overnight interest on $1 million is approximately 14.6%.
See also REPO.

OVERSOLD
Term used by technical analysts who (1) expected a security to go down in value, but (2) it went down too fast. An oversold technical situation is often manifested by a "gap," or "selling climax," in which the opening price is substantially below the closing price or the low of the previous trading day. Technical analysts expect an oversold condition to be corrected by a rise in the price of the security.

OVER THE COUNTER
General name for:
1 Any transaction in securities that does not take place on an exchange.
See also OTC MARGIN STOCK and OTC OPTION.
2 The communications network linking dealers in securities who make transactions that are completed by telephone or telex rather than in a centralized marketpace.

OVERTRADING
An NASD term for this situation: A dealer, who is also an underwriter, offers a client a higher price than is justified for a security if the customer will purchase a portion of a new issue. The spread on the new issue offsets the special price set for the client's shares. Thus, if a client is offered ½ point more than is justified, provided he buys a new issue with a spread of 1 point, the underwriter will come out ahead on the combined transactions.

OVERVALUED

A term used by fundamental analysts who feel that the present market price of a security, judged in terms of the company's earnings and the current price-earnings ratio, is not justified in terms of historical values given to the securities of that company. The analyst who gives a judgment of overvalued to a security expects the price of the security to drop in value.

OVERWRITING

Expression used of a call writer who estimates that the underlying security is overpriced and thus will decline in value. The call writer, therefore, does not expect the call to be exercised.

Overwriting, whether covered or uncovered, is speculative because the writer will, if the underlying security goes up in value, lose on an uncovered position or be unwilling to have the underlying stock called and will buy back the call at a loss.

P

P

As lowercase: appears in the option table of the newspaper to designate put options.

As uppercase: appears in the newspaper listings of corporate earnings to designate that the principal market for the security is the Philadelphia Stock Exchange.

PA

Used in newspaper reports about a company's earnings to designate that the principal marketplace for the security is the Pacific Stock Exchange. Normally printed Pa.

PACIFIC STOCK EXCHANGE

The Pacific Stock Exchange has trading floors located both in Los Angeles and San Francisco. The trading floors are interconnected electronically. The PSE trades in stocks listed on the exchange, in many securities traded on other exchanges, and in options listed on that exchange.

PAID-IN CAPITAL

The dollar difference between the aggregate par value of issued common shares of a corporation and the price at which they were sold. Paid-in capital is given on the balance sheet of the corporation.

Normally, paid-in capital is adjusted downward if a corporation repurchases its own shares and places the repurchased shares in the treasury.

Also called capital surplus.

PAINTING THE TAPE
Expression used if the speaker thinks that someone, or a group working in concert, is making transactions without a true change of beneficial ownership. The speaker has inferred from the flurry of transactions reported on the exchange tape that the transactions were made to give the impression (i.e., to paint the tape), of widespread activity in the stock—thereby causing others to buy or sell the security.

PAIRED SHARES
Normally, the common stock of two companies under common management sold as a unit. Usually, the certificates are printed back and front on the same piece of paper to facilitate transfer.

Also called Siamese shares or stapled stock.

P & L
An abbreviation for a profit and loss statement, which is a financial statement issued by a corporation to reflect its gross income and expenses and thus its profits or losses.

Also written P and L.

P & S
General industry term for the purchase and sale function of a broker-dealer. Although the function may include other aspects of the operations area, P & S normally is responsible for comparing and reconciling the terms of completed transactions to facilitate securities and money settlements.

Also written P and S.

PAPER
General industry term for shorter-term debt securities. Commercial paper is an obvious example, but bankers' acceptances and negotiable certificates of deposit often are included under the general term.

You also will see or hear the term short-term paper as a synonym for such debt securities.

PAPER LOSS
An unrealized loss on a security position. Paper losses become realized losses only if a long security is sold or a short position is covered.

PAPER PROFIT

An unrealized gain on a security position. Paper profits become realized only if a long position is sold or a short position is covered.

Generally, there are no tax consequences on paper profits until the position is sold or covered. However, tax advice is needed on paper profits if one leg expires in one tax year and the other leg in another year.

PAPILSKY RULES

Named for the plaintiff in a civil suit brought against an investment adviser and the broker-dealer affiliate.

The suit resulted in certain rule modifications by the National Association of Securities Dealers (NASD) regarding securities taken in trade by an underwriter, selling concessions made in exchange for bona fide research services, and the allocation of new issues to related persons.

PAR

From the Latin: equal. Used in the securities industry to represent any security whose market or offering price is the same as its face value at the time of redemption. For example, a bond with a face value of $1,000, offered at par, can be purchased at $1,000.

PAR BOND

A bond that is offered at, or whose current market price is, 100% of its redemption value.

PAR CAP

In connection with GNMA forward delivery contracts (TBA), under yield maintenance procedures, this means a seller is precluded from delivering substitute GNMA securities with an interest coupon rate that requires adjusting the contract's dollar price above the issue's par value. This would otherwise take place when the current coupon rate on settlement date is significantly lower than the rate prevailing in past months.

PARITY

Used of convertible securities if the value of the underlying common stock is equal to the market value of the convertible security. For example, if a bond is convertible into 50 shares of common stock, parity exists if the bond is priced at $700 and the stock is priced at $14 per share.

PARKING

A term used to cover fictitious practices. Parking occurs if:

1 A dealer sells a security to another dealer to reduce its net capital

requirement. Later, when a customer is found, the dealer buys back the security at a price that repays the other dealer for his cost of carrying the security.

2   An employer's transfering the registration of an employee to another employer so, at a later date, the former employee can be rehired without the need for a new registration examination.

PARTIAL DELIVERY

Industry expression for a delivery against a sale of less than the contract amount. For example, a selling broker of 1,000 shares delivers 500.

Also called a partial.

PARTICIPATE BUT DO NOT INITIATE

Instruction given on some very large orders to buy or sell. The instruction says, in effect, buy or sell, but do not initiate a new price— let market forces create the new price. Such instructions are given by institutional buyers or sellers that want to accumulate or distribute shares without disturbing the normal market forces, or by institutions that are not permitted by law to create an uptick, if buying, or a downtick, if selling.

PARTICIPATING PREFERRED

Preferred shares that offer a bonus dividend if, in any quarter, the dividend on common shares of the same issuer exceeds a stated dollar amount. Normally, any extra dividends declared by the company are shared equally by common and participating preferred shareholders.

Very few issues of participating preferred shares are outstanding.

PARTICIPATING TRUST

A type of unit investment trust that issues shares representing an interest in an underlying investment in a mutual fund.

Participating trusts are called plan companies and form the legal entity underlying a contractual-type mutual fund. Because some features come from the underlying mutual fund, and some from the plan company, investors in a fund through a participating trust receive two prospectuses: one for the plan company, one for the mutual fund shares.

PARTICIPATION CERTIFICATE

A security that represents an undivided interest in a pool of mortgages with the same interest rate and maturity date.

PARTNERSHIP

An association of two or more individuals who pool their money and talent to conduct a business. If the individuals are personally responsible for the liabilities of the partnership, they are called general partners. Individuals who contribute only money and who are not personally responsible for the liabilities of the partnership are called limited partners.

PARTY IN INTEREST
Term used in the Employee Retirement Income Security Act(ERISA) to identify a person who provides a service to a pension or other employee benefit plan. Service includes investment advice to a retirement plan; it also includes broker-dealers who make purchases, sales, leases, underwriting, or credit transactions for or with a retirement plan.

PAR VALUE
1 Used of fixed-income securities to designate the value of bonds at maturity, or the price at which preferred shares may be redeemed, unless a premium price is established. Also called the face value.
2 Used of common shares as an identifier. For example, the $10 par common shares.

This value also is used on the balance sheet to designate the stated value of outstanding common shares.

Par value is not a measure of market value for common shares.

PASSED DIVIDEND
1 Used of the dividend on cumulative preferred shares if omitted by a corporation. Such passed dividends form an arrearage that must be paid before any dividends may be paid on common shares.
2 Used of an expected dividend on common shares that is not declared by the board of directors. There is no obligation to pay passed dividends on common shares.

PASS-THROUGH SECURITY
A debt security that represents a fractional interest in a pool of mortgages. Abbreviation often is written P/T.

Payments on such securities, made monthly, are partially interest on unpaid principal balance and partially a repayment of principal.

Such securities are said to be modified if the originating mortgage bank partially reduces the interest rate on the underlying mortgages and uses the reduction as its fee for the pass-through service.

PAYDOWN
1 Used of a refunding of one debt by another if the new debt is smaller than the originally outstanding debt. For example, a

company borrows $8 million to refund bonds with a face value of $10 million.

2   Used of Ginnie Mae modified pass-through pools if the experienced reduction in the unpaid principal balance is greater than the anticipated reduction. For example, a GNMA pool, after eight years, should have a factor of .8532456; its experienced factor is .7894321.

PAYING AGENT

The person designated in an indenture or bond resolution to make principal repayment and periodic interest payments for an issuer of debt securities.

Normally, one or more commercial banks will be the paying agent(s), although it is not uncommon for the treasurer of the issuer to also be designated as a paying agent.

Also called the disbursing agent, although this term is more frequently used in connection with common stock dividends.

PAYMENT DATE

Date on which a cash payment, either dividend or interest, will be made by an issuer.

PAY-THROUGH BONDS

A hybrid debt security that combines some of the features of mortgage bonds and pass-through securities. The issuer guarantees its bonds with a pool of mortgages that it owns. Thus, the bonds remain as a liability on its balance sheet instead of as a sale of assets, which would occur if pass-through securities were issued. The monthly pro rata distribution of interest and principal, however, is similar to a pass-through security.

PAY UP

1   Term used of a customer who must supply additional funds because the cost of a purchase exceeds the proceeds of a sale. For example, a customer who swaps BBB bonds for AAA bonds of similar coupon and maturity normally must pay up to make the swap.
2   Term used of a borrower who must pay higher than prevailing interest rates because money is needed for a prior commitment.
3   As verb: pay up. As adjective or noun: pay-up.

PEGGING

Maintaining the offer price for a security by a bid at or slightly below that price.

When used of underwriting, pegging is legal. In other circumstances, pegging is a form of price manipulation and is illegal.

Also called stabilization.

PENALTY PLAN

A term used by critics of contractual mutual funds. Reason: because the purchaser has prepaid a large portion of the sales charge during early years of the contract, the purchaser will, in many cases, suffer a severe loss if the contract is not completed. Recent revisions of the Investment Company Act of 1940 have substantially reduced the penalties that will be suffered by an investor who discontinues a contractual plan.

PENALTY SYNDICATE BID

A stabilizing bid made by the manager of a syndicate, with the proviso that selling concessions will be withheld, and often a monetary penalty assessed, against those members of the account whose customers reoffer to the account manager securities just sold to them by members of the account.

PENNANT

Term used by technical analysts to describe a chart pattern for a security. The pattern roughly conforms to a triangle whose base is to the left of the chart and whose apex is to the right.

Pennant formations usually indicate a stock whose price may either rise or fall as the apex is reached; thus, no conclusive trend is indicated.

PENNY STOCKS

Wall Street expression for relatively low-priced, highly speculative securities. Although the term implies securities priced at less than $1 per share, the term is not limited to such shares. Many member firms have special margin maintenance requirements for such shares and often limit purchases of such shares to unsolicited orders by clients.

PER

Acronym for Post Execution Reporting on the American Stock Exchange. It is a computerized order routing system for member-firm market, limit, and odd-lot orders that transmits such orders and returns the details of executed orders. Similar in concept to the Designated Order Turnaround (DOT) system on the New York Stock Exchange.

PER CAPITA DEBT

Used by municipal bond analysts of general obligation bonds. Total bonded debt divided by the population of the municipality gives the per capita debt.

PERFORMANCE STOCK

A stock that is expected to rise in market value over the near or long term. Used as a synonym for a growth stock.

The term is not used of stocks chosen for income nor of stocks chosen for total return (i.e., a combination of steady income and some capital growth). Performance emphasizes capital growth.

PERIODIC PAYMENT PLAN

Common expression for a contractual mutual fund. The investor, through a contract, agrees to make monthly or quarterly payments to the plan company; in return, the investor receives certain benefits from the plan company, usually plan completion insurance and certain asset withdrawal privileges, and certain benefits from the underlying fund, usually a sharing in a diversified portfolio of common stocks and reinvestment privileges.

Normally, periodic payment plans have a 10-year or 15-year accumulation program, with a contract life that is twice as long.

PERIODIC PURCHASE DEFERRED CONTRACT

Term used of annuity contracts, either fixed or variable, whereby the investor makes monthly or quarterly fixed-amount payments. The contract has not been annuitized, thus payout is deferred pending an election by the annuitant of the payout method desired.

PERPETUAL WARRANT

A warrant to purchase a fixed number of common shares of a corporation at a fixed price that has no expiration date. For example, TriContinental Corporation, a closed-end management company, has perpetual warrants outstanding.

PHANTOM STOCK PLAN

A work-compensation incentive given to officers of a corporation. Under this plan, future bonus compensations are tied to the dollar value increase of the company's common stock. Thus, the bonus compensation will be computed as though the officers held a fixed number of the underlying shares; hence, the word phantom and the term phantom stock.

PHILADELPHIA PLAN

Used of equipment trust certificates wherein title to the leased equipment remains with the trustee until such time as all of the outstanding serial maturities for the issue are retired. At this time, title passes to the leasing issuer of the securities.

See also NEW YORK PLAN.

PHILADELPHIA STOCK EXCHANGE

The commonly used acronym for the Philadelphia Stock Exchange is PHLX. The exchange, founded in 1790, provides a marketplace for many local issues and for designated security options, and it serves as an alternate marketplace for many securities traded on the New York or other exchanges.

PICKUP

Term used of a swap of bonds with similar coupon rates and similar maturities at a basis price that is advantageous to the swapper. For example, a client sells 8-½% bonds of 2000 at a basis of 10.30% and buys 8-½% bonds of 2001 at a basis of 10.70%. The client has picked up 40 basis points of yield.

Pickup implies that the monetary adjustment between the purchase and sale prices is relatively small.

See also PICKUP BONDS.

PICKUP BONDS

Term used of bonds with a relatively high coupon and a relatively short callable date. If interest rates drop, the issuer usually will call the bonds at their premium price. The investor, therefore, will receive a return that is higher than anticipated because of the premium received when the bond is called.

PICTURE

Term used to describe the prices at which a dealer, or a specialist acting as either a broker or a dealer, is willing to trade. Often, size indications are included in the picture.

The term is slang and may be used as a synonym for quote and size. For example, "What's the picture on ABC?" "It's 19-½ to 20, 2,000 either way."

PIGGYBACK REGISTRATION

Term used if an issuer making a primary distribution of securities permits holders of shares purchased privately to include their shares in the offering. Such offerings are combined primary-secondary distributions, and the prospectus will disclose this fact and the names of the major sellers of securities previously purchased privately from the corporation.

PINK SHEETS
The National Quotations Bureau publishes each business day the list of securities being traded by over-the-counter market makers. Equity securities are published separately on long sheets colored pink; hence the name. Debt securities are published separately on long sheets colored yellow.

See also YELLOW SHEETS.

PIPELINE
Word signifying all of the procedures in a typical underwriting except the actual public offering. Thus, securities that are being underwritten but not yet sold are said to be in the pipeline.

The word also is used by mortgage bankers to describe mortgage contracts that have been negotiated but not yet closed.

PLACE
Industry jargon for a distribution of securities to a buyer through a public or private sale.

PLACEMENT RATIO
The percentage of new municipal issues of $1 million or more that have come into syndication within the past week and have been sold. Thus a placement ratio of 87% means that 87% of the dollar value of new municipal issues syndicated in the past week have been sold.

The Daily Bond Buyer compiles the placement ratio from municipal underwriters at the close of business each Thursday.

PLAN COMPANY
A sales organization registered with the SEC as a participating unit investment trust. The plan company sells contractual-type funds on behalf of the fund's underwriter.

Because the plan company's units and the shares of the underlying mutual fund are both registered with the SEC, the contractual plan purchaser will receive two prospectuses: one for the plan company, one for the mutual fund.

PLAN COMPLETION INSURANCE
Decreasing term life insurance sold at group rates to subscribers to a mutual fund contractual plan. If the planholder dies before the completed plan contract, the difference between the planholder's contributions and the plan amount is paid to the custodian bank. The bank, in turn, completes the plan with the insurance money and

holds the shares, together with shares already purchased, for the decedent's estate.

PLATO

Acronym for a computer-assisted instruction and testing procedure developed by the Control Data Corporation. Many industry regulatory examinations, including the branch office manager and the state blue-sky examinations, are taken at the Control Data Learning Centers on the PLATO system.

PLUS

Often written as a mathematical sign: +.

1   A fractional variation to designate a quote in 64ths; for example, 85.16+ means 85 and $\frac{33}{64}$th of par. The numerator is 2 times 16 plus 1; 64 is the denominator.
2   A designator for a transaction above the previous regular way transaction. For example, on the Quotron system, 45+ means that the last trade at 45 is higher than the previous trade.
3   In the stock column of the newspaper, a + in the change column means that the closing price of listed securities was higher by the stated amount over the previous day's close. For mutual funds and OTC securities, the change is measured from the previous day's bid price.
4   Used of the difference, if a positive number, between a closed-end investment company's offer price and the net asset value of the underlying share assets.

PLUS TICK

Expression signifying that a transaction in a listed security occurred at a price higher than the previous regular way transaction in that security. Thus, 74+ means that the prior regular-way transaction in the security was at 73-⅞ or below.

See also SHORT SALE and ZERO-PLUS TICK.

PLUS-TICK RULE

SEC rule requiring short sales of round lots of listed securities be made at a price that represents an advance over the last different regular-way price for that security on its principal exchange. Exception: If the last sale was itself an advance, a sale at the same price is a zero-plus tick and may be a legitimate short sale.

POINT

1   Used of equity securities: a $1 change in the market price, or the quote, of the underlying security. For example; an equity security

that went up 2 points means that its price per share increased by $2.

2   Used of bonds: a change of 1% of the par value of the bond relative to its market price. Thus, if the market price of a bond with a par value of $5,000 went up 1 point, the market value change was $50.

3   Used of bond yields: 100 basis points equals 1%.

See also BASIS POINT.

POINT AND FIGURE CHART

A method of plotting significant price changes in a security independently of time. On the graph, successive upward price changes are plotted on the same line with an X; if a price reversal occurs, successive downward prices are plotted on the same line with an O. Succeeding upward price movements, again using X, are plotted on the next line, and so on. The method will produce a trend in the stock's prices.

The method, because it abstracts from time, gives an insight into sentiment for the security; but it loses the momentum implied by a chart that measures price movements over time.

POOL

Commonly used expression if a group of debt instruments is gathered together and an undivided interest in the securities is represented by another security. For example, a bank issues mortgages on 50 homes with a $20,000 mortgage on each home. If the bank were to issue a security with a face value of $1 million, the security would represent a pool of mortgages.

POOLING OF INTEREST

Balance sheet term for the accounting procedure used if one corporation acquires another through merger or acquisition.

Principal concepts: (1) all assets and liabilities are merged; (2) if there is a difference between the cost of acquisition and the net tangible value of the acquired corporation, it is entered on the acquiring corporation's balance sheet as "goodwill." Present IRS rules permits this entry to be amortised over 40 years.

PORTFOLIO

Commonly accepted term for those assets of an individual or a legal person, such as a bank, trust company, pension or profit-sharing plan, or an investment company, which are invested in primary or secondary market securities. Generally, hard assets (e.g., gold, silver, art) and commodities are excluded from the term.

In the broadest sense, however, a person's portfolio is the sum of items of value which are (1) saleable and (2) needed for day-to-day use.

See also PRIMARY MARKET, SECONDARY MARKET, SECURITY.

PORTFOLIO MANAGER

A person who makes day-to-day investment decisions for another.

Commonly, the term is used of investment managers for mutual fund, pension or profit-sharing plans, or bank-trust companies.

However, anyone who manages the assets of another and who invests these assets in things that have resale value can be called a portfolio manager.

POSITION

1 As noun: the number of shares owned (long position) or owed (short position) by an individual or a dealer. A dealer's position is also called his inventory.
2 As verb: to acquire a net long or short inventory in a security. For example, "The dealer is trying to position the security."

POSITION BUILDING

Term used of account executives as they endeavor to establish net long (shares owned) or net short (shares owed) positions in the portfolios of their clients.

Position building, although it increases both the risk of selection and the risk of timing, decreases the number of security issues that the account executives must follow. The offset, of course, is that they must follow fewer issues in depth; thus, advice to buy or sell can be more timely in terms of short-term profits.

POSITION LIMIT

Maximum number of option contracts that a customer, or a group of customers working in concert, may hold in the same underlying security. Currently, the maximum for stock options is 2,000 contracts on the same side of the market. For example, long calls and short puts, or long puts and short calls.

The position limits on interest rate options vary with the kind of underlying instrument.

POSITIVE CARRY

Term that describes the use of borrowed funds to purchase interest-producing securities. If the income received is more than the income paid, there is a positive carry. For example, a person borrows money at 9% to buy bonds with a 10% coupon. Thus, the net gain is 1%.

POSITIVE YIELD CURVE

Term used to describe the yield versus time graph of securities of the same issuer, or of securities with a similar credit rating, in which longer-term securities have a higher yield than shorter-term securities. Thus, if 2-year Treasury bonds yield 8% and 4-year bonds yield 9% and 15-year bonds yield 11%, there is a positive yield curve.

Also called yield curve with an ascending slope.

POST

Location on the floor of an exchange where specific securities are traded, and where, in most cases, the specialist is available to receive bids and offers or to give a quote for specific securities.

Also called trading post.

POST 30

A numbered post on the floor of the New York Stock Exchange where relatively inactive listed preferred shares are traded. Bids and offers are entered in cabinets so contra brokers may have a market for trades. All of the stocks traded on Post 30 trade in round lots of 10-shares rather than 100-share units.

POT

Slang for that portion of the shares or bonds of a corporate issue returned to the account manager, as agent, for convenient sale to institutional buyers.

If sales are made from the pot, the members of the syndicate share in the spread in proportion to their takedown of the issue. Thus, on an issue of 1 million shares with 100,000 in the pot, a member of the account with a 10% participation (takedown) will share in 10% of the sales from the pot.

POT IS CLEAN

An announcement made by the manager of a syndicte to the account members that all the securities set aside for institutional sales have been sold.

POWER OF ATTORNEY

A signed document that empowers a second party to act on behalf of the signer.

If a brokerage account is managed by someone with power of attorney, it is important that it be specified whether the power of attorney account is general or limited. Persons with limited power of attorney may sell assets and reinvest the proceeds within the account. Persons with general power of attorney may deliver assets out of the account.

Brokerage accounts with limited power of attorney given to an employee of the brokerage firm are called discretionary accounts.

PRECEDENCE
Exchange trading floor term. It signifies that a broker (e.g., a buyer), is permitted to buy before other brokers despite the fact that other buying brokers also could complete the transaction.

As a general rule, precedence is determined by the time a broker makes a bid, then by the size of his bid relative to the number of shares being offered at that price.

PREEMPTIVE RIGHT
A privilege granted by the charter of some corporations to current common shareholders. It gives them the right to buy a portion of newly offered common shares that is proportional to their current common share holding. In this way, a common shareholder has the opportunity to preserve his or her proportional share of ownership in the corporation.

Because such newly offered shares are priced below the current market price, there is also a monetary incentive to subscribe to the new shares.

Most corporate charters do not grant a preemptive right to the shareholders.

PREFERENCE
Exchange floor term for who goes first in an auction impasse. For example, if two or more brokers, following an execution because of time priority, have orders that equal the remainder of the other side of the trade, they are on parity. Preference will be given to the broker who was the first to enter the group of brokers competing for a transaction (the crowd).

PREFERENCE SHARES
1 Often used as a synonym for any preferred shares.
2 Specifically used of preferred shares that give precedence to other preferred shares; thus, preference shares are junior in their claim on dividends and assets to other preferred shares of the same issuer.

PREFERRED DIVIDEND COVERAGE
The quotient found by dividing the net income after taxes of a corporation by the dollar amount of preferred dividends. Thus, if a

corporation's net income is $10 million and annual preferred dividends are $1 million, the preferred dividend coverage is 10 to 1, or simply 10 times.

PREFERRED STOCK
A form of equity security that has a fixed annual dividend, a stated call price related to its par value, and that, generally, has no voting right. Preferred stock has priority over common stock in the payment of dividends and in the distribution of assets if the company is dissolved. However, it is not a debt security and has no fixed maturity date.

PREFERRED STOCK RATIO
The ratio found by dividing the par value of outstanding preferred shares of a corporation by the total capitalization.

PREMIUM
1 The dollar amount by which the market price of a bond exceeds its par value. Used in a similar way if a preferred share's market price exceeds its face value.
2 A fee paid by a short seller to the lender of the security that is sold short.
See also CALL PREMIUM.

PREMIUM BOND
A bond whose dollar price exceeds its par or face value.

PREPAID CHARGE PLAN
Another name for a contractual mutual fund in which most of the total sales charge on the plan is paid in the first or in the early years of the plan.
See also FRONT-END LOAD and LOAD SPREAD OPTION.

PREPAID EXPENSE
The pro rata portion of a fully paid charge for a service if a portion of the service overlaps the end of a corporation's fiscal year. For example, a corporation pays a six-month premium for insurance in October. Its fiscal year ends in December. One half of the premium covers expenses for the first three months of the next year. This half of the premium will be listed on the corporation's balance sheet as an asset entitled prepaid expense.

PREPAYMENT
If a member firm pays a selling customer before the assigned settlement date, it is called a prepayment.

PREREFUNDING

If an issuer borrows, through a second bond issue, funds for the future refunding of an outstanding bond that is not yet callable, it is called a prerefunding. The outstanding issue that will be called at its earliest call date is said to be prerefunded.

The borrowed funds for the refunding normally are invested in treasuries that will mature at the earliest call date. For this reason, prerefunded bonds are normally rated AAA.

PRESALE ORDER

A buy order accepted by the manager of a municipal syndicate for a portion of the issue before the details of the offering are known.

ALthough such an order would be illegal for an offering under registration with the SEC, such orders are accepted for municipal securities because of their exemption.

PRESOLD ISSUE

An issue of municipals or governments that is completely sold before announcement is made of the price or coupon rate.

This would be an illegal practice on a registered corporate offering that requires a bona fide public offering. It is not illegal in the primary distribution of exempt securities.

PRICE CHANGE

When used of an individual security, price change is the net rise or fall in the market value of the security.

When used of a group of securities, the average of the price changes. For example, if security A rises 1 point and security B falls 1 point, the average change is zero: $+1 - 1 = 0$.

PRICE-EARNINGS RATIO

The price-earnings ratio is derived from the fraction which expresses the price in dollars as the numerator and the earnings per common share as the denominator.

Normally, the fraction is so rationalized that the denominator is 1. Thus, a common stock that is selling at $50 per share, and that has earnings per share of $5, has a PE of 10 to 1. Commonly, the shares are said to have a PE of 10, although technically this is a multiple of 10. The price is 10 times the earnings.

Also called the multiple.

PRICE GAP

Term used by technical analysts if a security's daily range does not overlap the daily range on the previous market day. For example:

yesterday's range for a stock was 38-½–39; today's range was 39-½–40. There was a gap of ½ point between 39 and 39-½.

Price gaps are usually considered indications of an oversold or overbought condition, and a consolidation can be expected in most cases.

The term also is used if successive trades exceed the minimum trading variations. Thus, successive trades at 40, 39-½, 39 exceed the normal variation of ⅛ and would be considered a gap.

PRICE RANGE

The high and low prices for a security over a defined time.
See also RANGE.

PRICE TALK

Term describing the preliminary discussions among underwriters about the range within which they will offer a negotiated issue or within which they will bid on a competitive issue.

Price talk is informal, with this exception: the preliminry prospectus of a corporate issue of common stock will state the maximum offering price if this is a first-time public sale of the security.

PRICEY

Industry slang for a bid that is underpriced, or an offer that is overpriced. For example, if the current market for a security is 35–36, a customer who insists either on a bid at 32 or an offer at 39 is pricey—he is currently unrealistic about buying or selling the security.

PRIMARY DISTRIBUTION

Term used to describe a sale of new securities by an issuer.

In the case of bonds, all sales by an issuer are primary. In the case of stocks, the sale of authorized and previously unissued shares is primary. Thus, a resale of Treasury shares that were previously issued but which are resold is a secondary.

PRIMARY EARNINGS

The quotient from dividing a corporation's net income after taxes, minus preferred dividends, by the number of common shares currently outstanding.

See also FULLY DILUTED EARNINGS PER SHARE (if a company's outstanding shares will be changed by the conversion of convertible securities, or by the exercise of rights, warrants, or stock options granted to corporate executives).

PRIMARY MARKET

General term for any market for assets where the proceeds of the sale go to the issuer. As such, the term includes:

1   The underwriting of original issues of securities.
2   Government securities auctions.
3   Opening sales of option contracts and commodity futures contracts.
4   An exchange, or the OTC market, which is the principal market for a specific outstanding security.

PRIME PAPER

Industry term for commercial paper that is given a rating of P by Moody's Investors Service.

The rating implies an investment grade security. The rating is further subdivided into:

P-1: Highest quality.
P-2: Higher quality.
P-3: High quality.
Ratings below P-3 are not prime paper.

PRIME RATE

A preferential rate of interest on short-term loans granted by commercial banks to their most credit-worthy customers. Theoretically, it is the lowest rate of interest for bank loans that are not backed by items of value pledged as collateral.

PRINCIPAL

Generally, anyone who buys or sells for his own account and risk.

Specifically, financial organizations that habitually buy or sell securities for their own account or who, as underwriters, purchase securities from an issuer for resale to the public.

See also PRINCIPAL AMOUNT (if term is related to an issue of debt securities).

PRINCIPAL AMOUNT

1   The face amount or par value of any debt security.
2   The face amount of a loan.

PRINCIPAL STOCKHOLDER

Generally, a stockholder who owns a large amount of a company's outstanding shares.

Specifically, under Section 12 of the Securities and Exchange Act of 1934, a person who holds 10% or more of the voting stock, including long calls on such stock, of a corporation registered with the SEC.

Also called control or affiliated persons.

PRINT

Slang expression for the records of securities transactions that appear on exchange tapes.

PRIORITY

Auction (trading) market term for the first member to bid or offer at the current highest bid or lowest offer. If a transaction occurs at that price, the contra broker must trade with the broker who has priority, regardless of the size of the bid or offer by the broker with priority.

In essence, therefore, in the auction market, the broker with priority always receives a full or partial execution if a trade occurs at his price.

PRIOR LIEN BOND

A debt security that gives priority to its holders over the claim of other bondholders.

The term is not used to distinguish secured bonds from unsecured bonds; for example, mortgage bonds as opposed to debentures. Instead, a prior lien bond would give priority to one secured bond over another.

Secured bonds with a prior lien over other secured bonds normally are issued by companies in financial difficulty and then only with the authorization of the holders of previously issued bonds who give their authorization to try to save the company.

PRIOR PREFERRED

The term identifies an issue of preferred stock that takes precedence over another issue of preferred stock in its claim on corporate assets in the event of dissolution of the company, or in its claim on earnings if dividends are declared.

PRIVATE PLACEMENT

A sale of securities to relatively few investors. As a general rule, the investors may not exceed 35 persons, although "accredited investors" are excluded from this number.

If a sale is truly private, the sale is an exempt transaction and need not be registered with the SEC.

See also ACCREDITED INVESTOR.

PROCEEDS SALE

National Association of Securities Dealers' term describing a customer sale in the secondary market with the proceeds of the sale to be used for a purchase in the secondary market.

The NASD rule for proceeds sales says that the swap must be

considered as one transaction and that the total sales charges or commissions must come under the 5% policy governing markups, markdowns, or commissions.

PRODUCTION RATE

The current coupon rate for issuance of pass-through securities of the Government National Mortgage Association (GNMA). It is an interest rate set 50 basis points (½%) below the prevailing FHA mortgage rate (i.e., the maximum interest rate at which the Federal Housing Administration will insure, and the Veterans Administration will guarantee, residential mortgages).

PROFIT

Generally, a positive difference between the current market value of a security and the investor's purchase price.

Specifically, the net positive difference between the proceeds of a sale and the investor's adjusted cost of acquisition.

PROFIT AND LOSS STATEMENT

A financial statement, prepared at least once a year by a corporation, that lists the firm's income, expenses, and net profit or loss over the period covered by the statement.

PROFIT MARGIN

Subtract the cost of goods sold from net sales to obtain operating income. Divide operating income by net sales to find the profit margin. For example, a company sells goods worth $10; it cost $8 to make the goods; the operating income is $2. The $2 divided by $10 gives a profit margin of 20%.

Also called the margin of profit, the margin of profit ratio, or the profit ratio.

PROFIT TAKING

Term explaining a drop in general market prices following a sharp rise in general market prices if there is no specific adverse economic or financial news. It is presumed that short-term traders have sold, thus pushing down the market, to capture short-term profits.

PRO FORMA

Latin: according to form or custom. In practice, the expression is used:

1 If a financial statement is currently unaudited but is sufficiently representative of the corporation's financial condition to be a reasonable and fair disclosure of the company's balance sheet.

2 If an action, done with due diligence and proper authorization, awaits only official approval. For example, the shareholders of a corporation have approved a stock split and application has been made for a charter revision. The application is pro forma because it will be approved.

PROJECT NOTE
Short-term municipal security issued by local housing agencies as temporary financing during the building of public housing. They are normally redeemed by the permanent bonds that form the long-term financing for the buildings. Project notes carry a U.S. guarantee through the Department of Housing and Urban Development (HUD).

Abbreviated PN on municipal bond offering sheets published by dealers and by Standard & Poor's in its daily BLue List.

PROPRIETORSHIP
A form of business organization comprised of one owner-person that is not incorporated. The owner has great flexibility in managing the business, but capital resources are often limited and personal financial liability for the debts of the organization is unlimited. Proprietors are self-employed and, as such, are eligible for Keogh account contributions.

PROSPECTUS
The printed summary of a registration statement filed with the SEC in conjunction with a public offering of nonexempt securities. The prospectus, which contains the material information about the offering of securities, must be given to the original purchasers of the security no later than the confirmation of their purchase.

PROTECTIVE COVENANT
General term for agreements and promises of a municipality to protect purchasers of an issue of municipal securities. These agreements are in the bond resolution made when the security is issued.

Typical content of the covenant: a promise to service and repair the facility built with the borrowed funds, adequate insurance coverage, the maintenance of books and records, and the assessment of adequate rates or tolls to cover interest and the repayment of principal.

PROXY
A form whereby a person, who is eligible to vote about corporate matters, transmits his or her written instructions, or transfers to another the right to vote in place of the eligible voter. Normally,

the corporate management transmits a form that is suited to the transmission of such voting instructions, but shareholders may request other forms of proxy if they wish to give special instructions. A proxy permits an eligible voter to vote without being present at the actual meeting.

PROXY STATEMENT
A statement of material information that must be provided by management, or any other person, who solicits the proxies of corporate shareholders. Such statements must be filed with the SEC for examination prior to their distribution to stockholders.

PRUDENT MAN RULE
Rule contained in the laws of many states governing the investment activities of persons who act as fiduciaries, such as trustees, executors, and administrators.

In general, the rule precludes speculative activities by fiduciaries and legislates as a norm the kind of investment actions that a prudent man would use in the conduct of his own financial affairs.

See also LEGAL LIST.

PUBLIC HOUSING AUTHORITY BONDS
Technical name for longer-term municipal bonds used to finance the construction of public housing and which are guaranteed by the full faith and credit of the United States government.

PUBLICLY HELD
Technically, any corporation whose shares are freely transferrable. Specifically:
1 Under SEC definition, a corporation with assets of $1 million or more and 500 or more holders of any class of equity security. Such corporations are required to make periodic reports to the SEC.
2 Under New York Stock Exchange rules, a member corporation whose outstanding stock is owned by 100 or more persons, not including members, allied members, or employees of that member corporation.

PUBLIC OFFERING
General term for a sale of securities by an issuer or control persons. Often called a distribution.

PUBLIC OFFERING PRICE
The price asked (offer) at the original sale (primary distribution) of a company's securities to the public.

See also INVESTMENT BANKER and UNDERWRITER.

PUBLIC SECURITIES ASSOCIATION
A trade association representing banks, dealers, and brokers who underwrite and trade municipals, governments, and federal agency securities.

PUBLIC UTILITY HOLDING COMPANY ACT
This act, passed by Congress in 1935, requires registration with the SEC for all publicly owned holding companies engaged in the electric utility business or in the retail distribution of gas.

PURCHASE ACQUISITION
Term used if one company acquires another for cash, or for Treasury stock purchased within the last two years, and the cost exceeds the net tangible assets of the acquired corporation. In this case, the difference between the cost and the asset value is considered goodwill on the acquirer's balance sheet. The goodwill will be amortized against future revenues over a 40-year period.

PURCHASING POWER
Term used of client general accounts that contain excess margin or other credits in the special miscellaneous account (SMA). Purchasing power is the dollar amount of marginable securities that may be purchased, or sold short, without causing a margin call. For example, Under current Regulation T 50% margin requirements, a client with an SMA entry of $1,000 could purchase marginable securities worth $2,000 without adding additional funds to the margin account.

PURPOSE LOAN
Name of a loan, collateralized by securities, if the money borrowed will be used to purchase, carry, or trade in securities subject to Federal Reserve Board credit regulations and limitations.

PURPOSE STATEMENT
A form that must be completed by a borrower and filed with the lender if margin securities collateralize the loan. In the statement, the borrower lists the purpose of the loan and attests that the loan is not made to purchase, carry, or trade securities subject to Federal Reserve Board restrictions.

PUT OPTION
A privilege that permits the holder of the put option to sell to the writer of the option a fixed number of shares at a fixed price within a specified time.

PUT TO SELLER
Industry jargon for the exercise of a put option by the holder, thereby obligating the seller of the option to purchase the underlying shares.

PV
1   Common abbreviation for par value.
    See also PAR VALUE.
2   In mathematical formulas for the computation of yield to maturity, PV stands for present value.

PX
Often used as an abbreviation for price on offering sheets or other communications about securities.

Q

Q
Signifies a company operating under federal bankruptcy law that will ultimately be liquidated or reorganized. Used uppercase before the security symbol on the consolidated A or B tapes and used lowercase following the name of the company on the newspaper reports of over-the-counter transactions.

QT
1   Acronym for a questioned trade between brokers. A trade is questioned if one or more of the details of the trade, for example, the details of amount and price of the contra broker, do not compare with the other broker's records.
2   Used commonly as an abbreviation in financial reports for the latest fiscal quarter.

Q-TIP TRUST
Industry jargon for a "qualified terminable interest" in a transfer of assets between spouses by means of a legal trust instrument. Under it, the grantor bequeaths income from the assets to the spouse, but upon that person's death, orders disposition of the property to one or more other parties.

QUALIFIED STOCK OPTION
Term describing a stock option granted before May 21, 1981. Under it, recipient could exercise the option at the less than market price

of the security. If the security was then held three or more years, the entire profit was a long-term capital gain. If sold before three years, the difference between the exercise price and the fair market value at the time of exercise was an ordinary income gain and a tax preference item. Only the amount above the fair market value and the ultimate sale price was eligible for capital gains.

QUALIFYING ANNUITY

A fixed, variable, or hybrid annuity approved for inclusion in an IRS-approved pension, profit-sharing, Keogh, or IRA retirement plan. Qualification permits the inclusion of pretax dollars in the annuity and the deduction of these dollars from the planholder's taxable income for that year. In effect, therefore, the dollars are tax sheltered until they are withdrawn from the qualifying annuity. When withdrawn, all withdrawals are taxable as ordinary income in the year received.

QUALIFYING COUPON RATE

Used in conjunction with Ginnie Mae contracts, whether cash, forwards, or options, if GNMAs with coupon rates below the current production rate are deliverable against the contract. There is, of course, an adjustment in the aggregate exercise price that takes into account the lowered coupon rate on the certificates delivered. Thus, current production GNMAs may be delivered at par, but GNMAs with coupons 4% below current production could only be delivered at 80% of par.

QUALITATIVE ANALYSIS

Term used by security analysts to describe value judgments about a security that are based on nonfinancial information. Thus, a buy-sell judgment about a security that is based not on the balance sheet or income statement but on the status of labor relations, the quality of management, or the employee morale would be qualitative.

QUANTITATIVE ANALYSIS

Term of security analysts to describe value judgments about a security that are based on financial information contained in the balance sheet or income statement of a corporation and on financial trends within a particular industry. The term does not necessarily exclude the use of qualitative judgments in arriving at a buy-sell decision by the analyst. The term does imply, however, that incidental market price movements on a short-term basis are excluded from the measurement criteria.

QUICK ASSET RATIO

A measurement of corporate liquidity that uses current assets minus inventory divided by current liabilities. Thus, if a corporation's current assets are $1 million and $300,000 represents inventory, its net quick assets are $700,000. If its current liabilities are $600,000 its quick asset, or acid-test, ratio is ⅞, or 1.16+. Under this criterion of corporate liquidity, ratios in excess of 1 are considered adequate. However, very high quick asset ratios may not be desirable; they may indicate that a cash-rich corporation is a candidate for a takeover.

Also called the acid-test ratio.

QUICK ASSETS

Commonly accepted term in financial statement analysis to mean current assets minus inventory. Thus, a corporation with current assets of $7 million and an inventory of $2.5 million has quick assets of $4.5 million.

Do not confuse quick assets, as computed above, with net quick assets. Net quick assets is defined as quick assets minus current liabilities.

QUID PRO QUO

Latin: one thing (quid) for (pro) another thing (quo).

The term is used extensively in the securities industry to describe any situation in which something of value is exchanged for another. The expression is not limited to sales for value received. It also is used if one party provides information or security research and the other party provides a trade that is profitable to the person providing the research.

QUOTE

A statement of the highest bid and lowest offer for a security. Thus, a quote of 8-½ to 9 represents a bid of 8-½ per share to a seller, and an offer of 9 to a buyer.

Quotes, by industry rules, are presumed to be firm for the accepted round-lot of trading. Quotes that are not firm must be so designated.

On exchanges, quotes normally will be accompanied by size; thus, the quote represents both prices and amounts available at those prices.

Also called the market.

R

RAIDER

1 Anyone who tries to buy control of a company's stock so he can install new management. Federal law places restrictions on raiders

if they become control persons; that is, holders of 10% or more
of a company's outstanding stock. The term raider is not generally
used if the purchaser is buying stock as an investment.
2 Bear raider: a person who tries to sell a company's stock, either
   long or short, with the intent of repurchasing it at a lower
   price.

RALLY

Industry term for a sharp rise in the price of a company's stock.
It also can apply to a sharp rise in bonds or preferred stock.

Rally does not necessarily imply a previous drop in security prices;
thus, a rally can follow a long sideways movement.

In every case, the term implies a sudden rise in prices.

RATE COVENANT

Agreement incorporated into the bond resolution for a municipal
revenue issue that promises to adjust rates for the use of the facility
in such a way that revenues are sufficient to provide for maintenance
and repair and for bond debt service. Thus, a rate covenant would
not provide for a sinking fund or for expansion of the facility; but it
would promise to repair, insure, and pay debt interest and principal
repayment.

RATE OF RETURN

1 Of an investment: the annual cash flow divided by the replacement
   cost. Commonly called current yield.
2 Of corporations: the annual net income, after preferred dividends,
   divided by the net common stockholder equity. Also called return
   on investment, or ROI.

If rate of return is not used as a synonym for current yield or return
on investment, the user normally so qualifies the term that the reader
knows the usage.

RATING

Judgment of creditworthiness of an issuer made by an accepted
rating service, such as Moody's, Standard & Poor's, or Fitch.

The judgment, based on rater's investigation of the risk of default
by the issuer, is stated in letters. Ratings of AAA, AA, A, and BBB
(S&P) are considered investment grade. Ratings of BB or below have
increasing risk of default. Similar ratings are given to preferred
stocks.

Letter ratings for common stock pertain to firm's history of
dividends and dividend coverage, but make no promise about future
coverage.

RATIO SPREAD

A person who holds long calls on a security and who writes more short calls than can be covered by the long calls. Thus, a ratio spread can be 2 for 1 if a person owns 1 long call for each 2 calls written. Ratio spreads can be bearish or bullish; that is, profitable if the market goes down (bearish), or profitable if the market goes up (bullish).

RATIO WRITER

Commonly accepted term for a person who owns an underlying security and who writes more call option contracts than stock he owns. For example, a person who owns 300 shares of XYZ writes six calls on XYZ. The person has a 2 for 1 ratio write. The ratio writer has a middle-risk position between the writer of three covered calls and the writer of six naked (uncovered) calls.

REAL ESTATE INVESTMENT TRUST

A trust, modeled after the diversification feature of investment companies, that invests in a diversified portfolio of real estate holdings. Such trusts, if publicly owned, must be registered with the SEC under the '33 Act.

See also EQUITY REIT and MORTGAGE REIT.

REALLOWANCE

A term used in corporate underwritings if the syndicate permits National Association of Securities Dealers' members who are outside the syndicate to receive a sales commission for sales made to their customers. Thus, if the sales concession on a registered offering is 50 cents per share, a reallowance of 25 cents per share could be made to other NASD members who are granted shares for sale to their customers.

RECEIVER

Technical term for the court-assigned person who sees to the details of a bankruptcy and thus effects either a liquidation for the benefit of bond and stockholders or oversees a corporate reorganization.

Full term: receiver in bankruptcy.

In practice, a receiver may or may not manage the corporation, but he is responsible for the control and preservation of the company's assets.

RECEIVER'S CERTIFICATES

Short-term debt securities issued by a court-appointed receiver to effect a corporate reorganization or liquidation. These securities take priority over all other debts of the corporation, including taxes due and unpaid wages. Thus, they are very low risk because monies received from the liquidation of assets will be used first to pay off these securities.

RECEIVE VERSUS PAYMENT

Instruction often added to sell orders entered by institutional clients.

Concept: The buyer will pay in cash when the seller, or his agent, delivers the securities. The contract is, in effect, made COD (cash on delivery), or RAP (receive against payment). Such contracts are made to obtain immediately usable funds or because the seller is obligated, by law, to have either the security or its cash value.

It is important that both buyer and seller agree that there will be a transfer of securities for cash on the settlement date.

RECLAIM

As verb: the act of recovering money or a certificate after an irregularity is discovered in the settlement of a security contract.

RECLAMATION

As noun: the privilege of either party to a security contract to recover money or a security from the contra party if an irregularity has occurred in the settlement process. For example, a buyer finds that the certificate delivered in settlement for a contract has been stolen. The buyer may make a reclamation.

RECORD DATE

Calendar date on which an issuer temporarily closes its register of holders to identify those holders who are eligible for a distribution of dividends, either cash or stock, interest or rights. The date is determined by the board of directors, and the register is closed at the end of business on that specified date.

RECOURSE LOAN

A financing arrangement frequently used in direct-participation programs (tax shelters) if the partnership borrows money to finance the business venture. In default, the lender has recourse not only against the assets pledged for the loan but also against the personal assets of the general partner.

REDEMPTION

Retirement of a security by repayment of the principal amount.

The term redemption also is used of bonds or preferred shares that are retired before the maturity date at a premium price.

The retirement of mutual fund shares through redemption at the net asset value when tendered by the fundholder also is included in this concept.

REDEMPTION PRICE

The dollar price at which a security may be redeemed by an issuer prior to its maturity date.

Usually, for bonds or preferred shares, the redemption price will be set at a premium above the par or face value of the security. For example, a bond with a face value of $1,000 has a redemption price, if called, of $1,050.

RED HERRING

Industry jargon for a preliminary prospectus. The name arises from the caveat, printed in red along the left border of the cover of the preliminary prospectus, warning the reader that the document does not contain all of the information about the issue and that some of the information may be changed before the final prospectus is issued.

Also called red herring prospectus.

REDISCOUNT

Term used if a member bank of the Federal Reserve System borrows funds from the Federal Reserve using eligible collateral which was, in turn, pledged to the bank by one of its borrowers. For example, a bank accepts collateral from a borrower. The bank is said to rediscount if it again pledges this collateral to the Fed for a loan.

REGISTERED COMPANY

A corporation that has filed a registration statement with the SEC and is now obliged to file certain periodic reports, including annual and quarterly reports and periodic reports of important matters that could influence stockholder activities.

REGISTERED COMPETITIVE MARKET MAKER

A member of the New York Stock Exchange who may initiate trades for his own or his firm's account. Such members are expected, in addition, to make bids or offers—either voluntarily or as requested— that will contribute to the general maintenance of the market if there is an imbalance of buy or sell orders. Thus, these members augment the dealer function of exchange specialists.

REGISTERED COMPETITIVE TRADER

A member of the New York Stock Exchange who may initiate trades for his own or his firm's account. These members attempt to make a profit from short-term trading, but are required to follow the rules of the specialists. Thus, 75% of their transactions must be stablilizing. This means that they should not buy above the sale price of the previous transaction nor sell below it. In addition, their bid-offer may not take precedence over an order from a public customer of a member firm at the same price.

REGISTERED EQUITY MARKET MAKER
American Stock Exchange term. Such ASE members perform a function similar to the registered competitive market maker on the NYSE. The ASE term is more restrictive, because both securities and options are traded on the ASE floor.

See also REGISTERED COMPETITIVE MARKET MAKER.

REGISTERED OPTIONS PRINCIPAL
A person engaged in the management of a broker-dealer's options business; that is, who supervises registered representatives and their contacts with the investing public. ROPs must pass a qualifying examination.

REGISTERED OPTIONS REPRESENTATIVE
An employee of a broker-dealer who engages in soliciting or accepting option business from the employer's customers. Such employees must apply for registration and must pass an examination to qualify for this position. Presently, the General Securities Examination qualifies a representative, although a supplementary examination is currently required if the representative will do business in interest-rate options.

REGISTERED OPTIONS TRADER
American Stock Exchange term for an ASE specialist in one or more classes of options traded on that exchange. Such members are required to maintain a fair and orderly market in the classes of option assigned to them.

REGISTERED REPRESENTATIVE
An employee of a broker-dealer who is a member of the National Association of Securities Dealers (NASD), a broker-dealer or a bank-dealer who is a member of the Municipal Securities Rulemaking Board (MSRB), or a member firm of an exchange who makes customer contacts to buy or sell securities.

Qualification is by the regulatory General Securities Examination; in some cases, however, limited registration is available.

As a general rule, persons who make buy-sell recommendations, who underwrite, who sell investment advice for a fee must be registered as representatives.

REGISTERED SECONDARY

Term for a sale of securities by an owner under an effective registration with the SEC.

Generally such registered secondaries are made by a control person or other holder of restricted securities:

1   As part of a combined primary-secondary offering under a prospectus issued by the corporation.
2   As a "shelf registration"; that is, an offering by the owner using currently filed disclosure documents of the issuer as his disclosure document in the sale of the securities to the public.

REGISTERED SECURITY

1   Any certificate that has the name of the owner inscribed on the certificate. For example, a registered bond or a registered stock.
2   Any stock or bond or other security whose public sale was registered with the SEC at the time of sale, or that—excluding such initial registration—was subsequently sold publicly in conformity with SEC rules. For example, a security originally sold privately is subsequently included in a registered secondary or a public sale under SEC rules 144 or 145.

REGISTRAR

In the securities industry, a person who:

1   Maintains the names and addresses of the security holders of an issuer.
2   Verifies that ownership transfers have been correctly effected; thus, no more new shares have been issued than have been properly cancelled.

Usually, a registrar is a commercial bank other than the transfer agent.

REGISTRATION FEE

A money fee charged by the SEC at the time that a public offering of securities is made.

See also SEC FEE.

REGISTRATION STATEMENT

Technical term for the documents filed with the SEC in conformity with the requirements of the Securities Act of 1933. The originally filed documents, before their final revision and amendments, are called the preliminary registration statement. The amended registration statement with the final details of the publicly sold issue is called the final registration statement.

REGULAR-WAY SETTLEMENT

Industry term for the normally accepted settlement date for secondary market transactions.

The generally accepted regular-way settlement is the fifth business day after the trade date. There are two exceptions: opening-closing transactions in listed options, and round-lot transactions in government and money market securities settle the next business day.

REGULAR-WAY TRANSACTION

The common secondary transaction in stocks and in corporate or municipal bonds. Settlement is due on the fifth business day following the stock trade date.

REGULATED INVESTMENT COMPANY

An investment company that meets IRS eligibility requirements as a regulated company. They (1) do not pay taxes on income received; instead, (2) the income, if passed through to the fundholders, is taxable to the fundholder. The net income passed through to the fundholders retains the "quality" it had when the fund received it; thus, long-term gains remain long-term gains, dividend income remains dividend income, and so on.

This latter concept is also called the conduit theory.

REGULATION A

An SEC-authored adjunct to the Securities Act of 1933 that sets a limit to the value of securities that may be offered publicly under an abbreviated registration statement. At present, issuers may complete an offering under Reg-A if the value of all securities issued in the previous 12 months does not exceed $1.5 million.

REGULATION G

Federal Reserve Board rule that governs the amount and type of credit that can be extended by anyone except broker-dealers or banks to customers who purchase, carry, or trade corporate securities.

REGULATION Q

Rule of the Federal Reserve Board that governs the rate of interest that banks may pay on time deposits. Deposits in excess of $100,000 and for more than 30 days are exempt from Reg-Q. This exemption gives rise to negotiable certificates of deposit.

REGULATION T

Federal Reserve Board rule that governs the amount and type of credit that a broker-dealer may extend or maintain if customers purchase, carry, or trade corporate securities. The extension or maintenance of credit by a broker-dealer for a customer who purchases or trades in exempt securities is not covered by Regulation T.

Usually abbreviated as Reg-T.

REGULATION U

Rule of the Federal Reserve Board that governs the amount and type of credit that a bank may extend to a customer who purchases, carries, or trades in corporate securities.

REGULATION W

Federal Reserve Board rule that governs commercial credit; that is, it governs down payments, and loan maturities for such consumer items as automobiles, household appliances, and revolving charge accounts.

REHYPOTHECATION

Technical term for the act of repledging securities originally pledged (i.e., hypothecated) as collateral with a broker-dealer for margin account loans. Thus, if a broker-dealer takes securities left as collateral for margin loans and repledges them with a bank to obtain money to finance a customer's margin account, this repledging is called rehypothecation.

REINVESTMENT RATE

1   The presumed rate of return that a fixed-income investor will receive if he is able to reinvest the cash flow from interest income at the same rate as that obtained when the security was purchased.
2   The actual rate at which the proceeds from the sale or maturity of a fixed-income investment can be reinvested.

REJECTION

Industry term if a buyer, or a buyer's broker, refuses to accept a security delivered in satisfaction of a trade.

RELATIVE VALUE

The comparative attractiveness of a security investment over another. The term may be used of one issue of securities over another of the same issuer based, for example, on call features, convertibility, or maturity, or it may be based on the valuation of securities of different issuers based on price, yield, liquidity, or risk.

RELEASE LETTER

Sent by the manager to the other participants in the syndicate, the letter contains final details of the offering, whether or not the offering will be advertised, the handling of the good faith deposit, the participation, and how the delivery of the certificates will be handled when they are ready for distribution. Normally, the expression is used of competitive bids for issues of bonds.

Also called the syndicate account letter and the release-terms letter.

RELIEF SPECIALIST

Exchange term for a member affiliated with a regular specialist who is both trained and authorized to substitute for the regular specialist if this is necessary.

REOPEN AN ISSUE

Used of government securities if the Treasury sells more of an issue that is already outstanding, with the same terms and conditions, at prevailing price levels. For example, rather than auction a new issue of notes with a new coupon rate, the Treasury reopens an older issue and sells notes with the same coupon priced to compete with current prices.

REORGANIZATION DEPARTMENT

Popular term for that portion of the cashiering function that handles the exchange of one security for another. For example, the execution of rights and warrants, conversions, tender offers, and exchanges of securities following mergers.

REPEAT PRICES OMITTED

Designation on the consolidated tapes. It means that the tape is late, and to save time, only the first transaction in a series of trades for the same security is printed. Thus, under a repeat prices omitted situation, a series of transactions that would appear as:

> ABC
> 54...2s...54...9s...54

appears as:

> ABC
> 54

REPURCHASE AGREEMENT

An agreement between a buyer and seller to reverse a trade at a specified time at a specified price. Such an arrangement is illegal if nonexempt securities are involved.

In the case of exempt securities, however, such agreements are frequently used by dealers in government and municipal securities to reduce the cost of carry. Thus, a government securities dealer can sell a security, with an agreement to repurchase at a fixed price, and thereby reduce his loan with his bank with the proceeds from the sale. The dealer pays a negotiated rate of interest to the buyer that makes it profitable to both parties.

RESCIND

In general, to cancel a contract; thus both parties are restored to the condition that existed before the contract.

Fraud, misrepresentation, lack of consent, failure to comply with the law, or inability of one party to make a binding contract give rise to the rescinding of the contract. Popular example: a minor contracts; the contract is rescindible. Another example: a registered representative solicits an order to buy a security that is not qualified for sale in the state of buyer.

The act of rescinding, viewed from the buyer's or seller's options, is called rescission.

RESERVE CITY BANK

A bank in the metropolitan area of a city where a Federal Reserve District Bank or one of its branches is located, for example; in the Fourth Federal Reserve District, the district bank is in St. Louis; the branches are in Memphis and Little Rock. Member banks of the Fed within metro St. Louis, Memphis, and Little Rock are considered reserve city banks.

Principal concept: reserve requirements for such city banks are slightly higher than the reserve requirement for rural banks outside these areas. Reason: checking activity will normally be greater.

RESERVE REQUIREMENT

The money that a member bank of the Federal Reserve System must keep on deposit with the nearest Federal Reserve District Bank. Cash in the vault of the member bank is included in the computation of the reserve. The required reserve differs for demand deposits and for time deposits.

Principal concept: The requirement must be in cash; thus, there is no possibility of loss of principal value.

RESISTANCE LEVEL

If the historical chart pattern for a security establishes a price at which sellers will tend to sell, this price is called the resistance level.

For example, a security over a period has traded between 12 and 16. Almost every time the price rose to 16, the price declined. Technical analysts would conclude that 16 is the resistance level. A substantial rise of the security above 16 is called a breakout.

RESTRICTED ACCOUNT
A margin account in which the customer's equity (i.e., approximate dollar value of customer's holdings if the securities were liquidated and debt to broker repaid) is less than the current Federal Reserve Board initial percentage requirement. For example, customer holds securities worth $50,000 in a margin account and has a $30,000 debit balance. The customer's equity is $20,000. The Fed's initial percentage requirement on securities worth $50,000 is 50%, or $25,000. Because the customer's equity is only $20,000 this margin account is restricted.

RESTRICTED LIST
A list, periodically updated, which broker-dealers provide to their sales personnel. The list gives the names of issuers and, in some cases, specific security issues, which may not be traded or which may be sold by customers only if the order to sell is unsolicited. Generally, the restriction arises from an upcoming public offering of securities that is currently in registration with the SEC.

RETAIL INVESTOR
Term used of individual investors as opposed to corporate or other institutional-type investors, such as banks, mutual funds, and pension funds. The distinction, however, is nonspecific in that most broker-dealers differentiate retail from institutional investors by the amount of revenue dollars generated from the accounts on an annual basis.

Accounts that generate a lower dollar amount of commission business are called retail; those with a higher dollar amount are called institutional.

RETAINED EARNINGS
Corporate balance sheet entry that shows the cumulative total of net earnings that were not distributed as dividends to stockholders.

Also called earned surplus.

RETAINED EARNINGS STATEMENT
A financial statement that often accompanies the annual report of a corporation. It gives a detailed record of dividend disbursements made in the current year from net earnings together with a summary of previous dividend payments.

Often called the accumulated retained earnings statement because it explains, over time, the retained earnings entry on the corporate balance sheet.

RETENTION

That portion of an underwriter's takedown it may sell to its customers. Normally, the syndicate manager will hold back some of the takedown to facilitate both institutional sales and sales by members of the selling group. The remainder forms the retention for the individual member of the syndicate. For example, an individual syndicate member may have a takedown of 10,000 shares. The manager holds 2,000 shares for institutional sales and selling group members. The syndicate member's retention is 8,000 shares.

See also TAKEDOWN.

RETENTION REQUIREMENT

Term from Regulation T of the Federal Reserve Board regarding disposition of proceeds of a long sale in a restricted margin account. Prior to February 1982, the broker had to retain 70% of proceeds in the account, thus lowering customer's debt to broker; the remaining 30% could be withdrawn from the account by the customer. In February 1982, the retention requirement was lowered to 50% and customer is now allowed to withdraw the other 50% of the sale's proceeds.

RETIREMENT

Used of debt securities or preferred stock if the issuer redeems, calls for early redemption, or exchanges an entire issue of securities so the issue no longer is outstanding. Redemption at the face or par value, plus any interest or dividends due, is the most common method of retirement of an issue, although a call prior to maturity is not unusual.

RETURN

Synonymous with rate of return.

Often used as a percentage to measure the total of dividends or interest on an investment plus any capital growth. In this latter sense, the term total return is used as a synonym. For example, a stock is purchased at $25 per share. One year later, its market value is $28 and $2 in dividends were paid. The total return, if the stock were sold, is $5 per share, or 20% of the original investment price of $25. Total return is a gross computation and does not include the tax consequences of the return.

RETURN OF CAPITAL

A distribution of cash by a corporation or a trust that does not arise from net income or retained earnings. For example, a utility distributes cash that represents depreciation on certain assets, or a unit investment trust distributes cash that represents the proceeds of the sale of portfolio securities.

A return of capital is not a taxable distribution; instead, recipient must lower the cost of acquisition of the security because part of original purchase price was returned. Later capital gains or losses will be computed from this adjusted purchase price.

RETURN ON EQUITY

Measurement used in financial analysis to judge the percentage of return on the equity capital employed in a business. Most common measurement: net income (before dividends) divided by stockholders' equity at the beginning of the firm's fiscal year.

The return on common equity is more specific. It uses net income minus preferred dividends divided by stockholders' equity after excluding the par value of outstanding preferred shares.

Common abbreviation is ROE.

RETURN ON INVESTED CAPITAL

Measurement used in financial analysis to judge the rate of return on all sources of long-term capital. Most commonly used formula: add interest paid on bonds to net income after taxes. Divide this by the par value of long-term bonds plus total stockholders' equity; that is, by the total capitalization of the company. The exact application of the formula may vary by industry classification of the company.

Common abbreviation is ROI.

REVENUE ANTICIPATION NOTE

Short-term municipal note issued by a state or municipality in anticipation of revenues other than those received from income taxes, or from the proceeds of a bond issue, that will be sufficient to retire the debt. For example, a note issued in anticipation of sales tax revenues could properly be called a revenue anticipation note.

A RAN is retired when the revenue is received.

REVENUE BOND

General term for a municipal security whose interest and principal will be paid from tolls, charges, rents, or other sources of income generated by the facility built with the money borrowed by the issue.

Almost any type of facility may be built with the proceeds of a revenue bond issue: bridges, airports, turnpikes, hospitals, dormitories, sports complexes—provided there is enabling legislation and the facility is used for the common good of the municipality.

REVERSAL

Term used by technical analysts in their charting of security price movements if a primary or a major secondary price trend is countered by a substantial change from the trend. For example, if a security's trend has been from $15 to $12 per share, a sustained rise above $13 per share would indicate a reversal of the trend.

Reversals are indicative only if they are sustained. Short-term price changes may negate the indication of a reversal. For example, a stock that dropped from $15 to $12, and then rose to $13, may rise in price (the reversal) but also may soon drop back to $11.

REVERSE ANNUITY MORTGAGE

Concept: an elderly property owner arranges to borrow against the collateral value of fully owned property. However, the annual payments will not deplete the value of the property during the person's lifetime. Thus, borrower can assure himself of constant income for his life and make provisions for disposal of the property's residual value after his death.

REVERSE A SWAP

Term used of a second transaction in bonds that reestablishes a client's original bond portfolio position. For example, a temporary change in the yield spread between treasuries and AAA corporates makes it profitable to sell Treasuries and buy IBM bonds. When the yield spreads return to their historical relationship, the client reverses the swap by selling the IBM bonds and repurchasing the originally held Treasury bonds.

REVERSE HEDGE

Term used of a customer who owns a common stock and sells short a convertible security that can be converted into the common stock. The customer is speculating that the premium over conversion parity will decline and the total position can be closed out at a profit. Technically, the combined position is not a hedge, as it would be if the customer were long the convertible security and short the common stock.

REVERSE REPURCHASE AGREEMENT

A customer delivers securities to a broker-dealer, receives cash, and promises to repurchase the securities at a later date at a fixed price. The difference between the cash received by the customer and the repurchase price represents, in effect, interest for the use of the money received. Usually, only government, agency, or municipal securities are subject to repurchase and reverse repos. The Federal Reserve Banking System is a frequent user of reverse repurchase agreements to fine-tune the money supply.

REVERSE SPLIT
Term used if a corporation reduces the number of outstanding shares by increasing the par value of the shares. For example, a company changes the par value of its common shares from $5 to $10. Outstanding shares will be turned in and the owner will receive half as many new shares, but the shares will have double the par value of the original shares. Used by firms whose shares are selling at very low market prices; thus, there will be fewer shares with a higher market value.

Also called a split-down.

REVOLVING LINE OF CREDIT
Term used in banking if a bank establishes a line of credit for a customer to be used when, as, and if needed. Often there is a commitment fee paid by the potential borrower.

Slang: a revolver.

RIGHT OF ACCUMULATION
Privilege offered by most open-end investment companies to current fundholders. The privilege becomes operative if the value of current holdings in any, or all, of the funds managed by the fund manager exceeds established breakpoints for fund purchases. For example; a fund's breakpoint is $25,000. A fundholder's shares are worth $22,000. A further investment of $4,000 will exceed the $25,000 breakpoint, and the $4,000 is eligible for reduced sales charges.

The prospectus of a fund describes how the right of accumulation applies to that fund.

RIGHT OF RESCISSION
Contract cancellation privilege because the purchase was made in contravention of existing laws.

See also RESCIND.

RIGHTS OFFERING
A privilege granted by some corporations to current common shareholders whereby they can purchase a proportionate number of new shares, at a price that is lower than current market prices, before the public is allowed to purchase the shares.

Commonly called a subscription, the rights offering is effected by delivering a prospectus and a security called "rights to present common shareholders." The shareholders may subscribe by delivering their rights and the required number of dollars to the company. Rights also may be resold if shareholder declines the rights offering.

RING

Term that describes the trading locations on most commodity exchanges and the location in the bond room of the New York Stock Exchange where commodities or bonds are bought and sold.

RISK

Common term for financial uncertainty. The term, if used alone, generally means capital risk; that is, the possibility that an asset will be sold at a price that is lower than the purchase price.

The term is often used in combination with other terms. Examples: inflationary risk, a change in the purchasing power of money; market risk, uncertainty due to price volatility or market illiquidity; interest-rate risk, a change in value because general interest rates rise.

RISK ARBITRAGE

General term for a long and short position taken in anticipation of, or upon the announcement of, a proposed merger. Normally, the speculator will buy shares of the company to be acquired and sell short the shares of the acquiring company on the speculation that the shares of the company to be acquired will go up, and the shares of the acquiring company will go down. The risk is that the merger will be cancelled. In this case, there can be substantial loss as the shares go back to original price levels.

RISKLESS TRANSACTION

NASD term for a broker-dealer who takes a position in a security only upon receipt of a firm order to buy entered by a customer.

Also called a simultaneous transaction. For example, a broker-dealer with no position in a security receives a firm order to buy 500 shares from a customer. Rather than make an agency transaction, the dealer buys 500 shares, marks it up, and sells to the customer.

Riskless transactions do not violate industry rules provided the markup conforms to industry standards. The use of a riskless transaction to conceal an excessive markup violates the accepted ethics of the NASD.

ROLL DOWN

The closing of an option position and the immediate establishment of a new position with a lower strike (exercise) price.

ROLL FORWARD

The closing of an option position and the reestablishment of another position with a longer time to expiration. Technically, if the new position has a higher-lower strike price, it is a roll up-down and forward.

ROLLING STOCK

Industry term used by transportation companies to designate movable equipment. In practice, the term includes railroad engines, freight and passenger cars, trucks, container cars, and, often, airplanes.

ROLLOVER

In general, the reinvestment of funds. Specifically, the term is used if:

1 Funds from a maturing bond or other debt instrument are reinvested in a similar security.
2 Funds in one qualified pension fund are reinvested in another. For example, an IRA rollover.
3 A security is sold at a profit and the funds are used to establish a new position in the same security at a new cost basis.

In practice, the term is not used if a capital loss or a negative cash flow is involved in the successive transactions.

ROLL UP

1 A tax-free exchange of a partnership interest for a proportionate share interest in a corporation. Because partnership interest was taxed annually, most of the cash flow from this exchange is considered a return of the owner's capital and is not subject to tax.
2 Used of options if an investor closes a current position and immediately establishes a position at a higher strike price. Often used even if the new, higher strike price has a longer period to expiration. Technically, this later strategy is a roll up and forward.

ROUND LOT

Term used for the generally accepted unit of trading in a security.

For stocks, the generally accepted unit of trading is 100 shares, although there are 10-share units for some inactive stocks and a trend toward 500-share units in institutional markets. Listed bonds trade in $1,000 par value units, but OTC bond trading round lots vary greatly according to the security. For example, governments trade in round lots of $100,000; corporate bonds in round lots of $250,000; and Ginnie Maes and CDs in round lots of $1 million.

ROUND UP

1 Industry practice to achieve a normally used price variation. For example; a stock goes ex-dividend. The specialist will, if the dividend is not a multiple of ⅛, round down to the next lower price that represents a multiple of ⅛. A dividend of 60¢ will be rounded up to ⅝, or $.625.

2 Customer instruction if a fixed dollar amount is invested. Round up means to buy a number of shares that leaves a debit in the account. The customer will pay the added amount. Round down means to leave a credit in customer's account by purchasing the closest share number under his deposit.

IRA and Keogh accounts should always be rounded down because the IRS does not permit debits in such accounts.

RTD

Abbreviation for rated.
See also RATING.

RULE 405

A New York Stock Exchange rule requiring that member firms and registered representatives learn the essential facts about customers, their agents, and specific securities transactions entered either by the customer or the agent.

The rule requires that responsible brokerage professionals know or, if they do not know, ask for the pertinent facts about customers, their accounts, and their transactions. The rule is so written that a brokerage professional cannot use "I did not know" as an excuse for an improper or unsuitable transaction.

See also KNOW YOUR CUSTOMER.

RULES OF FAIR PRACTICE

National Association of Securities Dealers' rules that outline and often state in detail the norms of ethical conduct for members and for registered representatives.

The Rules of Fair Practice, in more or less detail, deal with fair treatment, fair prices, proper disclosure, and the avoidance of conflicts of interest in dealings with other members and with investors.

The rules incorporate both federal securities law and civil law in some cases, and accepted industry practice in others. In all cases, violations of the Rules of Fair Practice subject the violator to severe penalties, ranging from censure to fines to suspension and expulsion from the NASD. If the law is violated, civil and criminal penalties may also apply.

RUN

Industry term for a market maker's current list of security offerings. In practice, the run for stocks includes bid-offer prices. For bonds, the run will usually include the par value of bonds offered with an offer price.

Government bills, notes, bonds, agencies, and money market securities may be represented by price ranges with actual prices given only after negotiation as to dollar amount and method of settlement.

RUNDOWN

Popular term for the dollar amounts available and their prices on the remaining bonds in a municipal serial issue.

RUNNING AHEAD

Term used of the improper activity whereby a registered representative enters personal orders to buy-sell a security before customer orders are entered.

Most member firms have internal controls that prohibit or limit such orders. For example, Merrill Lynch has a 48-hour rule. If that firm issues a research report to buy-sell a security, its employees may not buy or sell that security for two business days (48 real hours). This time restriction on brokerage employees places the firm's customers at an advantage and excludes "running ahead."

RUNNING THROUGH THE POT

Term used if the manager of a syndicate recalls some of the shares or bonds taken down by syndicate and selling group members for retail sales and includes them in the pot devoted to institutional sales.

Central concept: institutional sales seem to be going better than retail sales. If these securities can be sold to institutional investors, it will maintain the profitability of the syndicate and lessen the need to make a lot of retail sales to distribute all of the shares or bonds.

S

S

Used lowercase to signify:
1 On the consolidated tapes, a transaction that is a multiple of 100 shares. For example, 3s = 300 shares.
2 On the stock tables in the newspaper, following the name of the company, that a stock split or a stock dividend occurred that

increased the outstanding shares by 20% or more. For example, ABC s.

3   On the option tables in the newspaper, that a series (i.e., an issuer, a put or call, a strike price, and an expiration month) is not offered for trading on the exchange.

SAFE HARBOR

Financial term signifying that an action avoids legal or tax consequences. Implication: the action benefits the person doing the action.

SAFEKEEPING

Protective measures that a broker-dealer must employ to protect customers' fully paid securities. Such measures involve proper segregation, identification, or other means of protection. Forbidden by federal securities laws are commingling of customer securities with the securities owned by the broker, improper repledging or lending of customer securities without the specific written permission of the customer, improper record-keeping.

SALES CHARGE

The percentage fee charged by an open-end investment company, or by a unit investment trust, when shares or units are purchased. The fee is charged by the underwriter-sponsor of the fund and is shared by the underwriter and the dealer who makes the sale. Generally, the percentage fee decreases as the dollar value of the purchase increases. Funds that charge no fee are called no-load funds.

See also SALES LOAD; NO LOAD; FRONT-END LOAD; LOAD SPREAD OPTION; LETTER OF INTENT; and RIGHT OF ACCUMULATION.

SALES LITERATURE

Any communication by a broker-dealer for distribution to customers or to the public that describes the services provided by the issuer of the sales literature. Such sales literature must be truthful and must accurately describe the services provided by the broker-dealer. Industry rules require that sales literature be approved by a person within the firm who is appointed to do so.

SALES LOAD

Commonly used term for the percentage sales charge on open-end investment company shares.

See also SALES CHARGE.

SAME-DAY SUBSTITUTION

The purchase and sale of marginable securities with the same dollar value on the same day in a margin account. If such a substitution is made, there is no margin call and there is no release to the special miscellaneous account (SMA). In practice, any decommitment (reduction of customer risk) coupled to a commitment (increase of customer risk) is considered a same-day substitution if the dollar value is the same. For example, a purchase and a long sale; a long sale and a short sale.

SAUCER

Descriptive term for the graph of stock prices that approximates the shape of a saucer. If the rounded portion is on the bottom, which is the normal appearance of a saucer, the trend is considered upward. If the rounded portion is on the top, such as a saucer would appear that is upside down on a table, the trend is considered downward.

SAVINGS AND LOAN

A national- or state-chartered institution that accepts savings deposits from individuals. The funds are invested in real estate mortgages and similar financial instruments. These institutions are similar to banks, but they provide fewer services than full-service commercial banks.

Savings and loan associations and savings banks are generally grouped in the popular term "thrifts" or "thrift institutions."

Also called savings and loan association.

SAVINGS BANK

Generally, a state chartered bank, organized as a stock or mutual company, that accepts both time and demand deposits. Deposits are invested in mortgages, real estate, government bonds, and other securities as permitted by the state banking commissioner.

SBI

Acronym for share of beneficial interest. Term often is used of an equity security that represents an undivided interest in a pool of debt securities.

SCALE

Used, at the time of the initial offering of bonds with serial maturity, to designate the number of bonds, the maturity date, the coupon rate of interest, and the offering price of one of the serial maturities. For example, in an offering of $10 million of bonds maturing between 1987 and 1997, the scale for 1992 might appear:

$1,000,000 Jan. 15, 1992 10-½ PAR

The term also is used collectively of all of the bonds, their maturities, coupons, and prices for the entire issue.

SCALE ORDER

A single-order ticket that, in fact, contains multiple buy limit or sell limit orders at prices so staggered that the buyer or seller achieves an advantageous average price. For example, a buy limit order might contain the following instruction: "BUY 200 ABC 57, and 200 each half-point down. Total: 2,000 shares. "The buyer wants a total position of 2,000 with an average price midway between 57 and 52-½ per share."

Because of increased clerical work and the possibility of error, many member firms will not accept scale orders.

SCALPER

Slang for a market maker who places excessive markups, or markdowns, on transactions that involve minimum risk to himself. This activity violates the National Association of Securities Dealers' (NASD) 5% guideline for fair prices and commissions.

SCALPING

An unethical practice, which may also be illegal, whereby an investment adviser or research analyst recommends a security for purchase after buying the security for his own account. The subsequent purchases by persons who followed the recommendation pushes up the price of the security and permits the recommender to profit on the original purchase.

SCHEDULE C

A section of the National Association of Securities Dealers (NASD) bylaws that contains the criteria which certain persons associated with a member must meet to be registered as a principal, financial principal, or representative.

SCHEDULE 13D

A Securities and Exchange Commission form that must be filed within 10 business days by anyone who acquires 5% or more of an equity security registered with the SEC under the Securities Exchange Act of 1934. Purpose: to disclose the method of acquisition of the shares and the purchaser's intentions in terms of management or control of the company.

See also SCHEDULE 13G.

SCHEDULE 13G

A short-form version of Schedule 13D. The short form is to be filed by a person who, at the end of a calendar year, owns 5% or more of an equity security of a company registered under Section 12 of the Securities Exchange Act of 1934. The short-form filing is permitted if the person acquired the securities in the ordinary course of business and if the owner does not intend to change or influence control of the company. Broker-dealers, banks, and investment companies are typical filers of Schedule 13G. It is due within 45 calendar days of year's end.

SCIENTER

Latin: with knowledge, or knowingly. Used in cases of fraud. To gain a conviction under federal securities law, the Securities and Exchange Commission often must prove that the accused acted with knowledge.

SCRIP

A fractional share of stock distributed by a company on the occasion of a stock dividend, a split-up, or the spin-off of an asset. The recipient can hold the scrip, sell it, or, in most cases, purchase the remaining fraction of the share to have a full share.

SEASONED

Descriptive term often used of a new issue that was widely distributed to a large number of purchasers and that now trades frequently and with good liquidity in the secondary market. For example, "It is now a seasoned security."

SEAT

Used as a synonym for a membership on a national securities exchange. For example, "John Jones purchased a seat on the Philadelphia Stock Exchange."

In recent years some of the exchanges have permitted members to lease seats to others; the person who leases the seat is permitted to perform the functions of a member.

SEC FEE

A statutory fee of one cent per $300, or fraction thereof, levied on the sale of equity securities registered on an exchange, no matter where the transaction takes place. Traditionally, the fee is paid by the seller. Principal exceptions: registered new issues, listed options, private placements, the exercise of a warrant or a right, conversion of a convertible security, or a sale as a result of a tender offer or exchange.

SECO

Acronym for Securities and Exchange Commission Organization.

All broker-dealers registered with the SEC who are not members of the National Association of Securities Dealers (NASD) or a national securities exchange are identified as SECO members, thereby indicating that the SEC has direct jurisdiction over their activities.

SECONDARY DISTRIBUTION

Generically, any sale of securities, whether by an effective registration or not, made by a selling holder of the bonds or stocks. More specifically, a method of selling a large block of securities to investors by a previous holder. Such distributions may be "spot secondaries," if their sale is not SEC registered, or "registered secondaries," if the sale is registered. Such sales are made at a net price, with all sales charges paid by the seller. Secondary distributions, although they are made over-the-counter, are normally announced on the exchange tape before the transaction, and buy limit orders on the specialist's book at or above the price of the distribution will be executed at the distribution price.

SECONDARY MARKET

General term for the place where issued and outstanding securities are sold. The term includes both exchanges and the over-the-counter market. Distinguished from the primary market, which is the method of selling new issues so the proceeds of the sale go to the issuer.

SECOND MARKET

Occasionally used to designate the over-the-counter (OTC) market. Concept: the exchanges are the first market; the OTC is the second market; those dealers in the OTC market who specialize in the trading of listed securities are the third market.

SEC RULES

The following rules of the Securities and Exchange Commission often are used in the jargon of the industry. The rules, with their numbers, are identified in the following entries. This identification is not meant to be an explanation of the rule. Many of them are so complex, and have further SEC and legal interpretations, that advice of counsel is needed.

The order of the SEC rules that follow is numerical, as opposed to the letter-by-letter order in the rest of this glossary.

SEC RULE 10a-1

The so-called plus-tick rule. This rule prohibits the short sale of securities registered on an exchange unless the sale, wherever made, is effected at a price that is above the last different regular-way transaction on the principal exchange where the security is traded. Thus, under this rule, a short sale of ABC common stock, following transactions at 19½ and 19, could only be made at 19⅛ or above.

See also ZERO-PLUS TICK.

SEC RULE 10b-2

It forbids anyone from soliciting purchase orders for a security on an exchange while involved in a distribution (i.e., a sale) of that same issue.

SEC RULE 10b-4

The rule forbids the short sale of securities in response to a tender offer. Thus, a person could not sell borrowed securities to a person making a tender offer to buy.

SEC RULE 10b-6

It prohibits issuers, underwriters, broker-dealers, or anyone with an interest in a distribution of securities from purchasing, or inducing anyone else to purchase, the issue prior to the start of the public offering.

Underwriters, however, may accept indications of interest in such issues from prospective buyers, but no sales may be made.

SEC RULE 10b-7

The rule sets the terms and conditions under which an underwriter may use a stabilizing bid to facilitate a distribution of securities.

SEC RULE 10b-8

It prohibits the manipulation of the open-market price for a security by persons involved in the distribution of that security through a rights offering.

SEC RULE 10b-10

It regulates the preparation and distribution of purchase or of sale confirmations by a broker-dealer to customers. The rule sets forth the minimum information required, the necessary disclosures required, and the frequency of such confirmations to customers.

SEC RULE 10b-13

The rule prohibits persons involved in an exchange or tender offer from making other purchases of the same security, either publicly or privately, until the tender offer has expired.

SEC RULE 10b-16

This rule, which is the security industry's response to the truth-in-lending law, requires broker-dealers who extend credit to customers (e.g., a margin-account customer) to provide complete information about the financing terms, conditions, and arrangements.

SEC RULE 11A

A series of rules that govern the trading by exchange members for their own accounts.

SEC RULE 13D

This rule, which has subnumbers 1 through 7, require the filing of certain disclosures by anyone who acquires a beneficial ownership of 5% or more in any equity security registered with the SEC.

SEC RULE 13E

This rule, which has subnumbers 1 through 4, regulate the purchases by an issuer, or an affiliate of the issuer, of its own securities in the public marketplace.

SEC REGULATION 14A

It governs the preparation and distribution of proxy material to stockholders. It also sets forth the kind of information that must be included with the proxy statement, the supporting documents, the format, and the need for prior submission to the SEC of such material.

SEC RULE 15c2-1

This rule regulates the safekeeping of customers' securities left with a broker following their purchase in a margin account.

In substance, the rule prohibits commingling customers' securities with the broker's securities and prohibits the broker from hypothecating more of the securities than is justified by the customers' indebtedness to the broker.

SEC RULE 15c3-1

The "net capital" rule governing the liquid capital that a broker-dealer must maintain in terms of his aggregate indebtedness to customers. The rule dictates the minimum net capital and the ratio of debt-to-equity capital of a broker-dealer; but from the viewpoint of a member firm customer, the most important aspect is the coverage that a broker-dealer's net capital provides for customer indebtedness.

Although other measurement criteria may be used, the rule of thumb is that customer-related indebtedness may not exceed net capital by more than 15 to 1.

SEC RULE 15c3-2

It governs the use of credit balances left with a broker-dealer by a customer, if the credit balance may be freely withdrawn. The rule requires a broker-dealer to notify customers that such credit balances may be withdrawn at any time. If the customer does not request the withdrawal of these balances, the broker-dealer may use the credit balance in the conduct of its ordinary course of business. The customer, of course, retains his or her right to the money left on deposit with the broker-dealer.

SEC RULE 15c3-3

This rule regulates the handling of fully paid securities and money on deposit with a broker-dealer. In substance, the rule requires the proper segregation of customer securities that are fully paid and requires that, at least weekly, money on deposit be deposited in a special account for the benefit of all customers of that broker-dealer.

SEC RULE 17f-1

It requires that broker-dealers, banks, and transfer agents report promptly any knowledge of lost, stolen, counterfeit, or misplaced securities to a centralized computer service maintained for this purpose. This service, called the National Crime Information Center (NCIC), acts as a central clearing service for anyone who wishes to inquire about the report of a missing or stolen security.

SEC RULE 19c-3

This rule permits securities listed on an exchange after April 26, 1979, to be traded by exchange members on or off the exchange, as they see fit. Purpose: to establish an experiment for the widest possible market for listed securities.

SEC RULE 144

In substance, this rule permits a holder of unregistered securities to make a public sale of such securities, without the need for a formal registration statement, if certain conditions are met. The rule is complex and legal advice is needed, but as a rule of thumb, sales that represent less than 1% of outstanding shares during a 90-day period will not require a formal registration with the SEC.

SEC RULE 145

It sets forth the conditions under which persons who receive securities as a result of a reclassification, merger, consolidation, or transfer of corporate assets may sell these securities without the need for an effective registration statement.

SEC RULE 156

It prohibits the issuance or use of false or misleading sales literature in conjunction with the sale of investment company securities.

SEC RULE 174

This rule lists the circumstances under which a dealer must continue to deliver a prospectus in connection with secondary market transactions in securities that were recently registered.

SEC RULE 254

It sets forth the dollar limitations on sales made under the provisions of Regulation A. At present, issuers may sell securities worth $1.5 million or less—using a short-form registration and providing buyers with an offering circular—without the need for a full and formal registration with the SEC.

SEC RULE 433

This rule outlines the conditions under which a dealer may use a preliminary (i.e., a "red herring") prospectus.

SECTOR

A term used to describe bonds of the same class with similar ratings, coupons, and maturities. For example, the Salomon AA utility bond index or the Daily Bond Buyer 20-bond and 11-bond indices are based on the concept of sector. The presumption is that bonds in the same sector will have similar price and yield movements.

SECURED BOND

Term used of bonds if the issuer, in the bond indenture, has set aside certain identifiable assets as collateral for the prompt payment of interest and the repayment of the principal. In a default the bondholder, through the trustee, can lay claim to the asset. Generally, the asset has a greater value than the outstanding claim of the bondholder.

SECURED DEBT

As a general rule, this term is used as a synonym for secured bond.

SECURITIES ACT OF 1933

Federal law that requires adequate disclosure of the facts about new issues of securities sold to the public. The disclosure is made by the filing of a registration statement with the SEC and the delivery of a prospectus to the original purchaser. The law exempts many securities from such disclosure (exempt securities) and many transactions are not required to be registered. As a rule of thumb, however, public and interstate transactions of corporate securities come under the requirements of the Securities Act of 1933.

SECURITIES AND EXCHANGE COMMISSION

A federal agency, established by the Securities Exchange Act of 1934 as amended, that has five commissioners appointed by the President with the advice and consent of the Senate of the United States.

The powers of the commission include the interpretation, supervision, and enforcement of the securities laws of the United States. The commission has the authority to bring administrative proceedings against firms and persons registered with the SEC, but allegations of criminal violations of the law must be prosecuted by the Department of Justice.

SECURITIES EXCHANGE ACT OF 1934

This law, which is a keystone in the regulation of securities markets, governs exchanges, over-the-counter markets, broker-dealers, the conduct of secondary markets, the extension of credit in the purchase and sale of securities, the conduct of corporate insiders, and principally the prohibition of fraud and manipulation in securities transactions.

This law also outlines the powers of the Securities and Exchange Commission to interpret, supervise, and enforce the securities laws of the United States. Enforcement includes all but the civil and criminal aspects of the Securities Exchange Act of 1934.

SECURITIES INDUSTRY ASSOCIATION

It has two functions: to promote instruction of member employees and to lobby for the interest of the members of the association.

Many exchange member organizations and many NASD members belong to the SIA; to this extent, the SIA may be considered to be representative of the broker-dealers who buy and sell nonexempt securities.

SECURITIES INDUSTRY AUTOMATION
CORPORATION

Owned by the New York and American Stock Exchanges, SIAC operates automated communication systems that support trading, surveillance, and market data for these exchanges. These data, in turn, are provided to the National Security Clearing Corporation (NSCC), the Consolidated Tape Association (CTA), the Consolidated Quotation System (CQS), and the Intermarket Trading System (ITS).

SECURITIES INVESTORS PROTECTION CORPORATION

A nonprofit corporation, under the provisions of the Securities Investors Protection Act of 1970, that will provide protection to customers of insured members in the event of the member's insolvency. The upper limit of protection is $500,000 per customer account. Of this amount, no more than $100,000 may represent cash left with the member.

SECURITIES LOAN

Term refers to the lending of stock or bond certificates to another broker-dealer principally for use in the completion of short sales. The borrowing broker-dealer must fully collateralize the loan of the certificates with cash equal to the full market value of the certificates to protect the lending broker, or the broker's customer if the certificates, in turn, were borrowed from a customer.

Commonly called a stock loan.

SECURITY

An instrument, usually freely transferable, that evidences ownership (stock) or creditorship (bond) in a corporation, a federal or state government, an agency thereof, or a legal trust. The courts also have included evidences of indirect ownership in the definition. For example, rights, warrants, options, and partnership participations.

The term also is used of property, whether a security or not, pledged as collateral for a loan. For example, an issuer of bonds pledged its plant and equipment as security for an issue of mortgage bonds.

SEEK A MARKET

To try to get a transaction.

SEGREGATE

The act of segregating (i.e., keeping separate) customer securities from securities owned by the broker in its proprietary accounts.

In practice, fully paid securities owned by customers and that portion of margin-account securities, over and above the amount required to collateralize the broker's loan to the client, are segregated in accordance with federal law. In no case, may the broker hold more than 140% of the customer's debit balance in the form of collateral for the loan made in margin accounts.

Antonym for segregate: to commingle; i.e., to mix customer-owned securities and broker-owned securities and to use them in the conduct of business.

SEGREGATED SECURITIES

Industry term for customer securities that must be kept in a separate place and which may not be used by the broker-dealer in the conduct of the firm's business. Fully paid securities in cash accounts and securities in margin accounts—over and above the amount needed to collateralize the client's debit balance with the broker—must be segregated.

Normal practice: segregate securities in a separate vault on the broker's premises or leave them on deposit with an industry depository (e.g., the Depository Trust Corporation).

SELECTED DEALER AGREEMENT

Official term for the selling group agreement used by the underwriting syndicate in the distribution of securities. The selected dealer agreement sets forth the rights and responsibilities of selling group members, particularly the obligation to market the securities only at the public offering price established by the syndicate.

SELF-SUPPORTING

Term used in the analysis of municipal securities if the revenues generated by a project are sufficient to pay the debt service without any additional revenues from another source. For example, "The bridge tolls make the revenue bonds self-supporting."

SELL AT BEST

Instruction used by over-the-counter traders when using other broker-dealers to help them sell portions of a market order. In effect, the instruction directs the sale at the best available bid price.

SELLER'S OPTION

A securities contract that establishes the contract price for securities and, in the case of bonds, the amount of accrued interest to be paid by the buyer to the seller, but which permits the seller to deliver the securities to the office of the buyer at a later date, within the provisions of the contract. For example, a seller's option 60 establishes all of the details of the sale, but the seller may deliver the security to the buyer any time following the 5th business day up to and including the 60th calendar day following the trade.

SELLING CLIMAX

Term used by technical analysts of a downward price trend that is suddenly marked by an increase in volume and a dramatic price drop.

Generally, the selling climax is marked by a "gap" (i.e., a series of transactions with volume that are below previously established lows for the security).

Technical analysts consider a selling climax as an overreaction and use it to predict a rise in the security's value, at least to the point where the gap occurred.

SELLING CONCESSION

Industry term for the fee that will be paid to selling group members for each unit of the offering they sell. It is not unusual for the selling concession to be 50% or more of the underwriting spread on an issue. For example, bonds were purchased at 98-½ to be reoffered at par with a ¾-point concession. The gross underwriting spread is $15 (1-½ points), and a selling group member who sells a bond will receive $7.50 (¾ point).

SELLING DIVIDENDS

The unethical practice whereby a representative persuades a client to purchase investment company securities solely to obtain a soon-to-be-paid dividend. The practice is unfair because the dividend is already included in the net asset value for the fund; thus, the customer, in effect, is paying for the dividend with his own funds.

SELLING GROUP

Popular name for dealers who associate with the underwriting syndicate in the marketing of a distribution of securities. The selling group has no financial involvement in the distribution; instead, on an agency basis, it agrees to sell portions of the issue to its customers. If successful, selling group members receive a concession, or selling commission, for these sales.

SELL OUT

Industry term for the procedure whereby a broker-dealer liquidates client holdings that were purchased on behalf of the client but have not yet been paid by the client in accordance with the terms of the contract.

The term also is used if a buying broker fails to pay for securities bought from a selling broker. Sell outs are made at the best available market price, and the buyer is responsible for any financial loss suffered by the broker.

SELL-OUT PROCEDURE

The seller's remedy if the purchasing broker-dealer in a contract between two broker-dealers fails to accept and pay for the purchased securities without a legitimate reason for refusal. The selling broker-dealer can sell those securities at the best available market price without giving notice to the defaulting purchaser. The seller can also hold the buyer responsible for any financial loss resulting from his default.

Also called close-out.

See also BUY-IN PROCEDURE.

SELL PLUS

Instruction sometimes used on a market order for exchange traded securities. The instruction requests that the sale be made at a price higher than the last differently priced transaction in the security.

The instruction is used by selling clients who do not want to sell on downticks. The instruction is not used on orders to sell short; by federal law, such sales may not be made on downticks.

SELL STOP ORDER

An instruction that may be placed on orders to be transacted on an exchange. The instruction tells the broker to sell at the market when and if there is a transaction at or below the stop price designated on the order. For example, Sell Long 500 ABC 27 STOP. When and if there is a transaction at 27 or below, the broker is instructed to sell 500 ABC at the market.

Also called a stop-loss order. The American Stock Exchange permits such orders only if the customer also provides a limit price equal to the stop price. For example, Sell Long 500 LMN 29 STOP 29 LIMIT.

SELL THE BOOK

A seller's instruction: "Sell as many shares as you can at the prevailing best bid on the exchanges where the security trades.

The instruction includes sales at that price to broker-dealers in the crowd who are willing to accept the same price.

SENIOR REGISTERED OPTION PRINCIPAL

An officer or general partner specifically designated with overall authority and responsibility for customer options transactions and accounts.

The SROP may also be the CROP (the compliance registered option principal). In this latter capacity, the option principal has responsibility for advertising, sales literature, and training in option transactions for the member firm. In many firms, the SROP and the CROP are different persons.

SEPARATE ACCOUNT

Term used of variable annuities. Because the risk is borne by the investor in a variable annuity, the issuer may not commingle funds invested in the variable annuity with the general funds of the issuer; such funds are invested in a separate account. Although the separate account may contain individual securities, the most common investment is in a "market basket" of other securities having objectives similar to those set forth in the prospectus of the variable annuity.

SEPARATE CUSTOMER

Term used in conjunction with the protection offered under the Securities Investor Protection Corporation (SIPC). The maximum protection is by separate customer; thus, accounts that are bookkeeping formalities, such as cash, margin, and special bond account, are grouped as if they are in the name of the same customer. However, accounts with differing ownerships (e.g., an individual's account and a joint account with a spouse) are not grouped and are considered separate customer accounts for purposes of SIPC protection.

SERIAL BOND

An expression for a bond offering so issued that portions of the debt are redeemed each year.

Serial bonds always are identified as such, and the individual bond certificate designates the time of its maturity. Bonds that may be subject to premature redemption—either through a full or partial call or through the operation of a sinking fund—are not designated as serial bonds.

Serial bonds are a common form of municipal bond offerings.

SERIES E BONDS

Government savings bonds issued from the time of World War II until December 31, 1979. They have been replaced with Series EE bonds. Outstanding Series E bonds continue to bear interest, but by congressional action, bonds held for 40 years or more cease to bear interest, although these bonds may be exchanged for Series EE bonds or Series HH bonds.

SERIES EE BONDS

Nontransferable U.S. government bonds issued in denominations of $50 to $10,000. The bonds are purchased at 50% of their face value and mature at face value, although they continue to bear interest if held for a longer period. Since 1982, the interest rate has been pegged to the average interest rate on other Treasury securities and will vary accordingly.

No distribution of interest is made until the holder redeems the bonds. Holders may choose to pay income tax on the interest as it accrues, but most choose to pay the tax only when bonds are redeemed.

Commonly called savings bonds.

See also SERIES HH BONDS.

SERIES HH BONDS

Nontransferable U.S. government bonds that pay semiannual interest directly to the registered owner. Prior to 1982, Series HH bonds could be purchased directly. Now, these bonds are available only in exchange for Series EE bonds. The exchange is advantageous for holders of Series EE bonds because it continues the tax sheltering of the interest previously accrued, but not paid out, on the Series EE bonds until the newly acquired Series HH bonds are redeemed. However, current taxes are payable on the interest earned on the Series HH bonds acquired by exchange.

Commonly called current-income bonds.

See also SERIES EE BONDS.

SERIES OF OPTION

A class of option on the same underlying security with same expiration date and same exercise (strike) price. Thus, the Merrill Lynch January 50 calls form a series of option. The IBM March 80 puts would form another series of option.

Currently, the newspaper listing of option transactions uses "r" if no trades in an option series occurred; an "s" if a series is not available for trading.

SETTLE

Industry term for the completion of a securities transaction (i.e., a buyer pays for and a seller delivers the security purchased to the buyer).

In industry jargon, the term clear is commonly used as a synonym for settle if transactions between broker-dealers are being discussed. Thus, Brokers A and B cleared the transaction, but Broker A and his customer settled the transaction.

227

SETTLEMENT DATE

The date on which a securities contract, by prearranged agreement, must be cleared or settled.

In the primary market, only when-issued settlement is available; when the securities are available, a specific settlement date will be established.

In the secondary market, "regular-way settlement" is the normal contract: payment or delivery is due on the fifth business day after the trade date.

For listed options, regular-way settlement is the next business day, just as it is for government securities.

Contracts for same-day settlement (cash) or delayed-delivery settlement (seller's option) also may be negotiated in secondary market transactions.

SEVERALLY AND JOINTLY

Used of underwritings where the syndicate members agree to purchase an issue and are both individually (severally) and as an account (jointly) responsible for the purchase price of the securities.

Such underwriting accounts are called Eastern accounts and are commonly used in the underwriting of municipal issues.

SEVERALLY BUT NOT JOINTLY

Used of underwritings where the syndicate members agree to individually purchase a specific portion of the issue (severally), but they are not responsible as a group (but not jointly) for unsold securities.

Commonly used in corporate underwritings. For example, Underwriters A and B make such an underwriting agreement. A sells his total takedown; B only sells two thirds of his. Underwriter A has no obligation for the securities unsold by B.

When used of corporate underwritings, the term Western account is used of this financial arrangement.

SHADOW CALENDAR

Industry slang for issues in registration with the SEC for which no approximate effective date is available. The backup in the processing of the registrations often is the result of a backlog of work at the commission or because of unsettled market conditions.

SHARE

A unit of ownership of a corporation. The basic proportion of such ownership is established by the corporate charter, which states the number of authorized shares that may be issued. However, the practical value of such ownership is a function of the number of issued shares. Thus, a corporation with 10,000 authorized shares has only 5,000 issued shares. A person who owns 500 shares owns 10% of the company although, in theory, if the company issues the remaining authorized shares, he will own only 5% of the company.

SHAREHOLDER
A person, or other legal entity, who owns either common or preferred stock of a corporation. Usually, evidence of ownership is in the form of a certificate, issued by the company, that describes the number of ownership units, or shares.

The term shareholder is not used of owners of nonstock or mutual corporations. For example, the NYSE is a nonstock corporation. The owners of the NYSE are its members; they are not called shareholders.

SHAREHOLDERS' EQUITY
Used in financial statements to identify the net worth of a corporation (i.e., the residual value of a company after all liabilities are subtracted from all assets). The net worth is further subdivided into the par value of outstanding preferred and common shares, the paid-in capital (surplus), which represents what the owners paid above the par value when the shares were purchased from the company, and retained earnings (i.e., cumulative earnings not paid as cash or stock dividends).

Also called stockholders' equity.

SHELF DISTRIBUTION
Term used If an affiliate of a company, using the current financial reports made by the company to the SEC as an effective registration statement, intends to sell at various times and at various prices a fixed number of shares or bonds in the public marketplace. The sell orders are identified as part of a distribution, and buyers are informed that the purchased securities were part of the distribution.

SHELL COMPANY
Jargon for a corporation, usually without assets or a valid business operation, whose shares are offered for sale. Although such sales are not necessarily fraudulent, the value of the shares is questionable and are always high risk.

SHOP
1   As noun: the location of the office of a broker-dealer. For example, "His shop is very active these days."

2 As verb: the act of soliciting the highest bid or lowest offer for a security. For example, "We'll shop around for the best price." Also used in the expression "shopping the street."

SHORT
Used of a transaction in a client security account that causes both a credit and an obligation of future performance. For example, a client sells a borrowed certificate. The client is short because there is a credit of the proceeds of the sale and the client is obligated to return the borrowed certificate. Or a client sells a call or put; there is a credit and the client is obligated to deliver (call) or purchase (put) a specific security.

The term short is not used if there is a credit but no future obligation. For example, a client sells a security owned. There is a credit but no future obligation. This is called a long sale.

In commodity accounts, short is used of clients who obligate themselves to a future sale of the commodity.

SHORT AGAINST THE BOX
Descriptive term for an offsetting long and short position in the same security in a client account. For example, "The client is long 500 shares of Monsanto and short 500 shares."

The technique establishes a perfect hedge whereby the client can neither gain nor lose from that point onward. The technique can be used to transfer the tax consequences of the long position to a future tax year. It cannot be used to turn a short-term paper gain on the long security into a long-term gain because the short sale, if the long security was held one year or less, wipes out the holding period on the long security.

SHORT BOND
1 A bond sold short (i.e., sold and a borrowed certificate is used to complete delivery).
2 A bond, originally issued with a long maturity, whose remaining time to maturity is now relatively short. For example, a bond that was issued in 1959 with a 25-year maturity now, in 1983, has only one year remaining to maturity.

SHORT COUPON
1 Used as a synonym for a short-term bond (i.e., a bond whose remaining time to maturity is relatively short).
2 Used of a new issue of bonds whose first coupon payment will be less than six months of interest. For example, a bond issue is dated March 1. The semiannual interest payments are scheduled for

June–December 1. The first coupon will be short and will represent interest only for the three months between March 1 and June 1.

SHORT EXEMPT

Indication placed on certain short-sale orders sent to an exchange for execution. In practice, customer short-sale orders may be so designated if they are part of a bona fide arbitrage transaction. The designation informs the floor broker that the short sale need not be made on an uptick (i.e., the transaction is exempt from this regulation).

Member firm orders made to correct an error on the floor and specialist orders used to complete certain odd-lot buy transactions, also are short exempt.

SHORT HEDGE

Term for the strategy that fully or partially limits the downside risk of ownership. A short against the box provides a full hedge against downside risk. A short call against an established position provides a partial protection against downside risk. For example, a client long $1 million Ginnie Mae pass-throughs could provide a short hedge by selling 10 GNMA calls. If interest rates rise, both the GNMA pass-throughs and the calls will go down in value. Thus, the premium received when the calls were sold will partially protect the client from the drop in value of the GNMA pass-throughs.

The term also is used if a client reduces downside risk exposure by the use of commodity future or forward contracts.

SHORT INTEREST

The total short positions in listed securities. The short positions for individual member firms are provided to the exchanges. The exchanges, in turn, compile the total short positions and, about the 15th of each month, provide these figures to the news media.

Both the New York Times and The Wall Street Journal provide a representative listing of the securities with the largest short interest.

The short positions represent total shorts, and no differentiation is made between regular short sales and short positions against the box.

SHORT INTEREST THEORY

A theory that predicts an upward price movement in a security based on the total short positions in the security. Basic rule of thumb: if the short interest exceeds 1-½ to 2 times the average daily volume in the security, it is predictive of a price rise.

In recent years, because many covered call writers deliver borrowed stock if exercised, technical analysts place less credence in the total short position in a security. Instead, these analysts look more closely at the short positions established by specialists as an indicator of possible price rise in the security.

Also called the cushion theory.

SHORT LEG
Slang for the short option that forms part of a spread. For example, a client buys and sells a call to establish a call spread.

SHORT POSITION
1 Industry term for a client account in which completion of a sale was made by the delivery of a borrowed certificate. The client is said to have a short position because the client owes the security borrowed to the broker.
2 Industry term for a client account in which a client has written an option, either a put or a call, and has not yet made a closing purchase, has not been exercised, or the option has not expired.
3 Industry term for a client commodity account in which the client has contracted to sell the commodity at a future date for a fixed price.

SHORT SALE
Any sale that is completed by the delivery of a borrowed certificate. Short sales are made because the seller anticipates a decline in the price of a security.

Regular short sales (i.e., where the client has no other position in the security) are made to profit from a price decline.

Short sales against the box (i.e., where the client has an offsetting long position) are made to avoid a loss and to postpone the tax consequences of a long sale to a subsequent tax year.

SHORT-SALE RULE
IRS rule that pertains to the use of a hedge against a long position. Basic concept: a long put or a short against the box, if used as a hedge against a long position that has been held twelve months or less, wipes out the holding period of the long position. When the hedge is removed, the holding period of the long security begins anew. Tax advice is needed for married puts and hedges against positions that are long-term.

SHORT TENDER
A person who accepts a tender offer by the delivery of securities that are borrowed. This practice is forbidden by SEC Rule 10b-4; only long securities can be tendered under this rule.

SHORT TERM
For purposes of capital gains tax, a term of ownership of a security of 12 months or less.

See also LONG TERM.

SHORT-TERM DEBT
Debt securities with a relatively short time remaining to maturity. On corporation balance sheets, bonds with one year or less to maturity are listed among current liabilities.

In the analysis of corporations or municipalities, bonds with five or less years to maturity remaining are considered short term. The meaning of the term, therefore, depends on the context in which it is used.

SHORT-TERM GAIN
If a taxpayer purchases a capital asset and within one year or less sells it at a profit, the IRS considers the gain as short term. One exception: all profits on short sales are short term because it is a profit based on a sale followed by a purchase, rather than a purchase followed by a sale. Thus, the client has no holding period.

SHORT-TERM LOSS
If a taxpayer purchases a capital asset and within one year or less sells it at a loss, the IRS considers the loss to be short term. One exception: if a taxpayer hedges a long-term capital gain with a short sale against the box and, in covering the short position, suffers a capital loss, the loss is considered long term by the IRS.

SILENT PARTNER
Industry term for a limited partner in a direct participation program. The term is so used because limited partners have no vote in the management of the venture. For example, a partnership that will engage in the development of oil wells has one general partner who will manage the venture and 30 limited partners who will contribute capital. The limited partners, because they have no voice in management, are silent partners.

SIMPLIFIED EMPLOYEE PENSION PLAN
A hybrid that combines features of IRA and Keogh accounts. Under SEP, an employer may make contributions to the plan for employees who are 25 years or older and who have 3 or more years of employment. The contributions are vested, are not considered taxable income for

the employees, and are tax-sheltered until withdrawn by the employee, although employees may upon termination roll over their vested interest into another IRA plan. Contribution by the employer may be linked to firm profits; thus, in practice, they become combined pension and profit-sharing plans.

SINGLE-PURCHASE CONTRACT
Term used of an annuity, either fixed or variable, where the investor makes a lump-sum purchase. Such contracts, at the election of the investor, may provide immediate payout or future payout. Once the investor elects for the terms of the payout, the terms may not be changed.

SINKER
Industry slang for a bond with a sinking-fund provision.

SINKING FUND
A fund of money that a corporation must set aside annually to provide for the early retirement of portions of a bond issue or, occasionally, an issue of preferred stock. Generally, these funds are used to retire bonds in the year that the funds are set aside, although the bond indenture may provide for alternate bond redemption provisions. Sinking funds, if promised in the bond indenture, are obligatory on the issuing corporation.

Many municipal revenue issues also have sinking-fund provisions; these are not obligatory, however, unless the revenues are sufficient to maintain the facility and provide for debt service.

The abbreviation SF often is used by Moody's or Standard & Poor's bond guides in the brief description of a bond issue to designate that a sinking-fund provision is applicable.

SIPA
Acronym for the Securities Investors Protection Act.

See also SECURITIES INVESTORS PROTECTION CORPORATION (for an explanation of the protection provided by the act).

SIZE
1 Industry term for the quantity of shares or bonds available for purchase or sale. For example, (1) in asking for an OTC quote, a dealer may designate that he wants a "quote-large" (i.e., for more than the unit of trading) or (2) in response to a request for a quote, a specialist may give both the quote and the size. Thus, a specialist

could quote: "It's 19-½ to 20, 11 by 13." There are 1100 shares to be bought at 19-½; 1300 to be sold at 20.

2   Used in the expression "in size" or "available in size" to designate that large quantities are available for purchase. In practice, the term is not used of the buy side of the market.

SKIP-DAY SETTLEMENT
A negotiated settlement that calls for delivery and payment on the second business day following the trade date. Although such settlement may be called for in transactions for T-bills and bankers' acceptances, it is the usual method of trading commercial paper. Reason: dealers are willing to break up commercial paper into smaller lots to suit investor needs, and they want the chance to market the remainder of the "piece" to other investors.

SLD
1   Abbreviation for sold sale. This designation follows the symbol for a security on the consolidated tape if, for any reason, the report of the transaction is out of time sequence.

2   Used on the consolidated tape to designate a transaction that is out of sequence.

Also appears in SLD LAST SALE to designate a transaction that is significantly higher or lower than the previous sale and is not already explained by the tape symbol, OPD.

See also OPD.

SLD LAST SALE
Designation on the consolidated tape placed after the symbol for the security. The designation, which means sold last sale, signifies that the price designated is significantly higher or lower than the preceding transaction in that issue.

As a rule of thumb, the designation is used if the current price is one or more points away from a previous transaction of 19-⅞ or below, or two or more points away from a previous transaction of 20 or above.

SMALL BUSINESS ADMINISTRATION
A government agency. It provides small businesses with loans and management assistance. Monies borrowed by the SBA through bond issues are guaranteed by the full faith and credit of the U.S. government. Interest received from SBA securities is subject to federal income tax but not to state or local taxation.

SOFT DOLLARS

Jargon for a method of payment by means of directed underwriting credits and commissions from portfolio transactions. This payment for research and other brokerage services takes the place of payment in "hard dollars" (i.e., dollars that are a direct payment from the portfolio manager). For example, "The computerized analysis of your portfolio will cost $3,000 hard dollars, or $10,000 soft dollars."

SOFT MARKET

Description of a market for stocks or bonds that has very little demand. As a result, even slight selling pressure will cause prices to drop.

SOLD TO YOU

This is part of industry jargon used by over-the-counter traders when they reconfirm that their offer has been accepted by the contratrader. For example, the buying trader, "We buy 200 Pabst at 27." The selling trader, "We confirm, we sold to you 200 Pabst at 27."

SOVEREIGN RISK

The risk faced by an investor who invests funds in a foreign country. The risk refers to possible changes in currency values and changes in governments and laws that may be disadvantageous to the investor.

SOYD

Abbreviation for a method of depreciation of fixed assets called sum-of-the-years' digits.

SPECIAL ARBITRAGE ACCOUNT

A form of margin account in which a customer may receive advantageous credit terms if he purchases a security and, at about the same time, either (1) sells it in a different market or (2) sells an equal security in the same or a different market to take advantage of a difference in prices. For example, in a special arbitrage account, a client buys 5,000 ABC in market A at $21 per share and at the same time sells 5,000 ABC in market B at $21.50 per share.

SPECIAL ASSESSMENT BOND

A form of municipal general obligation bond so named because there is a special tax, or assessment, paid by users of the facility. The tax is sufficient to pay the bond debt service. Used for the construction of streets, curbs, sewers, water, and other public utilities.

SPECIAL BID

A bid made by a New York Stock Exchange member, publicized on the tape, for a block of stock at a fixed price. The buying member pays all transaction costs, including a special commission to the contrabroker. Special bids are seldom used.

SPECIAL BOND ACCOUNT

A form of margin account with a broker-dealer in which a customer may purchase, carry, or trade on advantageous credit terms: (1) U.S. government, government-guaranteed, or municipal securities, (2) nonconvertible corporate bonds listed on an exchange, (3) many nonconvertible corporate bonds that are unlisted but meet special qualifications published by the Federal Reserve.

The broker-dealer may set his own initial margin requirement, but customers are governed by the margin maintenance requirements set by the exchanges and the National Association of Securities Dealers (NASD).

SPECIAL CASH ACCOUNT

Technical term for what is popularly called a cash account. In such accounts, brokerage clients may purchase or sell long any security. Delivery of securities sold and payment for securities purchased must be made promptly and, in any event, be within seven business days following the trade date.

The special cash account does not permit the broker to maintain a creditor-debtor relationship with the customer, although debits of less than $500 do not require that the broker buy in or sell out the account. Regulation T gives the client seven business days following the trade date; industry rules require payment by the fifth business day following the trade.

SPECIAL CONVERTIBLE DEBT SECURITY ACCOUNT

A form of margin account in which a customer may finance the purchase or short sale of debt securities that are (1) convertible into a margin stock or (2) carry a warrant or right to subscribe to a margin stock.

Convertible preferred stocks are carried in the client's general margin account.

SPECIAL DEAL

An improper practice, prohibited in the National Association of Securities Dealers' Rules of Fair Practice, whereby an underwriter of investment company securities pays or gives anything of material value, other than the selling concessions granted in the prospectus, to an employee of another dealer in concurrence with the sale of the fund's shares. The NASD defines material value as something worth more than $25 in a one-year period.

SPECIAL DRAWING RIGHTS

Special drawing rights are used to settle international trade imbalances between governments. The special drawing rights, which are adjusted about once a year to represent changes in trading patterns between nations, are a statistically weighted composite of currencies of the world's leading trading nations. They are, in effect, a kind of money used between governments through bookkeeping transfers in the international banking system.

Sometimes called "paper gold."

SPECIALIST

A member of a national securities exchange registered by that exchange to maintain an orderly market in selected securities traded on that exchange. In fulfilling this function, specialists normally act as (1) brokers in opening the market and in the prompt execution of orders left with them by other members and (2) as dealers in buying or selling for their own account, to give market depth and reasonable price continuity in their specialty stock, and by taking the other side of all odd-lot transactions.

SPECIALIST'S BOOK

Popular name for the record-keeping device used by specialists to record orders left with them by other members. In some cases, the book is a loose-leaf notebook; in others, the actual order tickets are time-stamped and arranged by price or, in more modern instances, a computer bank will record customer buy or sell orders and the number of shares and the conditions or prices at which the orders are to be executed.

SPECIALIST UNIT

A group of three or more fully qualified specialists who work together to maintain an orderly market in specific stocks listed on an exchange. The units may be an association, a partnership, or a corporation.

SPECIALIZED MUTUAL FUND

Popular term for a mutual fund that concentrates its investments in a particular industry or a specific geographic area. Examples are the Energy Fund, the Chemical Fund, the Merrill Lynch Pacific Fund.

SPECIAL MISCELLANEOUS ACCOUNT
Regulation T of the Federal Reserve permits broker-dealers who carry margin accounts to keep a memorandum on the excess margin in a client's margin account. The memorandum is called the special miscellaneous account. The SMA gives the broker an insight into the dollars that may be available for cash withdrawals, purchases or short sales of marginable securities, or for the withdrawal of securities in the account. The SMA account, however, is not usable at the discretion of the customer. It is the broker's decision to permit the use of the SMA. Regulation T does prescribe the maximum use of the SMA.

SPECIAL OFFERING
Term designating a method of selling a large block by a NYSE member for its own or a customer's account. The offering, which is made on the consolidated tape, is for a specific number of shares at a fixed price. The seller pays all transaction charges, including a special commission to the buying brokers.

SPECIAL OMNIBUS ACCOUNT
Title of an account with one broker-dealer opened by another broker-dealer who is registered with the SEC. In this account, the second broker-dealer can transact for its customers without disclosing the names of the customers.

SPECIAL SITUATION
Industry jargon for a security that appears to be undervalued in price and which, because of a one-time event, seems due for a rise in price. The one-time event could be a change in management, a change in the fortunes of the industry or the company, a new product, or a tax-loss carryover that will improve the fortunes of the company.

SPECIAL SUBSCRIPTION ACCOUNT
A form of margin account in which a customer can obtain advantageous credit to acquire a margin security through the exercise of a right or a warrant. Member firms may grant a larger than usual loan for purchases in a special subscription account provided the customer, within one year by four equal quarterly payments, reduces the outstanding loan and transfers the securities purchased to the client's general margin account.

SPECIAL TAX BOND
A class of municipal revenue bonds so called because the bond debt service will be paid by an excise tax on certain luxury items, principally gasoline, liquor, or tobacco products.

SPECTAIL DEALER
Pun on speculator and retail. Slang for a broker-dealer who handles some retail client accounts but who seems to devote more time to speculative trading positions in its own account.

SPECULATION
Latin: speculare, to watch or to examine closely. In industry usage, the assumption of high risk, often without regard to current income or to the preservation of principal, to achieve large capital gains. As a general rule, the shorter the time in which one endeavors to achieve the desired capital gains, the more speculative the investment.

SPECULATOR
One who speculates.
See also SPECULATION.

SPIN-OFF
A distribution of stock made to shareholders by a parent company of shares in a subsidiary. The subsidiary thereby becomes an independent corporate entity. For example, Company A is the parent company of Company B. Company A spins off Company B by distributing its shares, on a pro rata basis, to its shareholders of record. Company B is now independently owned by the persons who own the shares distributed to them.

SPLIT
General term for the amendment of a corporation's charter whereby the number of authorized shares is increased (split up) or decreased (split down). The par value of previously authorized shares is so changed to reflect the split that the common stock account on the corporation's balance sheet remains the same before and after the split. A split requires stockholder approval.
See also SPLIT UP and SPLIT DOWN.

SPLIT DOWN
This amendment of the corporation's charter decreases the number of authorized shares and increases their par value proportionately. For example,

Before: 2 million shares authorized at a par value of $5.

After: 1 million shares authorized at a par value of $10.

Split downs often are used by corporations whose shares are low priced. The split down will decrease the number of shares and increase the market price.

Also called a reverse split.

SPLIT OFFERING

Term describing a public sale of a debt issue that is comprised of both serial and term maturity bonds and large-term maturity bonds of the same issuer. For example, an issue that is comprised of $40 million serial maturity bonds maturing between 1990 and 2000 and $100 million in term bonds maturing in 2007.

Split offerings are common in the issuance of municipal revenue bonds and some general obligation issues.

SPLIT RATING

The situation that results if one major bond rating service gives a higher or lower rating than another bond rating service to the same issue. For example, Moody's may rate a bond Aa but Standard & Poor's rates it A.

Split ratings are not uncommon for nonconvertible debt securities. They are usual for convertible securities because Moody's generally rates convertibles one grade below nonconvertible securities.

SPLIT UP

This amendment of the corporation's charter increases the number of authorized shares and decreases the par value proportionately. For example,

Before: 1 million shares authorized at a par value of $6.

After: 3 million shares authorized at a par value of $2.

Split ups often are used by corporations whose shares are highly priced, usually $80, $100, or more per share. The split up will increase the number of shares available and decrease the market price.

Also simply called a stock split because it is the most common split used by corporations.

SPONSOR

Term for the underwriter of investment company securities. In practice, the terms underwriter, sponsor, and wholesaler are used synonymously in the investment company industry.

SPOT COMMODITY

Industry jargon for commodity transactions that will result in actual physical delivery of the commodity, as opposed to a transaction for future delivery.

Futures contracts that are due to expire in the current month often are called spot commodities.

SPOT MARKET

Industry jargon for trades in commodities either for immediate delivery (the same or the next business day) or for trades in futures contracts that will expire this month.

SPOT MONTH
Industry jargon for the current month if a previously traded futures contract will become deliverable during the month.

SPOT PRICE
Industry jargon for the current price of a physical commodity, either agricultural, mineral, or a government security.

SPOT SECONDARY
Term designating a secondary offering of a stock or a bond that is being sold without an effective registration statement.

SPREAD
In the securities industry:
1   The difference between the bid and offer price for a security. For example, a security is bid 18, offered 19. The spread is 1 point.
2   The difference between the proceeds to the issuer and the public offering price on an underwriting. For example, "The syndicate bought the bonds at 98-½ and reoffered them at par. The spread is 1-½ points."
3   In listed option trading: a purchase and sale of options of the same class. For example, "Buy an Eastman Kodak January 85 call, sell an Eastman Kodak January 95 call."
4   The difference between yields on various fixed-income securities.

SPREADING
Used of option trading if a customer buys and sells options of the same class in an endeavor to profit from price change movements in the underlying stock and thus profit in the value of the premiums for the options. Spreads limit profits by limiting risk.

The term also is used of commodity contracts that partially offset risk in the hope of limited reward.

See also BEAR SPREAD; BULL SPREAD; CALENDAR SPREAD; VERTICAL SPREAD.

SPREAD LOAD
Term used of contractual-type mutual funds if the principal portion of the sales charge is paid over the first four years of the contract, with the remainder of the sales charge paid in equal installments over the remainder of the contract. Under current law, the maximum charge for sales may not exceed 20% of any year's contributions to the fund, and the total of the first four years' charges may not exceed 64% of one year's contributions. In practice, therefore, the sales charge will average 16% per year for the first four years. The advantages

or disadvantages of the prepayment of fund sales charges should be weighed against the benefits provided by the plan.

SPREAD OPTION

When used of conventional (OTC) options, a spread option is a long put and a long call with the same expiration time but with different exercise prices. Thus, it is the equivalent of a long combination in listed options. This gives rise to confusion, so the reader must note the context in which the term is used.

SPREAD ORDER

Used of orders for listed options if the client is endeavoring to put on a spread. Because there is much volatility in option premiums, due to the price movement of the underlying stock, spread orders usually designate the series desired and the net debit or credit to the customer. It is the net debit or credit that determines the client's strategy, e.g., with ABC at 48, a client enters this spread order:

Buy 10 ABC Jan 45 calls
Sell 10 ABC Oct 40 calls
Net debit 3-¼ points

The floor brokers will execute the spread if they can do so at a net debit of 3-½ points per contract.

SPREAD POSITION

Term used to describe the status of a client account in listed options if the client has both long and short options of the same class on the underlying security. For example, a client has the following option positions:

long 15 LMN Jan 55 calls
short 15 LMN Apr 50 calls

The client has a spread position in LMN options.

SRO

Acronym for a self-regulatory organization.

Commonly used abbreviation for an exchange, securities association, or clearing agency registered with the SEC. Principal concept: under the federal securities laws, such organizations are required to be self-policing and to moderate the activities of their members.

SS

Used on the consolidated tape, usually in a vertical configuration, to designate two things: (1) a security trades in 10-share units and

(2) that the number of units represented on the tape is not in round-lots, instead it represents the total transaction in shares. For example, the consolidated tape displays the following transaction:

UEP Pr

30 ss 97

Meaning: there was a sale of 30 shares of Union Electric Power preferred shares at $97 per share.

ST

Used on the consolidated tape, usually in a vertical configuration, to designate that an execution on the floor was at a guaranteed price; i.e., it was "stopped" by the specialist or by another member. For example, the consolidated tape shows:

MER

6s . . . 62. . . . 2s . . . 62ST

Meaning: there was a sale of 600 Merrill Lynch at 62, and that sale caused the specialist to also trade 200 MER at the price of 62 that was guaranteed to another floor broker.

STABLIZATION

The act of so pegging a price for a security with a bid that the price will not drop below the bid price. Stabilization, which normally is illegal, may be used in conjunction with a registered offering. Thus, the syndicate that is offering shares at $31 may stabilize the price with a bid at $31 or $30⅞ or $30¾. Stabilizing bids always are identified as such.

SEC Rule 10b-7 gives the guidelines for stabilizing bids.

STANDARD & POOR'S

A leading registered investment adviser that specializes in financial reports. The Standard & Poor's manuals, its stock and bond guides, and its Blue List (book), which gives daily municipal bond offerings by dealers, are common publications sponsored by S&P

In addition, the S&P Index of 500 Stocks is followed by many investors.

See also STANDARD & POOR'S INDEX.

STANDARD & POOR'S INDEX

A measurement of the value movement of 500 widely held common stocks. The index reflects the number of shares outstanding for each of the individual companies. It is considered as a measurement of average stock market performance and thus is used as a norm of above or below average price volatility of other securities.

The index contains 400 industrial issues and 100 other issues divided as follows: 20 transportaton, 40 financial, and 40 public utility issues.

Also called the S&P Index.

STANDARD & POOR'S RATING

A rating of credit risk assigned by Standard & Poor's to corporate and municipal bonds. The higher the rating, the lower the risk of default in the payment of interest and in the repayment of principal. The top four ratings, AAA, AA, A, and BBB, with their subdivisions, are considered investment grade and suitable for trust accounts and investments by fiduciaries. Bonds rated BB, B, and below are considered to be increasingly speculative.

STANDBY UNDERWRITER

Term used of an investment banker who agrees to purchase any shares that remain unsubscribed after they are offered to current shareholders through a rights offering. The investment banker is paid a fee to provide this service, and any unsubscribed shares are purchased by the investment banker at a price below the subscription price.

STANY

Acronym for the Security Traders' Association of New York.

STATED VALUE

A bookkeeping value assigned by the corporation to no par stock For example, a company has no-par stock outstanding. It assigned a stated value of $2 per share. Its balance sheet will appear:

Common stock: 1,000,000
shares outstanding at
$2 stated value. . . . $2,000,000

STATEMENT

Term describing the periodic reports by broker-dealers to their customers that summarize account balances and list securities transactions. Federal law requires that statements of account be sent quarterly to all customers who transacted or who have a debit or credit balance or a net security position with the broker. In practice, statements are sent monthly if there was a transaction in the account or if there are option positions.

SOP

In older literature, the abbreviation for the SEC's Statement of Policy.

The SOP governed the advertising and merchandising of investment company securities. The SOP was rescinded in 1980.

STATUTORY UNDERWRITER

Federal law defines an underwriter as a person who purchases a security from an issuer for purpose of resale. The term statutory underwriter describes a person who performs such an action, albeit inadvertantly, and thereby subjects himself to the penalties of the law for those who sell unregistered securities. For example, a registered representative fails to exercise proper diligence in the sale of securities by a control person. The representative and his firm could be penalized, as a statutory underwriter, for violations of the Securities Act of 1933.

STATUTORY VOTING

A procedure, outlined in a corporations charter, whereby shareholders may cast one vote for, or one vote against, each of the candidates on the slate of candidates proposed for the board of directors. Shareholders, however, may not concentrate their vote (number of shares times number of candidates) on any one of the candidates. End result: holders of 50+% of a corporation's shares will control the election of the board of directors. Most corporations provide for statutory voting.

See also CUMULATIVE VOTING.

STEENTH

Abbreviation for one sixteenth. Commonly used to designate bids or offers quoted in 16ths. For securities quoted in dollars, a steenth is 6-¼ cents per share; if a security is quoted in bond points, a steenth is $.625 (62-½ cents) per $1,000 of face value. Popular usage: "It's quoted a quarter to a steenth." Meaning: the bid is one quarter (¼), the offer is ¹⁄₁₆th higher (⁵⁄₁₆). The quote could also be 4 to 5 steenths (i.e., ⁴⁄₁₆ bid and ⁵⁄₁₆ offered).

STICKY DEAL

Industry jargon for an underwriting that will be difficult to market. The difficulty may arise from market conditions, the company, or economic factors. For example, "At $45 per share, this could be a sticky deal." Basic idea: the underwriter is measuring his risk against the risk the investor will assume.

STOCK

Term used of an investment represented by an ownership certificate. For example, "I own stock in ABC corporation," or "We own 200 shares of stock."

Basic meaning: any capital contribution to a business venture. For example, "I own livestock"; "I've got to restock my shelves"; "I've got to take stock of my investments"; and, from long ago, "public stock" (the name for the first public bond issue of the United States).

In practice, therefore, as a noun the word stock means a transferable evidence of ownership of a corporation; but in other contexts, stock may mean a debt or an action.

STOCK AHEAD

Trading floor expression. "Stock ahead" would be relayed to a registered representative who asks about the status of a client's unexecuted limit order. Meaning: there were other executions at the client's limit price, but the client's order was not executed because other brokers had prior limit orders at the same price. For example, "If the best bid for a stock was $18, and your client's bid for 100 represented the 28th of 36 round-lot bids for the stock at that price, transactions for 1,500 shares at $18 would execute many orders but would not execute your client's order." If you asked about your client's order, the response would be, "Stock ahead."

STOCK BUSINESS

Term used in municipal bond underwriting if a dealer or a dealer bank buys part of a municipal issue for its own account to make short-term profits by a later resale of the bonds.

Also used in the expression "going for stock" to designate that part of an underwriting was bought by members of the account for future bond sales.

STOCK DIVIDEND

A distribution of additional shares to current shareholders made by the issuing corporation in lieu of a cash dividend. The distribution, which requires approval of the board of directors but not the shareholders, conserves cash within the corporation. The shares, which normally come from authorized but unissued shares, are bought with retained earnings. The distribution is not a taxable event for the recipients until the shares are sold.

STOCK LIST

A function of each of the registered exchanges that examines the eligibility of companies for listing on that exchange, the possibility of unlisted trading, and whether a listed security should be delisted from trading.

Also called the stock list department.

STOCK POWER

A form of assignment and power of substitution used in the sale and transfer of securities. The form, which is a separate piece of paper, duplicates the transfer form on the back of registered securities. If signed, witnessed, and guaranteed by a member firm or a commercial bank and attached to a stock or registered bond certificate, it will be accepted by the transfer agent and the certificate will be registered in the name of the new owner.

Also called a stock/bond power.

STOCK RECORD

Also called the stock record department in many firms.

This function monitors the movement of all securities, both stocks and bonds, within the firm. The stock record department identifies by name the securities it controls and the owners and audits on a day-to-day basis the location of these securities.

STOP-LIMIT ORDER

An instruction on a stop order to buy or sell. If there is a transaction at the stop price or higher (buy stop limit), or at the stop price or lower (sell stop limit), the customer wants to buy or sell at the designated limit price given on the order. For example, Buy 400 LMN 52 STOP 53 LIMIT. Explanation: the customer wants a limit order entered at 53 as soon as there is a transaction at 52 or above.

The American Stock Exchange permits such orders only if the stop and limit prices are the same.

STOP ORDER

An instruction by a customer on an order to buy or sell. The instruction requests that a market order to buy or sell be executed once a given transaction price is attained in the security. For example, Buy 800 ABC 28 STOP. Any transaction at 28 or above elects (activates) the stop and the order now becomes a market order to buy at the best available price.

Stop orders may not be entered for over-the-counter transactions.

Also called a suspended market order because the execution is suspended until a transaction in the public market elects the order.

STOP-OUT PRICE

Term used of Treasury security auctions. It is the lowest price accepted in the auction. This price plus the highest price are used to determine the average price. Noncompetitive purchasers—$500,000 or less for T-bills and $1 million or less for T-notes and bonds—pay the average of the competitive bidder prices.

STOPPED OUT

Industry jargon used on an exchange floor if a customer's order is executed at the stopped (guaranteed) price given by a specialist or other member. For example, a broker with a market order to buy is guaranteed a price of $53 per share. If the next transaction is at $53 per share, that also is the price that the broker's client will receive. The client has been stopped out. His transaction will appear on the tape with the symbol ST following the price.

STOPPED STOCK

Term used to describe the guarantee that a specialist or other member gives to a broker with a public order to buy or sell. The guarantee of a specific price or better permits the broker to seek a better price without the fear of missing the market. For example, a broker with a market order to buy is stopped at 52 by a specialist. This means that the broker will not pay more than 52 for the stock.

STRADDLE

When used of listed stock options, a straddle may be either long or short. A long straddle is a long call and a long put on the same underlying security at the same exercise price and the same expiration month. For example, 1 long ABC Jan 50 call and 1 long ABC Jan 50 put. A short straddle is a short call and a short put on the same security at the same exercise price and the same expiration month.

When used of commodity positions, a straddle is a purchase of a commodity future with an expiration in one month, and the sale of a commodity future with an expiration in another month.

STRAIGHT BOND

Any bond that is not convertible into another security.

STRAIGHT-LINE DEPRECIATION

A conservative accounting procedure that apportions a corporation's cost of a qualified asset over its useful lifetime in equal annual amounts. The amount to be depreciated is the cost minus the estimated scrap value at the end of useful life. The annual amount of depreciation is subtracted from fixed assets on the balance sheet and from operating income on the income statement. Because depreciation is part of the cost of doing business, it reduces the company's tax liability.

See also CASH FLOW.

STRAP

A form of conventional option that couples one put and two calls on the same security at the same exercise price with the same expiration date. The premium is less than it would be if the options were purchased separately.

The term is not used of listed options; instead this would be a long straddle and a long call.

STREET

Popular term for Wall Street and the surrounding financial area. In recent years, the term has included all elements of the financial community, no matter where located. For example, "Here's what I hear on the street."

STREET NAME

Popular term for a security registered in the name of a broker-dealer. For example, "The security is in street name." Securities owned by the broker-dealer are in street name, and securities owned by customers that have been deposited with the broker-dealer normally are registered in the name of the broker-dealer to facilitate transfer when the security is sold.

Customer-owned securities in street name are said to have the broker-dealer as the nominee and the customer as the beneficial owner; i.e., the owner of the security and all of the rights pertaining thereto.

STRIKE PRICE

Popular name for the exercise price of a put or call option.

Also called striking price.

STRIP

A form of conventional option that couples one call and two puts on the same security at the same exercise price with the same expiration date. The premium is less than it would be if the options were purchased separately.

The term is not used of listed options; instead this would be a long straddle and a long put.

STUDENT LOAN MARKETING ASSOCIATION

Nicknamed "Sallie Mae," this government-sponsored private corporation purchases, holds, services, and sells student loans made by banks and other institutions to qualified students of colleges, universities, and vocational schools.

Bonds issued by Sallie Mae are backed by the full faith and credit of the U.S. government.

SUBCHAPTER M

That section of the Internal Revenue Code that sets forth the conditions under which investment companies and real estate investment trusts may distribute income, whether from dividends, interest, or capital gains, to their shareholders without incurring a federal tax liability for the company or trust.

See also CONDUIT THEORY.

SUBCHAPTER S CORPORATION

A relatively small corporation that qualifies and chooses to be taxed as a partnership under Subchapter S of the Internal Revenue Code. Under this option, taxable income and certain liabilities of the corporation flow through to the individual proprietors as part of their tax reports.

SUBJECT

Term used of a quote made by a dealer, whether a bid or an offer or both, that must be reviewed before a final decision to buy or sell is made. Examples: (1) all orders received by underwriting syndicates are subject to prior sale; thus, they are subject until confirmed; (2) requests for quotes made in excess of the common unit of trading will be given as subject until the dealer has more information about the trade.

Common industry practice requires that dealers identify quotes given as subject if further negotiation of the details of the contract is required.

SUBJECT MARKET

A quotation on which a broker-dealer is unable to trade until he confirms the acceptability of the bid and asked prices with the party he represents.

SUBJECT QUOTE

Industry term for a bid or offer, or both, that requires further negotiation before a firm quotation will be made by a dealer.

See also SUBJECT.

SUBORDINATED

Latin: subordinare, to be below. Term used of debt securities if the bondholder not only gives precedence to secured creditors but also to general creditors of the issuer. For example, an issuer has outstanding mortgage bonds and has accepted deposits from customers. The issuer then sells subordinated debentures. Holders of the subordinated debentures will receive payment after all other creditors are paid. However, they will be paid before the corporate owners are paid.

SUBPOENA DUCES TECUM
Latin: under penalty of law (I order you) to bring with you. . . . In effect, this court order requires that the recipient produce such records as are pertinent to a trial. Such orders may also be issued by the SEC in its investigation of violations, or allegations thereof, of the securities laws of the United States.

SUBSCRIPTION PRIVILEGE
This privilege allows a common shareholder to buy, on a pro rata basis, newly issued shares at a favorable price before the shares are offered to the general public. The privilege also may extend to an issue of convertible bonds or preferred stock. The privilege normally has a fixed period within which it must be exercised; the time usually is 30 to 60 days.

The evidence of the subscription privilege is known as a subscription right.

Also known as preemptive right.

SUBSCRIPTION RATIO
The company-established number of subscription rights needed by a shareholder to subscribe to a single share, or to a convertible bond, under the subscription privilege.

SUBSCRIPTION RIGHT
A security that evidences the number of rights granted to a shareholder on the occasion of a subscription to new common shares or new convertible securities. The practice is to issue one right for each common share held. The common shareholder may buy one new share, as determined by the subscription ratio, by sending the rights and the required dollar price to the company. For example, the subscription ratio is 4 rights for each new share; the subscription price is $40 per share. A stockholder who receives 40 rights may purchase 10 new shares if he sends the 40 rights and $400 to the company.

Subscription rights may be sold to other persons who wish to subscribe to new shares.

SUBSCRIPTION WARRANT
A security normally given in conjunction with the purchase of another security. For example, a bond or a preferred stock that permits

the holder to buy one or more common shares of the issuing corporation at a fixed price for a designated time.

Subscription warrants are similar to subscription rights with these exceptions: they are generally valid for longer periods and, at the time they are granted, the subscription price is higher than the current market price for the common stock. Thus, immediate exercise will not be profitable for the recipient.

Also known as a warrant.

SUBSTANTIVE

Adjective often used in connection with the term interest or the term matter to designate a proposed corporate activity that will affect shareholders or facts that will influence investor decisions. For example, "The next annual meeting of the XYZ Corporation will propose matters of substantive interest to investors."

The term is legal; most unsophisticated persons would use the term important in its place.

SUBSTITUTION

1 The sale of one security and the purchase of another in a client account.
2 The withdrawal of one security from a client margin account and the deposit of a second security to collateralize the client's debit balance.
3 The action of an attorney whereby he permits a second attorney to exercise his function in the process of securities transfers. For example, a client provided his broker with a signed stock power that also permits power of substitution.

SUMMARY COMPLAINT PROCEEDINGS

Under the National Association of Securities Dealers' (NASD's) Code of Procedure, the district business conduct committees may permit the respondent in a trade practice complaint to plead guilty to relatively minor infractions of the association's Rules of Fair Practice. Under such summary complaint proceedings, the respondent waives the right of appeal; but the maximum penalty is censure and a fine of $1,000.

SUM-OF-THE-YEARS'-DIGITS METHOD

An acceptable accounting method of accelerated depreciation. In it, the annual depreciation is found as follows: (1) determine the amount to be depreciated; (2) add the ordinal numbers of the years of useful life (e.g., 5 years is $1 + 2 + 3 + 4 + 5 = 15$); (3) multiply the amount to be depreciated by the reverse of the ordinal year (e.g., first year is 5, second year is 4), and divide by the sum of the years.

To illustrate: if $15,000 is to be depreciated over 5 years, the depreciation in year 2 would be:

$$\$15,000 \times \frac{4}{15} = \$4,000$$

SUNDRY ASSET
Balance sheet entry used for an item of value owned by a corporation that will be held for a relatively long time but not used in the day-to-day operation of the corporation and thus does not fit neatly into current or fixed assets. For example, raw or undeveloped land or an investment in another company could be listed under sundry assets.

As a general rule, such intangibles as good will and prepaid expenses are not listed under sundry assets; instead, a separate entry is made on the balance sheet for such items of value.

SUNSET PROVISION
Slang for a feature incorporated into a law that, unless positively reinstated by legislature, will expire at a specified future date. For example, the new tax law provides for the limited tax exemption of dividends from utility stocks reinvested in new shares of the same issuer under a sunset provision that expires in tax year 1985.

SUNSHINE LAW
Colorful expression that describes the public's right of access to the meetings and records of certain governmental agencies involved in investigatory, reporting, and rulemaking processes.

Most activities of the SEC and the Commodities Futures Trading Commission (CFTC) are subject to sunshine laws.

SUPERRESTRICTED ACCOUNT
Term formerly applied to margin accounts that were margined at less than 30% of the market value of the securities in the account. The term superrestricted was dropped from Regulation T in February 1982.

SUPERVISORY ANALYST
Designation applied by the NYSE to an employee or principal of a member firm who qualifies to review and approve research reports designed for public distribution. Qualification is achieved through a special NYSE examination.

SUPPORT LEVEL

Based on the previous trading history of a security, this is the price level at which buyers have tended to purchase a security in volume, and thus have overcome the downward pressure from sellers. For example, "On five occasions in the past year, when the price of ABC has dropped to 35 or so, the price has consistently risen." A technical analyst would consider 35 as the support level.

SUSPENSE ACCOUNT

A record maintained by a broker-dealer for money or security balance differences until such time as they are reconciled.

SWAP

Industry jargon for the sale of one security and the purchase of another. The term, which basically describes a substitution, tends to be used with a qualifying phrase that describes the reason for the swap. For example, the client made a maturity swap, or a quality swap (higher rated for lower-rated bonds), or a yield swap (a higher yield for lower-yielding bonds), and so on.

SWAP ORDER

Instruction from a customer to sell one security and purchase another on the same day. As a general rule, the instruction is absolute and has no contingent conditions. Most member firms will not accept a swap order unless it can be executed in full within the member firm. For example, a swap of one unit investment trust for another. Instead, the firm will require two orders: one to sell and, when executed, another order to buy.

SWEETENER

Industry slang for an issue of securities that adds a special feature to induce the purchase of the security. Thus, the addition of convertibility to an issue of bonds or preferreds, or a subscription right that permits the purchase of shares at a price below the current market price, would be considered as sweeteners.

SWIFT

Acronym for Society for Worldwide Interbank Financial Telecommunications. The automated communication network facilitates the transfer of currencies and financial information.

SWITCHING

1 Used synonymously for swap.
2 Used to describe the result of high-pressure selling methods by a

mutual fund salesperson, whereby a holder of a mutual fund that was purchased with a sales charge is persuaded to sell the previous mutual fund holding and to purchase another mutual fund with a sales charge so the salesperson achieves the sales commission. Nothing prevents a holder of a mutual fund from redeeming shares of the fund and, on an unsolicited basis, reinvesting the money in a second fund. Many firms, however, require the fundholder to state in writing that the switch was unsolicited.

SWITCH ORDER
Often used synonymously for a contingent order. For example, Sell 500 ABC at 55; when sold, BUY 1000 LMN at 27.

SYNDICATE
Industry term for the group of investment bankers who guarantee the issuer its money by purchasing the securities and, in turn, agree to reoffer the securities at a fixed price to the public.

The term account often is used synonymously.

The term is also used of groups of investment bankers who bid for a competitive issue but who are not successful. The term is not used of broker-dealers who act as agents of the issuer or as agents of the underwriters (e.g., members of the selling group).

SYNDICATE ACCOUNT
The financial status of a syndicate. The syndicate letter, sent by the syndicate manager before the underwriting, describes the conditions under which the syndicate will operate. For corporate offerings, this agreement is a formal document called the agreement among underwriters. After the underwriting, the syndicate account letter releases the members of the syndicate from the terms of the agreement and permits syndicate members to make sales at prices different from the established public offering price. In every case, there will be a final financial report to members of the syndicate.

SYNDICATE MANAGER
Term applied to the leading underwriter in an account. The manager organizes the syndicate, forms a selling group when needed, allocates member participation, confirms subject orders received by the account, makes stabilizing transactions, and provides the final financial accounting for the account. If an underwriting is negotiated, the manager normally receives a fee for his services. It is common in competitive underwritings to have co-managers for the account (i.e., more than one manager).

T

T

Appears after the name of a company in the newspaper report of corporate sales and earnings to designate that the primary marketplace for the company's securities is the Toronto Stock Exchange.

TAG ENDS

Slang: means that only small amounts of an offering of debt securities are available from the syndicate. The remainder of the issue has been sold.

TAIL

1 In a U.S. Treasury auction: the difference between the average bid and the lowest bid price accepted.
2 In a competitive underwriting: the decimals that follow the point bid. For example, in a bid of 98.7542 for a bond, .7542 is the tail. There is no limit on the number of decimals that can be used.
3 In Ginnie Mae terminology: a certificate that, when issued, does not bear a round-dollar face value. For example, a certificate with an original face value of $52,431.56.

See also GOVERNMENT NATIONAL MORTGAGE ASSOCIATION (GNMA).

TAILGATING

Slang: a registered representative, following the purchase of a security for a customer's account, purchases the security for her own personal account. Practice is questionable if the customer gave the impression that he had special reliable information and the registered representative not only buys but also recommends the security to others.

TAKE

Term used by dealers and exchange members to indicate that, as buyers, they are accepting another dealer's or member's offering price, thereby completing a transaction.

TAKE A POSITION

Action whereby a dealer or a customer establishes a net inventory, either long or short, in a security. For example, the dealer sold 10,000 shares, thereby taking a net short position of 2,500 shares.

The term also can imply that the position was taken as a longer-term investment. For example, the Williams brothers took a major position in the stock of the ABC company.

TAKE DOWN

1 As one word: takedown is the dollar discount given by the manager of a municipal syndicate to syndicate members when they take bonds from the account. For example, the bonds have a public offering price of 100 and the syndicate member's takedown price is 98.75.

2 As two words: take down is used in corporate underwritings to signify the number of shares or bonds for which a syndicate member is financially responsible. For example, member A's take down is 150 bonds.

TAKE OUT

1 Slang: for the dollar amount an investor removes from an account if he sells one security and purchases another at a lower cost.

2 A trader's bid for the remainder of a seller's holdings that he has been selling piecemeal. Purpose: to remove overhanging supply from the marketplace.

3 Also called a backup bid if a Ginnie Mae dealer offers to finance a mortgage banker's loans offered for sale at a GNMA auction. The dealer gets the right to repurchase them later at a specified price.

TANDEM PLAN

Arrangement whereby GNMA (Ginnie Mae) buys selected mortgages above their market value and concurrently uses FNMA (Fannie Mae) to sell them in the secondary market to minimize the loss. GNMA, in effect, is subsidizing selected housing projects with a minimum cash outlay.

See also GOVERNMENT NATIONAL MORTGAGE ASSOCIATION (GNMA) and FEDERAL NATIONAL MORTGAGE ASSOCIATION (FNMA).

TANDEM SPREAD

Term for a strategy that resembles a spread, but involves the purchase of one security and the short sale of another. Concept: there is a historical price relationship between the two securities. If the spread between the prices widens, the investor will have a gain; if the spread narrows, the investor will have a loss.

TAPE RACING

Unethical practice of transacting personal business in an issue with prior knowledge of and before executing a customer's large order in that security. This ploy attempts to profit from the price momentum generated by execution of the customer's order.

TAP ISSUE
An offering of securities with the same terms and conditions, albeit at different prices, as a previous issue of bonds. The issuer, in effect, is tapping the same market as with the previous issue. U.S. Treasury notes occasionally are tap issues.

See also REOPEN AN ISSUE.

TARGET COMPANY
A company whose shares are being secretly acquired by someone who intends to gain control. No public announcement is made until the purchaser reaches the 5% level of outstanding stock; at that time the purchaser must file the information with the SEC. Term also is used once the information becomes public.

TAX AND LOAN ACCOUNT
Demand deposits owned by the U.S. government at commercial banks. The depositors are corporations or persons who owe social security payments or withheld taxes from employees' income. Banks may use these deposits, subject to reserve requirements, until such time as the U.S. government withdraws them.

TAX ANTICIPATION BILL
Treasury bill periodically issued by the U.S. government to raise money in anticipation of the quarterly payments of corporate taxes.

Special feature: the bills, which mature several days to a week after the due date for corporation income taxes, will be accepted at face value on tax due date if a corporation uses the bills to pay its quarterly taxes. The corporation, in effect, receives a few extra days of interest and is thereby motivated to purchase the bills.

TAX ANTICIPATION NOTE
Short-term municipal security issued to raise money for the interim financing of municipal expenses. The TAN will be paid off with taxes received from taxpayers and corporations.

Used extensively by cities and other municipalities to provide a reasonably level income for salaries and other expense items that will be offset by income taxes due annually or quarterly.

TAX-EXEMPT SECURITY
General name for municipal securities. Reason for name: the interest income received from municipal securities is exempt from federal

taxation—although it is not necessarily exempt from state or local taxation.

The term is not used of securities that pay interest income subject to federal taxation but which is exempt from state or local taxation. For example, the interest income paid by U.S. government securities is exempt from state and local taxes but not from federal taxation.

TAX-LOSS CARRY-FORWARD

Dollar amount of a net capital loss, in excess of the $3,000 annual deduction permitted on a tax form for such losses, that may be carried into the next, and subsequent, tax years. Such losses, which retain their identity as short- or long-term capital losses, are included in the capital computations for gains or losses on the purchase and sale of assets in the next tax year. There is no time limit for the carry-over of tax losses for an individual taxpayer.

TAX SHELTER

General term, inappropriately used, that describes an investment of aftertax dollars that will provide the investor with current deductions based on depreciation of an asset, or a tax credit based on the investment tax credit or on the depletion allowance.

The term also implies a possible capital gain with preferential tax treatment.

Technically, the term tax-advantaged investment is appropriate. Specifically, a tax shelter is an investment that keeps current income untaxed until it is used. For example, Keogh and IRA accounts, which permit deductions from current income, are tax sheltered.

TAX STRADDLE

General term for a strategy whereby a client with a realized short-term capital gain could take offsetting positions in commodity futures contracts. Purpose: take a short-term loss in the same tax year as the realized short-term gain—thus, no tax on the net position—but get a long-term gain in the next tax year on the remaining position. The Economic Recovery Tax Act (1981) requires that the remaining position be considered a completed transaction (i.e., marked to the market for tax computations). As a result, tax straddles are no longer an effective strategy for negating a gain in one tax year and postponing it to the next.

TAX UMBRELLA

Term to describe prior and current losses sustained by a corporation. Concept: such losses may be carried forward to shelter future profits of the corporation.

TBA

Acronym for to be announced. Used in the jargon of the GNMA market if settlement for a future contract in GNMAs can be satisfied by presently existing certificates at a price that subsequently will be decided.

TEAR SHEET

Slang for individual stock comments published by Standard & Poor's. Term arises because S&P publishes stock reports in a loose-leaf binder. Many brokers, in response to customer requests, tear these sheets from the binder and send them to customers.

TECHNICAL ANALYSIS

A method of predicting stock price movements over a short term—generally, four to six weeks. The prediction is based on current stock price trends and relationship of the present trend to prior trends, and it presumes trading volume will corroborate the trend. Technical analysts use charts of price movement to predict future price movements.

Technical analysis is an endeavor to predict investor psychology; as such, it has all the shortcomings of statistical sciences, such as sociology, economics, and statistics.

TECHNICAL SIGN

A movement in the price of a security which, if accompanied by normal volume of trading, indicates a short-term trend in the price.

TELEPHONE BOOTHS

Exchange and industry term for the communication facilities maintained by member firms In practice, the booths are located on exchange floors. They permit the firm and its employees to receive orders to buy or sell securities, to return the details of executed orders, and to retain records of unexecuted orders. Also, incoming orders may be routed for possible execution to the firm's employees (floor brokers) or to other members ($2 brokers or specialists).

TEMPORARY SPECIALIST

An exchange member appointed temporarily to take over the duties of a specialist for a limited time. The temporary specialist has the same obligations and financial responsibilities as the regular specialist.

TENANT

In the securities industry, a part owner of a security. Accounts with tenants are called joint accounts and are variously designated on the certificates and on the brokerage records of the account.

See also TENANTS BY THE ENTIRETIES; TENANTS IN COMMON; and JOINT TENANTS WITH RIGHT OF SURVIVORSHIP.

TENANTS BY THE ENTIRETIES

A form of joint ownership used in several of the states as the equivalent of joint tenants with right of survivorship.

Often abbreviated ATBE on registered securities and brokerage account records.

TENANTS IN COMMON

A form of joint ownership of property whereby the portion owned by a decedent passes to his or her estate for probate rather than to the possession of the other party, or parties, to the account.

Often abbreviated TIC or TEN COM on registered security certificates and brokerage account records.

TENDER

1 To submit a formal bid for a security. For example, to tender a bid in a Treasury offering of bills, notes, or bonds.
2 To submit a security in response to an offer to buy at a fixed price. For example, when ABC made an offer to buy the security at $29 per share, the client tendered his shares.

TENDER OFFER

Public announcement of intent to acquire, at a fixed price, any or all of the securities of a company. Notice of the announcement first must be filed with the SEC. The acquisition also may be by exchange rather than by a cash offer. Used often in the takeover of another corporation.

TENNESSEE VALLEY AUTHORITY

U.S. government agency, established in 1933, to develop the Tennessee River and the area surrounding it. Both power and development and nonpower activities are financed through the sale of bonds and notes.

As agency securities, they may be bought and sold through government securities dealers.

TEN PERCENT GUIDELINE

Term used in the analysis of municipal debt issues. A rule of thumb: total bonded debt of a municipality should not exceed 10% of the market value of real estate within the municipality.

TERM BOND

Generally, a longer-term bond with a single maturity date. The expression does not exclude the possibility of an early call or the application of a sinking fund.

In the municipal securities industry, the expression is used of longer-term maturities, in opposition to shorter-term maturities that will be redeemed serially.

Most corporate and U.S. government bonds are term bonds.

TERM CERTIFICATES

General expression for certificates of deposit with maturities from two to five years. Normally, interest is paid semiannually.

TERM FEDERAL FUNDS

Excess reserves of commercial banks loaned at a negotiated rate of interest for longer periods than the customary overnight basis.

TERM LOAN

Loan made by a commercial bank for a defined period. For example, a loan made for a period of 90 days, or three to five years.

TERM REPO

A repurchase agreement that has a longer life span than the normal overnight agreement.

TESTAMENTARY TRUST

Legal document that empowers a person or an organization to administer assets for the benefit of one or more persons. The document becomes operative upon the death of the person who establishes the trust.

THEORETICAL VALUE

Any evaluation that is based only on mathematical computation and which does not take into account market factors that may affect its worth. Used frequently of rights once a company announces a subscription but before the rights have been distributed to shareholders of record. Accepted computation of theoretical value of a right:

$$\frac{\text{Market price} - \text{subscription price}}{1 + \text{Number of rights required to subscribe to 1 new share}}$$

THIN MARKET
Slang for a lack of liquidity for a security. In effect, there are few buyers and sellers at current price levels.

THIRD MARKET
Commonly used expression for over-the-counter dealers who specialize in the buying and selling of listed securities. Also used of transactions made by or with such dealers.

Third-market transactions in NYSE- and ASE-listed securities are reported on the consolidated tapes of those exchanges.

THIRD-PARTY ACCOUNT
Brokerage account carried and operated in the name of a person other than the owner. For example, Bill Jones carries and manages a brokerage account in his name that is actually the account of his brother-in-law. Such accounts are forbidden by industry regulation.

Do not confuse with power-of-attorney accounts, which are managed by a third party but which are owned and are held in the name of the person who gave such authorization.

THIRD-PARTY CHECK
A check payable to someone other than the current holder. For example, a check payable to Bill Smith and endorsed by him that is now held by Tom Jones. Normally, brokers will not accept such checks, even if endorsed by Tom Jones, in payment for security purchases.

THIRTY-DAY VISIBLE SUPPLY
Calendar of new municipal securities, both negotiated and competitive, that will come to market within the next 30 days. Published each Thursday by the Daily Bond Buyer.

Also called visible supply.

THREE-HANDED DEAL
Slang in municipal security underwriting: the issue will combine serial maturities with two term maturities. Four-handed and five-handed deals expand the number of term issues accordingly.

THRIFT INSTITUTION
Expression, used singly or collectively, to describe a savings bank, a savings and loan association, or a credit union.

Also called thrifts.

THROWAWAY OFFER
A bid or offer that is nominal only and is not intended to give a price at which transactions can be made. Such bids and offers are approximate and must be identified as such.

THUNDERING HERD
Nickname for Merrill Lynch & Co. Used because of the size of the firm and the number of sales personnel it has registered.

TICK
Slang, probably derived from the early ticker tapes, used to designate a transaction. Now more commonly used to designate the numerical relationship of successive prices in the same security.

See also PLUS TICK; DOWNTICK; ZERO-PLUS TICK.

TICKER
Commonly used expression for the mechanism, whether mechanical or electronic, that displays successive security transactions, their prices, and often the volume of the trades.

TICKER SYMBOL
The designation in letters used for individual security issues. Because these designations are previously agreed upon, they can be used to relay orders to buy or sell the specific security and to relay completed transaction information.

TIER
Popular designation of a class or group of securities. The term has no official standing. For example, "We are seeing a lot of activity these days in second, rather than first, tier companies."

TIFFANY LIST
Slang for the issuers of the highest-quality commercial paper.

TIGHT MARKET
General description of an active, highly competitive market characterized by narrow spreads between bid and offer prices.

Also used of the market for an individual security or class of security. For example, "There is a tight market for the five-year Treasury notes with spreads of ⅛ and ¹⁄₁₆ prevailing."

TIME DEPOSIT
Term for a bank deposit in which funds are pledged for a fixed time, usually at a fixed rate of interest. Chief concept: the bank can refuse the early withdrawal of the funds or impose a penalty for such a withdrawal.

Often used as a synonym for a savings account, although the expression time deposit is a broader term.

TIME DRAFT

Industry term for a post-dated instrument that transfers money from a buyer to a seller. Because the instrument is post-dated, the seller will not have the use of the money until the date specified. Used in distinction from a sight draft, which is payable as soon as it is received.

TIMES FIXED CHARGES

Term used by security analysts to describe the coverage of bond interest and, after taxes, of preferred stock dividends provided by the income of a corporation.

Also called times fixed charges earned and fixed charge coverage.

TIME VALUE

Term designating that portion of an option premium over and above the intrinsic value of an in-the-money option. For example, a call at 50 has a premium of 5. If the underlying stock is at 52, the call has an intrinsic value of 2, and the time value is 3.

Also called the net premium. If an option is at- or out-of-the-money, the total premium is the time value, and no adjustment is made for the amount the option is out-of-the-money.

TIP

Slang for a recommendation to buy, sell long, or sell short that is supposedly based on qualified information, often unknown to the investing public. Of itself, the term is neutral; the context will determine if the implication of inside information is given.

TIPPEE

Slang for the recipient of inside information.

TITLE XI BONDS

Reference to a section of the Merchant Marine Act of 1936 and bonds issued under the provisions of the section. Qualifying bonds are backed by the full faith and credit of the U.S. government.

TOEHOLD PURCHASE

Slang for the purchase of less than 5% of the outstanding stock of a company prior to the public disclosure to the SEC that the purchaser owns 5% or more of the shares.

TOMBSTONE

Slang for the newspaper advertisement of a public distribution of securities. The advertisement, which may be made before or after the fact, is basically a public relations event for the underwriting syndicate.

Called a tombstone because the announcement is factual and refers the reader to the prospectus, the offering circular, or the official statement for details of the issue.

TOPPING A BID

Term used if someone makes a bid higher than the then-prevailing bid. In effect, topping a bid means to improve the market.

TOTAL CAPITALIZATION

Redundancy for the capitalization of a corporation (i.e., the aggregate of fixed debt with a maturity of one year or more, the par value of outstanding preferred stock plus the par value of common stock, the paid-in surplus, and the retained earnings).

TOTAL COST

The out-of-pocket cost of a security purchase. It includes the contract purchase price, the commission, if any, and—depending on the context—the accrued interest.

The term should not be confused with basis (i.e., the cost of acquisition that is used to compute profit or loss for tax purposes).

Many investment situations require an adjustment of total cost to find the basis for tax computations. For example, a client purchased a municipal bond at 103 and held it to maturity. His total cost is $1,030 plus accrued interest; his basis is $1,000 because he is required to amortize the $30 premium over the life of the investment.

TOTAL RETURN

Mathematical consideration of yield that factors in both current cash flow from the investment and an ultimate capital gain or loss in terms of invested dollars.

Called yield to maturity on bonds if the current cash flow is reinvested at the same rate.

Most popular usage: an equity investment that sacrifices some current yield—and thus reduces fully taxable income—for an ultimate capital gain that receives preferential tax treatment.

Also called total rate of return.

TOTAL VOLUME

Aggregate number of shares traded not only on the principal exchange but also on other marketplaces. For example, if ABC has trades for 100,000 shares on the ASE, but 25,000 shares trade on the other exchanges and on NASDAQ, the total volume is 125,000 shares.

TO THE BUCK

Slang expression used by traders in the U.S. government securities market. Term designates the offer side of a quote if the bid side is close to the offer and the offer is a round point. For example, the quote is 96-28/32 bid, 97 offered. Traders would quote "28 to the buck." The person who requested the quote would know that it means 96-28/32 bid, 97 offered.

TRADE

1   As noun: a synonym for a transaction. For example; the trade took place at 28-1/2.
2   As verb: used generically to signify any investment action that results in a buy-sell transaction. For example; "We traded it at 54."
    Used specifically to designate the actions of a person whose business involves the buying and selling of securities. For example: "Bill trades securities in the over-the-counter market." In this latter sense, the verb may be used of the principal and his agent.
3   As verb: used to designate the act of frequent buying or selling of securities. For example, "I do not want to trade; I want to invest." To trade is not pejorative, but it implies frequent buying and selling.

TRADE DATE

The calendar day on which a securities transaction occurred. The designation is factual and is readily identifiable. For example, the trade date was September 29.

Do not confuse trade date with settlement date: the date payment and delivery are due; or with dated date: the calendar date from which accrued interest will be computed on new issues of bonds.

TRADER

Term for a person or organization who:
1   Buys and sells securities for personal profit. For example, "Bill is a trader in securities."
2   Completes transactions in securities for an employer. For example, "Mary is a trader for Salomon Brothers."

TRADE THROUGH

Term used if an exchange member executes a transaction on the floor if a more advantageous price is available through the Intermarket Trading System (ITS). Such trades are unethical unless the volume of the trade is such that it is to the customer's advantage to complete the entire transaction on the floor at one price.

TRADING AUTHORIZATION
Industry term for the document whereby the owner of an account gives power of attorney to an employee of a broker-dealer to make buy-sell transactions for the client.

TRADING DIVIDENDS
The act of buying-selling equity securities by a corporation to increase the number of annual dividends subject to the 85% exclusion of dividend income from corporate taxation.

Trading dividends is possible because the IRS requires only a 16-day holding period for a corporate holder to be eligible for the preferential exclusion privilege.

In practice, trading dividends is highly sophisticated because most corporate preferred securities tend to be priced in such a way that both seller and buyer share the advantages of the 85% dividend exclusion for corporate holders.

TRADING ON THE EQUITY
Term describing the issuance of funded debt by a corporation. For example, a corporation with equity of $5 million issues bonds with a face value of $2 million. The corporation is trading on the equity in that the interest on the bonds, as a percent, may be less than the percent return on total capital ($7 million). Thus, the corporation is leveraging its total investment.

Trading on the equity increases the risk of bankruptcy because the fixed-interest charges on debt may exceed the return on total capital.

See also LEVERAGE.

TRADING PAPER
Used as a noun (paper) and an adjective (trading) to designate highly negotiable, short-term certificates of deposits. Concept: trading paper is a highly desirable investment for corporate funds until more attractive investment opportunities arise. And, if none arise, they are safe until they mature.

TRADING PATTERN
Generally, a trading pattern is two parallel lines on a stock-trend chart that enclose all transaction prices for that stock over a certain period. The slope of these lines indicates the general trend of that stock.

TRADING POST
Industry term for specific locations on exchange floors where individual securities are traded. Chief concept: exchange-listed

securities are not traded at random on exchange floors; instead, there is a designated location, and a designated specialist, for the orderly maintenance of the market in listed securities. About 100 stocks are traded at each of the 20 NYSE posts.

TRADING RING
Designated area on the floor of the NYSE where exchange-completed trades in listed bonds must occur. Recently, this area was transferred from the old bond room of the NYSE and now is included in the same trading room as the New York Futures Exchange.

TRADING ROTATION
Procedure used to open trading in the various series of options for individual securities and for the various months in commodity futures contracts. After the rotation is completed, trading in the individual contracts may continue. This differs dramatically from the single execution price for the first trade in other listed securities on exchanges.

TRADING THROUGH THE FUND'S RATE
Term used of a debt security if its yield to maturity is less than the federal fund's rate. The federal fund's rate, which is particularly sensitive to interest-rate changes, is basically a market rate that changes with supply and demand for excess reserves. Trading through the fund's rate often is a leading indicator of a change in Federal Reserve monetary policy.

TRADING TO TOTAL VOLUME
A criterion used to judge the specialist's willingness to provide liquidity and, thus, an orderly succession of prices.

In practice, the specialist's buy-sell activities as a dealer are divided by twice the reported share volume to give the ratio of trading to total volume. Reason for doubling stock volume: the specialist can act only as a buyer or a seller on an individual transaction.

TRADING UNIT
Popular name for a round lot.
See also UNIT OF TRADING.

TRADING VARIATION
Minimum permissible price variation between trades if a subsequent trade does not occur at same price as the previous trade. On stock exchanges, the usual trading variation is ⅛ point. Exception: options with premiums below $3 per share may trade in minimum variations

of $\frac{1}{16}$ point. Corporate and municipal bonds generally trade in variations of $\frac{1}{8}$. Government notes and bonds generally trade in minimum variations of $\frac{1}{32}$, although shorter-term bonds may trade in variations of $\frac{1}{64}$.

TRANSACTION

Used synonymously for a trade (i.e., a completed agreement between a buyer and a seller).

Generally, the terms means that a buyer accepts a risk and the seller removes a risk. In options, in commodities, and in the description of a person who is short, distinguish between opening transaction (one which places the investor at risk) and closing transaction (one which results in a net zero position; i.e., the person is no longer at risk).

TRANSFER AGENT

An institution, which generally is a commercial bank but may be the issuer itself, responsible for the cancellation of certificates that are sold, gifted, or bequeathed and the reissuance of new certificates to the new owner. The transfer is effected by cancellation of the old certificate and the issuance of new certificates in the name of the new owner.

TRANSFER AND SHIP

Instruction by the owner of a security to a brokerage firm holding the security to have it registered in his name and to send it to his address on the broker's new account form. Such instruction may be given at the purchase, or at any future time, if the security is fully paid. Separate instructions are required if the owner wishes the security registered in the name of another person. For example, to give the security to another person.

TRANSFER TAX

A tax levied by the state of Florida on transactions in equity securities that are actually executed within that state, regardless of the residence of buyer or seller.

TREASURIES

General name for all negotiable debt securities of the U.S. government.

TREASURY BILL

General name for short-term debt obligations of the U.S. government that (1) will mature within one year and that (2) are issued at a discount from their face value.

Minimum denomination: $10,000 plus variations of $5,000. Format: book-entry only. Primary market price determination: competitive auction, unless the amount is less than $500,000. Secondary market: extremely liquid, active market featuring same-day or next-day settlement.

Many foreign governments issue similar short-term debt securities.

Special tax considerations apply if T-bills are sold before maturity and the sale price exceeds the ratable value based on a straight-line accretion from purchase price to face value.

TREASURY BILL AUCTION

An auction, conducted weekly by the U.S. Treasury, in which persons desiring to purchase more than $500,000 of short-term government obligations may enter competitive bids at a discount from the face value.

Non-competitive bidders ($500,000 or less) are awarded bills at the average discount paid by competitive bidders.

See also TREASURY BILL.

TREASURY BOND

Longer-term debt security of the U.S. government. Maturity: more than 10 years from issue date. Minimum denomination: $1,000 and multiples thereof. Format: bearer, registered, or book-entry. Interest: paid semiannually. Primary market price determination: by an auction unless tender is for $1 million or less. Secondary market: active, highly liquid market priced in points and 32ds with same-day or next-day settlement available.

Treasury bonds frequently are callable five years before term maturity.

TREASURY CERTIFICATES

Short-term U.S. government debt securities formerly issued with maturities of six months to one year. The securities no longer are issued publicly, although they occasionally are issued to facilitate transfers from the Federal Reserve to banks.

Also called certificates of indebtedness.

TREASURY STOCK

Stock, formerly outstanding, reacquired by the issuing corporation, usually by repurchase. Such stock may subsequently be resold, or it may be retired (i.e., by stockholder vote it is removed from the number of authorized shares). The number of shares of stock in the treasury normally is designated on the balance sheet of the corporation. While held in the treasury, such stock receives no dividends, either cash or stock, and has no voting privilege.

TREND

An up or down movement in the market price of a security, or for the market in general, over an extended time period. Generally, a consistent movement for six or more months, or longer, is called a primary trend.

Movements in the opposite direction to the primary trend are called secondary trends.

The term also is used of the direction, up or down, of yields on classes of fixed-income securities.

TRENDLINE

A straight line drawn to connect top or bottom prices in an established price trend of a security. Generally, a straight line is used beneath prices if the trend is upward; above the prices, if the trend is downward.

Technical analysts use the trendline to estimate when a trend reversal has occurred. For example, if the general trend has been consistently downward from $40 to $30 per share, the trendline will connect the $40 with the $30 price, and a substantial movement of the price above $30 is considered a sign of a trend reversal.

TRIANGLE

Term of technical analysts to describe the historical pattern of stock price movements that, in general, could be described as a triangle— with the base at left and the apex at right when looking at a chart of the stock's price movements. For example, a stock went from $50 to $30, up to $45, down to $35, and now to $40 per share.

Also called triangle formation or, depending on the degree of geometric symmetry of the pattern, a flag, coil, wedge, or pennant.

TRIPLE EXEMPTION

Term used to describe a municipal bond providing interest income to a holder that is exempt from federal, state, and local taxation.

As a general rule, interest income from bonds issued within the state in which the holder-taxpayer is a resident has a triple exemption.

The term triple tax exempt, as a feature for any holder, regardless of the state of residence, normally is reserved for municipal bonds issued by the Commonwealth of Puerto Rico or by the District of Columbia because this feature is provided in the federal tax law.

TRUST

As noun: a legal instrument whereby a person or organization administers assets and their use for the benefit of one or more designated persons. For example, John Jones placed the assets in trust, to be administered by the First National Bank, for the benefit of his wife.

TRUSTEE

The person, or organization, administering a trust in accord with the specific instructions of the person who established the trust. Legal advice is needed for the establishment of a trust, and securities industry personnel dealing with a trustee should have evidence of the trust, its legality, and the restrictions on the activities of the trustee.

TRUST INDENTURE ACT OF 1939

Federal legislation that requires nonexempt issues of corporate debt securities with a face amount of $1 million or more to be issued under an indenture (deed of trust).

The indenture must specify the amount of debt, date of maturity, interest rate, and method of disbursement; also it must appoint a trustee, usually a bank, to safeguard the interests of bondholders. Generally, the registration statement and prospectus of corporate debt issues highlight main points of the trust indenture for the bondholder.

TRUTH-IN-LENDING LAW

Federal law that requires a lender to specify the terms of the loan and its conditions to the borrower. SEC Rule 10b-16 instructs broker-dealers how they are to implement the provisions of the law.

TURKEY

Slang: a poor and unsuccessful performance. Used of the security that loses money for investors or of an offering of securities that loses money for the underwriters.

TURNAROUND

1   Of a corporation: a change for the better in the company's financial affairs.
2   Of a security: a change from a declining price trend to an upward price trend.
3   Of an investor's strategies: a change from one position to another, especially if it is marked by short-term trading.

The expression day trading is more commonly used, although the word does not exclude a change of investment objectives. For example, "Bill did a turnaround from income to growth as an investment objective."

TWENTY-DAY PERIOD

Industry term for the statutory waiting period between the filing of a registration statement with the SEC and the normal issuance of an effective date—the date on which a public sale may be made. The 20 days may be extended by the SEC if it requires more time for a full examination of the registration statement; or, upon request, it may shorten the 20-day period.

Often called the cooling, or cooling-off, period.

TWENTY-FIVE PERCENT RULE

Rule-of-thumb measurement in municipal bond analysis. In general, a municipality's bonded debt should not exceed 25% of its annual budget.

TWENTY-PERCENT CUSHION RULE

Rule-of-thumb measurement in the analysis of municipal revenue bonds. In general, the revenue of a facility built with bonds should exceed by 20% the budget for operations and maintenance and debt service. Reason: the 20% is a cushion for unexpected expenses.

TWISTING

Alternate name for churning, especially if it involves the persuasion of a customer to change from one mutual fund to another with an additional sales charge.

Also called switching.

TWO-DOLLAR BROKER

Jargon for an exchange member who, acting as a broker's broker, transacts orders for member firms when their regular brokers are too busy, are ill, or are on vacation. Term arises from formerly charged fee of $2 per 100 shares in the transaction. Fee is now negotiable.

TWOFER

Slang for one long call at a lower exercise price and two short calls at a higher exercise price, all having the same expiration date. Equivalent, in terms of risk, to a two-for-one ratio write.

See also RATIO WRITE.

200-DAY MOVING AVERAGE

A popular technical indicator that moderates, over time, wide market swings on a daily, weekly, or monthly basis. Concept: instead of charting daily, or even weekly, price movements, chart an average of the previous 200 days. The chart is made daily; each day, the average is based on today's price plus the prior 199 days. Thus, each day the price farthest away is so eliminated that only 200 prices are averaged.

Proponents contend that this method gives a better indication of trend. Other technicians follow 20- , 30- , 50- , and 100-day moving averages.

TWO-SIDED MARKET

Term used to signify a market maker's willingness to provide both a firm bid and asked price for the accepted round-lot in a security. Typical in the markets for over-the-counter stocks and government securities.

The municipal bond secondary market is usually a one-sided market—the offer price only—and persons who wish to sell must ask for a bid price.

Often called a two-way market.

TYPE OF OPTION

Generic term for any option privilege. For example, by type, options are puts and calls. Specifically, puts are a class of option (i.e., the right to sell at a fixed price), calls are a second class of option (i.e., the right to buy at a fixed price).

U

U

Used lowercase in the newspaper report of stock transactions. It signifies that the intraday high is a new high for the last 52 weeks. For example, u67 means that the trade at $67 per share is the new high. Next day, the new high will replace the old high in the 52-week range. For example, 65 43 becomes 67 43.

U-4

A uniform application form used by industry regulators to register security agents, representatives, and principals. When completed, the form provides the exchanges, the NASD, and the states with information about the educational, legal, and business and personal history of applicants for registration.

See also U-5.

U-5

A uniform notification document whereby securities industry employers can notify the exchanges, the NASD, and the states to terminate the registration of agents, representatives, and principals no longer associated with them.

UNCOVERED OPTION

Term describes the status of an opening sale of an option if the writer does not have a corresponding position in the underlying stock (long position in the case of a short call; short position in the case of a short put) or the client does not have a long option that protects the short position.

Also known as a naked option.

UNDERBANKED

Industry slang for a proposed underwriting if the investment banker is finding it difficult to attract other members into the syndicate to share the risk of the underwriting.

UNDERBOOKED

Industry slang for a proposed underwriting for which there is limited interest on the part of the investing public, as shown by the small indications of interest received by the members of the syndicate.

UNDERCUTTING AN OFFERING

Attempting to sell securities at a price that is lower than the best prevailing offer.

UNDERLYING DEBT

Used in municipal finance to describe the liabilities of lower municipalities for which the residents of a higher municipality have some responsibilities. For example, county residents have some liability for the general obligations of cities and towns within their county's jurisdiction. The county can be said to have underlying debt.

UNDERLYING SECURITY

1 The stock subject to purchase (a call) or to sale (a put) if the holder of an option chooses to exercise the option.
2 The common stock that a corporation must deliver to a person who chooses to exercise a stock option, to subscribe to a rights offering, to exercise a warrant, or to convert a security that is convertible.

UNDERVALUED

A judgment about the current market price of a security. The judgment states, in effect, that current corporate earnings, or market trends, or industry price-earnings ratios should justify a higher price for the security.

UNDERWRITE

General term for the process whereby investment bankers purchase a new issue of securities from the issuer and resell the security to the investing public. The term implies that the investment banker is at risk between the time of purchase and resale.

The term also is used more loosely of some security distributions where the investment banker acts as the agent of the issuer and has no financial risk. For example, a best-efforts underwriting.

UNDERWRITER

General industry term for a person who facilitates the public sale of securities by an issuer.
1 Used as a synonym for an investment banker.
2 Used of the sponsor, also called the wholesaler, of investment
   company securities.
Specifically, an underwriter is any person who purchases securities from an issuer for purposes of resale.

UNDERWRITING AGREEMENT

The contract between an underwriting syndicate and the issuer, or seller, of a security. The agreement sets forth the terms of the issue, the amount of money guaranteed, the fixed public offering price, and the details of final settlement of the account.

Also called the purchase agreement.

UNDERWRITING GROUP

The investment bankers who make a contractual agreement among themselves and with the issuer of securities to buy and distribute a block of securities.

Used generically of the group before the final agreements are signed, or of groups that do not win a competitive bid.

Also called a syndicate.

UNDERWRITING RECAPTURE

Used of a broker-dealer who is a member of a syndicate or selling group and who, in turn, sells part of the underwriting to an institutional portfolio that it manages or controls. If the broker-dealer passes the securities along to the institution at its cost, the institution, in effect, recaptures the underwriting compensation because it acquires the securities below the public offering price. This practice violates NASD rules prohibiting rebates to nonmembers.

UNDERWRITING SPREAD

The dollar difference, often stated in points per share or bond, between the price paid to the issuer by the syndicate and the price at which the securities are offered to the public. For example, if a syndicate buys shares from the issuer at $19 and sells the shares to the public at $20, the underwriting spread is $1.

UNENCUMBERED

Term used of an asset that is fully owned and has no lien or other creditor claim against it. Securities in a client's cash account are unencumbered. So also is an asset that was previously used as collateral but the outstanding debt has been paid in full. The asset is now unencumbered.

UNIFIED CREDIT

Term used to describe the once-in-a-lifetime credit that may be applied against an individual's gift or estate taxes. At present, the unified credit is rising annually. Tax advice is needed.

UNIFORM COMMERCIAL CODE

A nationwide statute designed to standardize commercial customs, usages, and practices. There are local modifications, some exceptions in transactions among the members of certain trade associations, and it has not been adopted by the state of Louisiana.

UNIFORM GIFT TO MINORS ACT

Law, standard in form in all states, whereby someone of legal age can serve as a custodian for a minor's assets. The law provides for a simplified procedure without extensive paperwork or cost.

Also used in the securities industry as a qualifier to describe securities purchased or sold under the provisions of this law, or accounts conducted for such purposes. For example, "I opened a UGMA account for my son."

UNIFORM PRACTICE CODE

Rules and procedures established by the National Association of Securities Dealers (NASD) to regulate the business details of executing, clearing, and settling over-the-counter transactions in nonexempt securities. For example, the time of settlement, good delivery, ex-dates, and other transactional details.

Within the 13 districts of the NASD, the Uniform Practice Committees settle disputes at the local level and interpret the Uniform Practice Code.

UNIFORM SECURITIES AGENT STATE LAW EXAMINATION

At the present time, approximately 20 states require a specific examination of persons who wish to become registered representatives or principals as securities agents in those states. The exam (designated Series 63 by the NASD, which administers it) can be taken on the PLATO system provided by the Control Data Corporation or at local testing centers.

States that do not require the USASLE exam accept the Series 7 General Securities Representative Examination as their qualification for registration.

UNISSUED STOCK

Term describing that portion of a corporation's authorized common or preferred shares that has never been exchanged for money, goods, or services. The term does not include treasury shares.

The board of directors may sell unissued shares. One exception: if a corporation has outstanding stock options, convertibles, rights, or warrants, the appropriate number of unissued shares needed to satisfy their exercise must be set aside (i.e., escrowed) until these options expire.

UNIT

1 Term used to describe securities sold as a "package." For example, a company offers two common shares and one convertible preferred share as a unit.

    Bonds and warrants are frequent unit offerings.
2 Term describing a group of exchange specialists who are responsible for maintaining a fair and orderly market in a specific number of securities.

    Exchange rules require that specialist units maintain a common set of business records, although the form of business enterprise (corporation, partnership, association) is not predetermined.

UNITED STATES GOVERNMENT SECURITIES

Generic name for the nonnegotiable and the negotiable securities of the United States. Series EE and HH bonds are nonnegotiable and may only be redeemed by the U.S. government Treasury bills, notes, and bonds are negotiable and enjoy an active secondary market.

The U.S. government also issues certificates of indebtedness for interbank and interagency transfers of funds. These certificates are not publicly issued.

UNIT INVESTMENT TRUST

A trust, registered under the Investment Company Act of 1940, that may take two forms:
1   A fixed trust: the most popular form. Such trusts assemble a portfolio of securities. Units are sold which represent an undivided interest in the underlying portfolio. Unit holders receive a proportional share of net income and, as underlying securities are sold or mature, a return of principal.
2   A participating trust: the legal form for contractual-type mutual fund agreements. The unit holder receives benefits both from the trust and the underlying mutual fund.
All unit investment trusts are redeemable securities.

UNIT OF TRADING

Commonly accepted minimum quantity for which transaction contracts are made in exchange marketplaces. Term also is used of over-the-counter quotes and markets. Also called a round-lot.
Units of trading:
1   Stocks: 100 shares, although smaller units often are set.
2   Corporate bonds: 250 bonds is typical. Exchange transactions: 1 bond.
3   Municipals: 25 bonds is typical.
4   Governments and agencies: 50 bonds is typical.
Transactions less than the unit of trading are called odd-lots.
See also DIFFERENTIAL.

UNLISTED SECURITY

Any security that has not been admitted to trading privileges on an exchange.

In general, equity securities that have not been qualified for trading on an exchange are called over-the-counter securities.

Also called unlisted stocks or unlisted bonds.

UNLISTED TRADING

With the permission of the SEC, a security may be traded on an exchange without an application by the corporation for listing.

UNSECURED DEBT

A bond that has no specific collateral backing. The good faith and credit rating of the issuer back the bond.

Such bonds are typically called debentures, although shorter-term debt issues often are called commercial paper or notes.

UNWIND A TRADE
1 To reverse a previously established transaction: a purchase is unwound by a sale; a short sale by a short cover.
2 To cover a transaction made in error. For example, a broker-dealer makes a sale but the client actually entered an order to buy. The broker-dealer is short the security sold—this will have to be unwound to rectify the situation. The client's buy order is unexecuted. This, too, will have to be rectified.

UP-AND-OUT OPTION
A form of conventional over-the-counter put option. The option holder has the privilege of selling a fixed number of shares at a fixed price for a fixed time. However, if the underlying shares rise above a predetermined price, the option is cancelled. Thus, if the price goes up, the option is out.

UPSTAIRS MARKET
Industry term for the in-house trading facilities of a broker-dealer, whereby transactions for listed securities are completed within the broker-dealer's firm and are not transmitted to the exchange floor. For example, a broker-dealer gets an order to sell 5,000 XYZ. The broker-dealer, rather than send the order to the exchange floor, finds a mutual fund that wants to buy 5,000 XYZ at a negotiated price.

UPTREND
A generally upward movement in the price of a security.
See also TRENDLINE.

UR
Acronym for under review. Often used on corporate and municipal calendars if one or more of the bond rating services continues to have the issue under review and has not yet assigned a bond rating.

V

VALUE CHANGE
Used only of groups of securities to indicate price changes of the individual securities weighted to represent the number of shares outstanding. For example, security A has 1 million shares outstanding

and it goes up $1 per share; the same day, security B, which has 2 million shares outstanding, goes down 50 cents. Change up: + 1 million. Change down: − 1 million. The net value change of the two securities was zero.

Measurements of value change for a group of securities weighted to represent outstanding shares are called indices.

VALUE DATE

Used synonymously with settlement date for Eurodollar and foreign currency transactions.

Generally, value date is the second business day after the trade date on spot transactions.

On forward trades, it is a negotiated date in the future.

VARIABLE ANNUITY

A life insurance investment contract, purchased either lump-sum or by installments, that features an investment in an underlying portfolio of debt and equity securities. Because these securities are in a separate account and are not guaranteed from principal loss by the insurance company, their value and the income they derive may vary. Holders who annuitize their contracts may select different payout plans, but the amount paid out will vary with the value of the separate account.

VARIABLE RATE MORTGAGE

A 20- to 30-year amortizing loan made on real estate. The interest rate is not fixed. Instead, the rate is adjusted every six months according to a prestated interest rate norm. As a general rule, the rate may not vary more than ½% in any year, nor more than 2-½% over the life of the mortgage. Because the mortgage is amortizing, the monthly payments made by the mortgagee will vary with the changes in the interest rate.

VARIABLE RATIO WRITING

An option writing technique whereby a holder of the underlying shares writes more calls than he has round lots to cover the short options. For example, a person with 3 round lots of ABC writes 6 calls. He has a 2-for-1 ratio write. The strategy accepts a middling risk position between that of the naked call writer and the covered call writer.

More commonly used term: ratio write.

VAULT CASH

Cash on hand in the vault of a bank. Concept: member banks of the Federal Reserve System are required to maintain a statutory reserve (i.e., a specified percentage of time and demand deposits that they have accepted). This statutory reserve may take two forms: (1) money on deposit with the Federal Reserve and (2) cash in the vault of the bank. The latter is called vault cash.

Neither 1 nor 2 is subject to capital risk; hence, they are truly a reserve against the deposits made by the clients of the bank.

VENTURE CAPITAL

Industry term for an investment in a new, untried business venture with all of the financial risks inherent in such an enterprise.

Companies specializing in such investments are called venture capital companies and, as part of their compensation for such investments, usually demand a large portion of the equity ownership. Thus, if the risky enterprise prospers, they will be richly rewarded.

VERTICAL LINE CHARTING

Chart of a stock's price movement that uses a vertical line to represent the high and the low, with a horizontal line to represent the closing price. Line may be used of daily, weekly, monthly, or average prices over a period. As the information is charted, a trend may appear that will give indication of appropriate timing for purchase or sale of the security.

The completed chart also is called a bar chart.

VERTICAL SPREAD

An option strategy whereby a client has long and short options of the same class, with the same expiration month, but with different strike prices. For example, long a July 60 put and short a July 50 put.

Also called a price, or money, spread.

See also BULL SPREAD and BEAR SPREAD (to clarify strategy).

V FORMATION

Description of a vertical line chart if the stock price pattern has the configuration of the letter V (bullish), or an inverted V (bearish).

Also called V bottom or V top.

VI

Used lowercase in the stock or bond tables in the newspaper to designate that the corporation is undergoing reorganization under the bankruptcy laws of the United States.

VOIDABLE

A transaction that can be annulled at a later date because, at the time of the transaction, it did not conform to the law. For example, a contract made by a minor.

See also RESCIND.

VOLATILE

Description of a stock, or a bond, or a market in general, whose price is subject to wide, rapid fluctuations.

VOLATILITY

Relative measure of a security's price movement during a specific time.

See also VOLATILITY RATIO.

VOLATILITY RATIO

Measurement of relative price movement of a security during a specific time. Normal measurement: subtract the low for the year from the high for the year. Divide the remainder by the low for the year to obtain the percentage of volatility for the year. For example, the yearly range for a stock is 50 high, 30 low. The difference is 20 points. Divide 20 by 30 to get a volatility ratio of 2 to 3, or 66%.

VOLUME

The number of shares or bonds traded during a specific time. For example, the daily volume or the weekly volume.

Normally, volume figures are given for the principal marketplace for the security, although a wider base of measurement can be used.

Also used of total stock or bond trading. For example, 12 million shares were traded yesterday on the ASE.

VOLUME DELETED

Announcement on the consolidated tape that only symbols and prices will be given, unless the transaction is for 5,000 or more shares. Normally done when the tape is two or more minutes late in its reporting of securities transactions.

VOLUNTARY ACCUMULATION PLAN

Name for an informal and flexible program whereby a mutual fund owner, at various times and with varying amounts of money, may continue to purchase shares of the fund.

Also called an open account.

VOLUNTARY ASSOCIATION

A membership organization that is not incorporated. However, there is continuing existence of the business enterprise. Membership in the organization is similar to membership in a partnership in that there is unlimited financial responsibility in the case of insolvency of the organization. For example, the NYSE was a voluntary association until 1971 when it became a not-for-profit corporation.

VOLUNTARY UNDERWRITER

Legal designation of an individual, partnership, or corporation that purchases a security from the issuer or an affiliated person and offers the security for public sale under an effective registration statement.

Antonym: statutory underwriter (i.e., a person who inadvertantly becomes an underwriter because he purchases securities that are not registered and resells them publicly).

VOTING TRUST CERTIFICATE

A registered certificate, issued by a bank under a trust agreement, to evidence the delivery of common shares into a voting trust. The certificate can be sold or transferred and has all the rights of ownership except the right to vote. This right is retained by the trust.

VTCs often arise when a company is in financial difficulties, or in proxy contests, and wants to so concentrate voting power that rapid changes in company management can be made as needed. Normally, voting trusts have a defined lifetime (e.g., five or seven years).

W

WASHINGTON METROPOLITAN AREA TRANSIT AUTHORITY

A government-assisted municipal agency created by Maryland, Virginia, and the District of Columbia to finance and operate mass transit facilities in the metropolitan District of Columbia. There is a federal guarantee on the bonds.

Interest income is subject to federal taxation and also may be subject to state and local taxation.

WASH SALE

1　A sale resulting in a disallowed capital loss because the seller purchased the same, or a substantially identical, security within 30 days prior to or 30 days after the sale at a loss. Tax advice is needed.
2　Popular name of the manipulative practice of buying and selling

similar amounts of a security—at the same price through the same broker-dealer without a true change of beneficial ownership—to give the impression of trading activity.

See also PAINTING THE TAPE.

WATCH LIST

Industry term for a security that is under surveillance to avoid illegal or unethical practices. A security may be on the watch list because of wide swings in price, a sudden flurry of buying or selling, or because a broker-dealer is about to underwrite the security and employee transactions in that security are not allowed. A watch list may be initiated by a broker-dealer or by an exchange or other self-regulating organization.

WATERED STOCK

Term for the practice of issuing additional shares of stock to represent the same amount of capital. For example, shares that are donated to corporate officers without an offsetting inflow of cash to the corporation's balance sheet.

Also called diluting the shares.

WEDGE

Alternate designation of the chart pattern called a coil, pennant, or triangle.

Also called a wedge formation.

See also TRIANGLE.

WESTERN ACCOUNT

Term describing a corporate underwriting agreement in which syndicate members sign a contract with the issuer as a group but limit their individual liability to the specific quantity of shares or bonds that they individually underwrite.

In practice, the term often is used of corporate underwritings, although it is infrequently used of municipal underwritings that have similar responsibility features.

Also caled a divided account.

See also EASTERN ACCOUNT.

W FORMATION

Term used to describe the appearance of the chart pattern of a security's price movement if, in general, it is similar to the letter w, either right-side up, or upside down.

See also DOUBLE BOTTOM and DOUBLE TOP.

WHEN DISTRIBUTED

Transactions made on the proviso that the contract is valid when, as, and if the underlying securities are distributed. For example, a company has proposed to distribute shares in a subsidiary, or shares of another corporation, subject to stockholder approval. Shares that may be distributed often will begin trading on a when-distributed basis.

See also WHEN ISSUED.

WHEN ISSUED

A transaction that establishes the contract price but not the settlement date. The settlement date will be determined when the securities are available.

Frequently used in primary transactions for corporate and municipal bonds, often used for new issues of stocks. Full term: when, as, and if issued.

When issued transactions also take place in government securities between the auction date and the preestablished settlement date.

See also WHEN DISTRIBUTED.

WHIPSAW

Slang for the financial effect of a rapid upward price movement followed by a rapid downward price movement if a person is exposed to risk on both the up and down sides.

Usually used as a past participle: whipsawed. For example, "Writers of short straddles in ABC were whipsawed as the price shot up then dropped like a rock."

WHITE KNIGHT

Slang for a person or corporation who saves a corporation from an unfriendly takeover by, in turn, taking over the corporation.

WHITE'S RATING

A system of classifying municipal bonds developed by White's Tax-Exempt Bond Rating Service. The system is based on municipal trading markets, rather than on the credit rating of the underlying issuer. The classification, available on a subscription basis, endeavors to give an insight into appropriate yields for specific municipal securities.

WHOLE LOAN

Jargon for an unpooled, individual residential mortgage that is not part of a mortgage pool used to back a pass-through or a participation certificate.

WHOLESALER
1 Used as a synonym for the underwriter-sponsor of a mutual fund.
2 A broker-dealer who is eligible for discounts and selling concessions in his transactions with other broker-dealers.

WHOOPS
Nickname for securities of the Washington Public Power Supply System (WPPS). Term is important because of the large dollar volume of such securities (over $7 billion of 1982), the controversy over nuclear power, and a partial U.S. government guarantee of portions of this issue.

WIDE OPEN
Industry slang for an upcoming underwriting that has shares or bonds available for additional syndication because the present members of the syndicate have not subscribed fully to the available securities. The situation may exist because there are too few participants in the syndicate or because a lack of indications of interest has caused some prior participants to withdraw from the account.
See also UNDERBANKED.

WIDGET
1 The plastic tube used to hold messages and other information that are transported from place to place on the NYSE floor by its pneumatic tube system.
2 Term, used jocularly, of an item manufactured by a hypothetical corporation. For example, "Today, I want to talk about XYZ Corporation. Let's say that they make widgets. . . ."

WINDFALL
Used in the financial sense to describe a sudden and unexpected gain. For example, the sudden rise in world oil prices caused a windfall for well owners. Also used as an adjective. For example, Congress is proposing a windfall profit tax.

WINDOW
A time within which a person may do an action without additional cost or other adverse effects. For example, by signing a letter of intent, a mutual fund purchaser has a 13-month window within which to purchase a sufficient dollar amount of the fund to achieve the reduced sales charge for larger purchases.

WINDOW DRESSING
Pejorative term for an activity done for show and which produces little lasting effect. Used in the securities industry of activities that

are showy and temporary. For example, "The fund sold most of its speculative securities just in time to put in a window dressing of blue chips for its annual report."

WINDOW SETTLEMENT
Term used to describe the physical delivery against settlement of securities with the contra broker of the trade.

Term is descriptive: most broker-dealers have a specific location, usually a window, at which selling brokers can deliver securities and receive payment by check for the delivery.

In practice, window settlement is uncommon; most security transactions are cleared through continuous net settlement by a recognized depository. For example, at SIAC, the Securities Industry Association Clearing (Corporation) or through the facilities of the Depository Trust Company.

WIRE HOUSE
1   Used factually of an exchange member firm that maintains a communication network linking its own branch offices, or its own offices and those of other nonclearing members.
2   Used descriptively of any large member firm. Also used collectively. For example, "Most of the wire houses are competing for the few retail clients that remain."

WIRE ROOM
An operating area or function within a broker-dealer that is responsible for the transmission of customer orders, by changing them into floor tickets, so the orders may be executed in the appropriate marketplace.

Also called the Order Room, or, more popularly, Wire and Order.

WITHHOLDING
1   Action by a disbursing agent whereby a statutory portion of dividends and interest paid by a domestic corporation to holders who are nonresident aliens is withheld in payment of U.S. taxes. Under present tax laws, the practice will apply to all distribution to U.S. citizens and resident aliens in July 1983.
2   Action by a broker-dealer whereby portions of the securities in an offering are sold to employees and members of their immediate family. The Rules of Fair Practice prohibit such actions if a hot issue is involved.
See also FREERIDING.

WITHHOLDING TAX AT THE SOURCE

Requirement of domestic issuers to withhold a portion of dividends and interest from nonresident aliens and foreign corporations in payment for the U.S. tax on these distributions. The percentage to be withheld is generally 30%, but the percentage often is reduced, or eliminated, depending on the tax treaty in effect between the United States and the alien's country of domicile.

WITH OR WITHOUT

Instruction on an odd-lot limit order. Meaning: use an effective sale in the round-lot market or the quote for the stock, whichever comes first, to make this transaction. May be used for odd-lot buy or sell limit orders. The price to the customer must conform to his limit.

Not used of odd-lot market orders. Here, the customer may use buy on offer, or sell on bid, if he does not want to wait for an effective sale.

WITHOUT AN OFFER

Expression often used to complete a one-sided quote. For example, a dealer may quote a security as 15 bid without an offer. Meaning: the dealer is willing to buy the security at 15, but the dealer is unwilling to sell—either because he does not have the security or is unwilling to sell short.

WITH RIGHT OF SURVIVORSHIP

A form of joint account that permits assets in the account to pass to the ownership of the remaining party if 1 party dies. Often abbreviated JTWROS, or W/R/O/S.

See also JOINT TENANTS WITH RIGHT OF SURVIVORSHIP.

WOODEN TICKET

Slang for the unethical practice of confirming the execution of an order to a customer without actually doing so. The practice is deceptive and, in effect, the broker-dealer is relying on a change to his advantage in the market price so the actual transaction, when later made, will provide the broker-dealer with a larger profit.

WOR

Acronym for we offer retail: that is, at a net price to the buyer because all transaction costs are borne by the seller.

WORKING CAPITAL

General term for the remainder obtained if current liabilities are subtracted from current assets of a corporation.

Also called net working capital.
See also NET CURRENT ASSETS.

WORKING CONTROL

The ability to dictate corporate policy by a person, or persons, who have less than 50% ownership of a corporation. Persons with more than 50% ownership always have control of a company. In practice, because of the dispersion of shares among many holders, minority holders often may be able to effectively control the corporation.

WORKOUT MARKET

A range of prices within which a broker-dealer feels that a transaction may be made. For example, a client wants to sell a block of stock. He asks a broker-dealer for an approximation of the sale price. The response: "I feel that it is 20 to 22, workout." The broker-dealer's estimation is that the block can be sold somewhere between $20 and $22 per share.

WRAPAROUND ANNUITY

An annuity contract that provides a tax shelter from dividends, interest, and capital appreciation, but in which the subscriber designates the specific securities upon which the security will be funded. The insurance company assumes no principal risk until such time as the contract is annuitized.

Also called an investment annuity.

WRAPAROUND MORTGAGE

A mortgage loan built around two components: an assumable mortgage from the previous seller and a new loan from the carrying bank. The recipient of the wraparound mortgage has a lower average rate of interest than would be available if the entire mortgage amount were covered by one interest rate.

WRINKLE

Slang: a feature of a security that may be advantageous to the holder. For example, a company offers to exchange outstanding 11% bonds with new 10% bonds with this wrinkle: the holder may tender the bonds at par five years from the day of the exchange. Obviously, this feature would be profitable to the holder if, five years from now, interest rates were substantially in excess of 10%. He could redeem at par and reinvest at higher interest rates. Meanwhile, the company has saved 1% of its interest costs each year.

WRITE OUT

Exchange floor slang if a specialist decides, within exchange rules, to trade with an order that is on his book. Rule: specialist must summon broker who entered order. This broker writes the order, with the specialist as other side of the trade, and thus broker earns the commission for the completed trade. Broker's client will, in turn, trade with the specialist using normal industry channels to complete transaction. There is no additional charge to client for this procedure.

WRITER

Common term for the person who sells an option contract, thereby obligating himself to the performance agreed upon in the contract: to sell (if a call was written), to buy (if a put was written).

WT

Used on the exchange tape and in other industry literature as an abbreviation for a warrant.

See also SUBSCRIPTION WARRANT.

X

X

1 Used in the newspaper tables to designate a security that is trading exdividend.
2 Used on the Quotron System to differentiate the number of shares bid and offered. For example, 10 × 11 signifies that 1,000 shares are bid at the prevailing quote and 1,100 shares are offered.

XCH

Used of a transaction between broker-dealers that will be completed outside the regular clearing facilities. The term means: ex-clearing house.

XD

Abbreviation for exdividend (i.e., the buyer of the security will not receive the next payable dividend).

Y

YANKEE BOND
Industry slang for a bond of a foreign issuer that is denominated in dollars and that has been registered for sale in the United States.

YELLOW SHEETS
A listing, published each business day by the National Quotation Bureau, of unlisted corporate bonds and their market makers. So called for the color of the paper on which the listing is made.

YEN BOND
A bond, originally issued outside the United States, that is denominated in Japanese yen. Such bonds are not registered for sale in the United States, although after the bond is "seasoned" (traded for a reasonable period outside the United States) it may become eligible for trading here.

YIELD
General term for the percentage return on a security investment. Although the context often will qualify the term, investors should be careful to use the term with a qualifier so the precise meaning is clear. For example, nominal (coupon) yield, current yield, yield to maturity, or yield to average life, and so on.

Often called rate of return.

See also DIVIDEND.

YIELD ADVANTAGE
Term describing the difference, if any, between current yield on a convertible security and current yield on the underlying common stock. For example, a convertible preferred has a current yield of 7% and the current yield on the common stock is 4-½%. The yield advantage is 2-½%.

Added insight: the percentage premium over conversion parity paid on the convertible divided by the yield advantage will give the number of years to repay the premium paid for the convertible. For example, a premium of 8% over parity will be repaid in 4 years if the yield advantage is 2%.

YIELD CURVE
General term for the graph depicting yields on the y-axis, and time to maturity on the x-axis, for fixed-income securities of the same class (e.g., corporates, utilities, governments, municipalities, and so on).

Yield curves may be ascending (long-term bonds yield more than short-term); descending (short-term bonds yield more than long-term bonds); or flat (both yield approximately the same).

A knowledge of the configuration of the yield curve and its trend is essential to intelligent fixed-income investing.

YIELD EQUIVALENCE

Term used in the completion of GNMA contracts: spot, forward, or option.

In effect, yield equivalence permits a seller to deliver various GNMA securities—each one, after all, represents a different pool—so the buyer gets the agreed-upon yield. This is accomplished by so adjusting the contract purchase price that the yield is maintained. For example, a contract to deliver a 12% GNMA at 90 may be effected by delivering a 10% GNMA at 77, if the yield will be 13.21% on either security.

See also YIELD MAINTENANCE CONTRACT.

YIELD MAINTENANCE CONTRACT

Trading in GNMA securities permits the basic contract to center on yield. Thus, a contract may be settled with the specific rate designated in the contract, or with other rates, provided the yield to the buyer is that agreed upon. This will require a price adjustment if securities with differing rates are delivered against the contract.

YIELD TO AVERAGE LIFE

Term used by money market funds—and often by dealers in unit investment trusts—to designate the simple interest that a new investor will receive, based on present cash flow and the average life of the securities in the portfolio. The yield is an estimate and presumes no portfolio changes.

Term should not be confused with the yield to average life used of GNMA securities. In this case, the yield is the anticipated compound rate of return and presumes the reinvestment of the cash flows as received.

YIELD TO MATURITY

A measurement of the compound rate of return that an investor in a bond with a maturity of more than one year will receive if: (1) he holds the security to maturity and (2) he reinvests all cash flows at the same market rate of interest.

YTM is an approximation and presumes a flat yield curve. However, it is used extensively in comparing fixed-income investments, in making fixed-income portfolio decisions, and in financial planning if an investor does not want to spend investment income but, instead, is looking for an increase in net worth.

The YTM is greater than current yield when the bond is selling at a discount, less when it is selling at a premium.

Z

Z
1 Used in the stock tables next to the volume figure. Meaning: this is the total volume, do not multiply by 100. For example, z220 means 220 shares, not 22,000 shares, were traded.
2 Occasionally used in the report of closing mutual fund prices in the newspaper if the fund did not supply the bid-offer prices by press time.

ZERO COUPON
Descriptive term for a debt security that (1) is issued at a discount from its face value, (2) matures at face value in more than one year, and (3) promises no other cash flow than the payment of the face value at maturity. The security may or may not be redeemable prior to maturity, depending on the indenture.

The difference between purchase price and the adjusted cost of acquisition, over time, is interest income. Tax advice is needed for the computation of the annual accretion of the adjusted cost of acquisition.

In general, zero coupon corporate bonds should be purchased by individual investors only in tax-sheltered accounts.

ZERO-MINUS TICK
Designation of a transaction price for a security that is (1) the same as the previous round-lot price, but (2) the previous round-lot price was lower than the next prior price. For example, transactions occur at:

$$21.....20.....20$$

The last transaction at 20 was made on a zero-minus tick. It was at the same price as the previous transaction, but both transactions were lower than the prior transaction at 21.

ZERO-PLUS TICK
Designation of a transaction price for a security that is (1) the same as the previous round-lot price, but (2) the previous round-lot price

was higher than the next prior price. For example, transactions occur at:

$$30......31.......31$$

The last transaction at 31 was made on a zero plus tick. It was at the same price as the previous transaction, but both transactions were higher than the prior price of 31.

Short sales may be made only on a plus tick or a zero-plus tick.